MW01031107

I AM
NOT
YOUR
VICTIM

DISCARD
Orland Park
Public Library
Aileen S. Andrew Memorial

Sage Series on Violence Against Women

Series Editors

Claire M. Renzetti
St. Joseph's University

Jeffrey L. Edleson
University of Minnesota

In this series . . .

I AM NOT YOUR VICTIM: Anatomy of Domestic Violence
by Beth Sipe and Evelyn J. Hall

WIFE RAPE: Understanding the Response of Survivors and Service Providers
by Raquel Kennedy Bergen

FUTURE INTERVENTIONS WITH BATTERED WOMEN AND THEIR FAMILIES
edited by Jeffrey L. Edleson and Zvi C. Eisikovits

WOMEN'S ENCOUNTERS WITH VIOLENCE: Australian Experiences
edited by Sandy Cook and Judith Bessant

WOMAN ABUSE ON CAMPUS: Results From the Canadian National Survey
by Walter S. DeKeseredy and Martin D. Schwartz

RURAL WOMEN BATTERING AND THE JUSTICE SYSTEM: An Ethnography
by Neil Websdale

SAFETY PLANNING WITH BATTERED WOMEN: Complex Lives/Difficult Choices
by Jill Davies, Eleanor Lyon, and Diane Monti-Catania

ATHLETES AND ACQUAINTANCE RAPE
by Jeffrey R. Benedict

RETHINKING VIOLENCE AGAINST WOMEN
edited by R. Emerson Dobash and Russell P. Dobash

EMPOWERING SURVIVORS OF ABUSE: Health Care for Battered Women and Their Children
edited by Jacquelyn Campbell

BATTERED WOMEN, CHILDREN, AND WELFARE REFORM: The Ties That Bind
edited by Ruth A. Brandwein

COORDINATING COMMUNITY RESPONSES TO DOMESTIC VIOLENCE: Lessons From Duluth and Beyond
edited by Melanie F. Shepard and Ellen L. Pence

CHANGING VIOLENT MEN
by R. Emerson Dobash, Russell P. Dobash, Kate Cavanagh, and Ruth Lewis

SAME-SEX DOMESTIC VIOLENCE: Strategies for Change
edited by Beth Leventhal and Sandra E. Lundy

MASCULINITIES, VIOLENCE, AND CULTURE
by Suzanne E. Hatty

LOCKED IN A VIOLENT EMBRACE
by Zvi Eisikovits and Eli Buchbinder

I AM NOT YOUR VICTIM

Anatomy of Domestic Violence

Beth Sipe
Evelyn J. Hall

SVAW
Sage Series on Violence Against Women

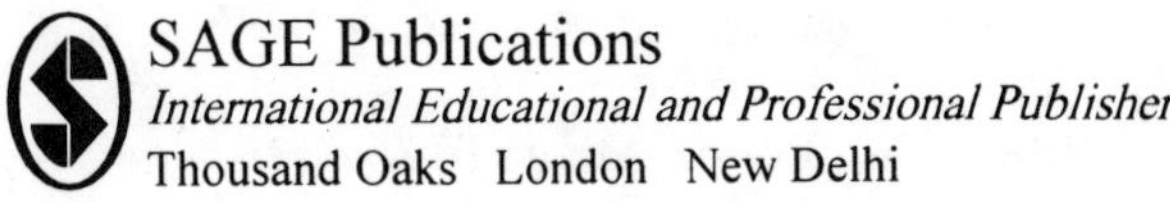

SAGE Publications
International Educational and Professional Publisher
Thousand Oaks London New Delhi

For information address:

SAGE Publications, Inc.
2455 Teller Road
Thousand Oaks, California 91320
E-mail: order@sagepub.com

SAGE Publications Ltd.
6 Bonhill Street
London EC2A 4PU
United Kingdom

SAGE Publications India Pvt. Ltd.
M-32 Market
Greater Kailash I
New Delhi 110 048 India

Printed in the United States of America

Library of Congress Cataloging-in-Publication Data

Sipe, Beth.
I am not your victim: Anatomy of domestic violence / authors, Beth Sipe, Evelyn J. Hall.
p. cm.—(Sage series on violence against women; v. 1)
Includes bibliographical references.
ISBN 0-7619-0145-0 (acid-free paper).—ISBN 0-7619-0146-9 (pbk. acid-free paper)
1. Sipe, Beth. 2. Abused wives—United States—Biography. 3. Domestic violence—United States. 4. Abused wives—Services for — United States. I. Hall, Evelyn J. II. Title. III. Series.
HV6626.S57 1996
362.82′92′092—dc20 [B] 96-4470

This book is printed on acid-free paper.

04 05 10 9 8 7

Sage Production Editor: Diana E. Axelsen
Sage Typesetter: Andrea D. Swanson

Dedications

Evelyn: I walked into your office with the sole purpose of having my story told to help other abused women. It was too late for me; I had no reason to live. You helped me to realize that not only did my children need me, but I deserved to live a life without abuse.

Amber: You walked into my life with a smile and a kind word. You proved not only to be my legal advocate, but also to be a true friend.

Bill: At the time I walked into your office, I didn't trust any men. You proved me wrong. You proved to be fair, honest, and, most of all, compassionate.

My children: For without your love, I would not have found the strength or the courage to survive.

Beth Sipe

To all the courageous women who have suffered abuse, to Temporary Assistance for Domestic Crisis, and to all my colleagues and friends who supported me in this project.

Evelyn Hall

Disclaimer

All names in Beth's story have been changed with the following exceptions: Beth Sipe, Sam Sipe, Beth's parents, William Smith, and Evelyn Hall.

Contents

Commentaries

Prologue

This book, Beth Sipe's autobiography, began as an assignment she did for her defense attorney, William (Bill) Smith. In longhand, Beth wrote about 250 pages, documenting sixteen years of extreme spousal abuse—physical, emotional, social, economic, and sexual—as well as destruction of property and pets. To this, we added information from incident reports, medical records, defense briefs, court documents, and more than 300 hours of interviews. Included also are passages from the couple's correspondence with one another.

Although the task of assembling an autobiography began as one aspect of Beth's defense preparation, it became an important therapeutic exercise for her as well, giving her a focus at a time when she found concentration most difficult. When Beth began therapy on April 26, 1988, she appeared totally beaten down, withdrawn, and profoundly depressed. She was painfully thin and ashen, her facial features were taut, and her affect flat. Therapy provided her with validation, support, encouragement, and information. The idea that the autobiography might become a book seemed to give her renewed energy, determination, and hope that she could, indeed, have a future.

From the beginning, Beth's goal in sharing her story was that others might learn and benefit from it. As her therapist, I agreed that her story had many valuable lessons, not only for other battered women but also for professionals working with domestic violence issues. For me personally, however, there was concern that a dual relationship might develop in the process. To guard against undue influence, we drew up a formal contract that specified Beth could stop the process to publish at any time prior to signing with a publisher. Whether or not the manuscript was ever published, our work on it was to have major therapeutic value for Beth. It has been over five years since her therapy ended, and Beth remains steadfast in her desire to tell her story publicly.

To understand Beth's story, it is helpful also to understand something about the dynamics inherent in the cycle of violence. As originally identified by Lenore Walker (1979), the cycle has within itself a number of subpatterns that interlock synergistically, making the cycle extremely difficult to interrupt. Confusion, imbalance of power, isolation, appeasement, secrecy, separations/reunions, alcohol/drug usage, becoming "other-focused," and child abuse are all subdynamics.

Strengthening these dynamics is the social programming of gender characteristics and roles. Barnett and LaViolette (1993) stated that the best predictor of a woman becoming involved in a violent relationship is growing up in American society. Women are usually recognized and praised for their nurturance, selflessness, patience, passivity, and flexibility (Barnett & LaViolette, 1993; Caplan, 1985; Jones & Schechter, 1992; Walker, 1979). They are encouraged to view men as dominant, as well as to derive their identities from relationships with men. A major part of love then involves being needed.

In contrast, men are programmed to set and pursue their own goals, particularly careers. From childhood, they are encouraged to view violence and sexual prowess as evidence of masculinity. Traditionally viewed as the providers in the family, many men are taught that they are entitled to special male privileges. Such privileges are often translated as the right to control all aspects of their families' lives. Titles such as "lord and master" and "king of his castle" lend authority to perceived rights of control.

Abusive men absorb these messages about traditional gender roles quite literally and, by adulthood, these messages have congealed into rigid beliefs—some conscious and others beneath the level of awareness. Batterers insist that their mates adhere to the notion of women as caretakers, supporters, nurturers, and subservient pieces of property. They believe that men are "always right" and free to enforce their beliefs with abuse and violence (Pence & Paymer, 1993).

Confusion is one of the first dynamics to appear in a violent relationship; it is created by an abusive partner's initial attack, whether verbal, physical, or a combination of both (Jones & Schecter, 1992). Stunned at first, the victim becomes absorbed with trying to integrate loving words with an abusive attack. Because there is no rational explanation for the abuse, she often becomes ambivalent, loses self-confidence, and feels ashamed. Initially, abusive men present themselves as the most romantic, loving suitors, appealing to women in general (Browne, 1987). They rarely become abusive until after some kind of commitment has taken place—for example, moving in together, becoming engaged, getting married (Forward & Torres, 1986). Having made such a commitment, a woman will rarely end the relationship after the first attack. Even with an early indication of trouble, the belief remains that "he'll change."

In most cases, after the first attack, the abuser expresses remorse and resumes romantic, loving behavior. Viewing this expression as indicative of "the real man," the victim perceives it as tangible evidence that he values and loves her. At this point, the three-stage cycle of violence—buildup of tension, acute abusive incident, and period of contrition (Walker, 1979, 1984)—has completed one revolution. Once the cycle occurs, it is certain to be repeated and to escalate in terms of frequency and severity. The more times it is completed, the less time it takes to complete. The longer the cycle goes uninterrupted, the more severe the violence becomes. Situations where episodic abuse is followed by long periods of loving behavior can give rise to the Stockholm syndrome in a battered woman. She becomes emotionally bonded to her abuser as a survival tool, much as hostages bond to their captors. The bond may be even stronger in a battered woman because her captor is the man she loves and trusts (Graham, Rawlings, & Rimini, 1988). With many repetitions, the contrition (or honeymoon) stage becomes shorter, until the only respite for a woman is merely the cessation of the violence.

With one completion of the cycle of violence, an imbalance of power has been created in the man's favor. Knowing he has the ability and willingness to hurt her, the fear created by even one physical attack greatly intensifies the impact of nonphysical forms of abuse, such as name calling, threats, accusations, and gestures (Pence & Paymer, 1993). Women usually acquiesce, but in cases where a woman does fight back, she quickly learns that the violence becomes greater. The batterer believes that his violence works to "correct" his partner's misbehavior, and because he rarely, if ever, receives negative consequences for such action, he does not see a need to change it. In many cases, he is actually able to convince his partner that *her* behavior is causing the abuse. Both become other-focused. Almost automatically, the victim will begin a pattern of appeasement, believing that if she obeys and tries harder to please her partner, she can avoid further abuse. Doing so, however, she unwittingly abandons herself, denies her own reality, and takes on responsibility for the abuse. At the same time, the batterer is looking for signs of "misbehavior." According to Ewing (1987), this imbalance of power is a major factor in binding the couple to each other.

Isolation also supports the cycle of violence. In some cases, a batterer will overwhelm his partner with attention, wanting to spend every free minute with her. At first, she may feel flattered and reassured but, without realizing it, she becomes isolated from a support system of family and friends. Methods abusers use to isolate include criticizing those close to her, withholding phone messages, creating embarrassing scenes in front of others, forbidding her to see "outsiders," and/or physically restraining her from outside contacts. He may contact her at work so often that she is fired. He may forbid her to work at all, disable her vehicle, or deny her any access to transportation. In some cases, he may even create geographic isolation by moving his partner far away from family and friends. As the cycle of violence escalates, a victimized woman may find that others turn away from her and that she has less energy to resist the efforts to isolate her.

Secrecy is yet another dynamic involved in the cycle of violence. Both partners keep the secret. He wants to maintain his reputation as a "nice guy" to protect his career status. Because she is ashamed, a battered woman hides the abuse and begins to cover up or lie about the bruises and injuries. She sees her partner's violence as separate from the "real" man and often the instances of abuse are never even discussed by the couple.

Closely related to secrecy is denial and minimization of the abuse. Both partners participate but for different motives. He uses this dynamic to avoid responsibility for perpetrating the violence, whereas his victim excuses and rationalizes the violence to maintain her hope that the abuse will end.

Frequently, a battered woman will flee her home during or immediately following an attack. Her escape may last a few hours, days, weeks, or months. Any communication with the batterer usually includes his impassioned apologies, expressions of love, pleas for her to return, and sincere promises to change. If she does not return quickly, however, his conciliatory messages often turn to veiled or open threats.

On the average, a battered woman returns six to seven times before ultimately ending the relationship. Her reasons for returning usually involve love for her partner, concern about separating the children from their father, and lack of any viable long-term living alternative (Barnett & LaViolette, 1993). Sometimes, the violent behavior is even more terrifying during separation and, in fact, this can be the most dangerous time for a battered woman (Montemurri, 1989). Her partner may escalate his abuse to include stalking, intense harassment, vandalism, assault, rape, kidnap of her and/or the children, threats to kill, attempts to kill, and murder. Separating and returning only reinforces the batterer's violence, and he becomes convinced that his aggression accomplishes the goal of keeping his partner under control.

Many times, alcohol and/or drug abuse also accompanies domestic abuse. Although alcohol or drugs, in themselves, do not cause the abuse, they do loosen inhibitions and moral restraints. Substance abuse also depletes the family's resources, at times leaving family members without necessary food and shelter.

Battered women frequently develop symptoms of Battered Women's Syndrome, a specific form of posttraumatic stress disorder (PTSD) (American Psychiatric Association, 1994). PTSD is defined as a cluster of symptoms that almost anyone subjected to trauma outside the range of usual human experience would develop. These include, but are not limited to: intrusive recollection of the trauma(s), psychic numbing of emotions, flashbacks, appetite and/or sleep disturbance, hypervigilance, exaggerated startle response, disturbed concentration, unpredictable irritability or anger, the Stockholm syndrome, anxiety, and depression. She may also experience symptoms of learned helplessness, passivity, indecisiveness, and chronic physical illnesses that can range from frequent colds, flus, and allergies to chronic urinary, vaginal, and gastrointestinal problems. In the most serious cases, ulcers and eating disorders have been related to the abuse.

Adding to the enormous scope of this domestic tragedy, child abuse is a frequent occurrence in households of partner violence. As with partner abuse, violence against the children usually starts with verbal abuse, swats, and slaps, escalating to beatings that require hospitalization. Not only do these children grow up also experiencing the symptoms of PTSD at increasing intervals in their lives, but the violent example of family life has a profound effect on the lives they lead as adults. They are at risk for repeating the violence they've witnessed and suffering from chronic PTSD; they may experience addiction, vocational confusion, and dysfunctional relationships (Jaffe, Wolfe, & Wilson, 1990).

All of these dynamics of domestic violence are dramatically illustrated in Beth's story, and it is hoped that this commentary is helpful as a framework within which to view her experiences. With the agreement to publish this work, Sage has expanded it to include a multidisciplinary examination of Beth's experience. Following the main body of the book are commentaries that provide public health, legal, advocacy, military, and mental health views of this case study in particular, and domestic violence in general.

Beth's Story

1

A Fine Romance

On a cold, wintry night in January 1971, I first met Steven Sipe. Susan, a good friend of mine, had been pestering me for weeks to meet him, but my standard reply to her was, "I'm not interested." On that particular night, I went out with Susan and my sister, Nancy, to the 18-Club, a hangout mostly for young people. Soon after we arrived, Steven, or Sam as he liked to be called, came over to our table with one of his buddies.

They introduced themselves politely enough, but to me, Sam seemed cocky and obnoxious. They were both Air Force guys, stationed in Blytheville, Arkansas, about fifteen miles from Steele, Missouri, where I lived. I deliberately gave him the cold shoulder, but for some reason, Sam and his buddy hung around us all night. Sam acted smug and superior, mouthing off things like, "All you southerners are racists and that's stupid." Many of his words still echo in my mind. "You girls from the South have never seen anybody like me," he bragged, "You just don't know what you're missing until you've had a lover like me; I'm the greatest." As soon as I could get Susan alone, I made it clear to her that I did not like Sam and certainly did not want to date him.

Up to that point, I would say my life had not been easy, but it was not terrible either. I was born April 6, 1951, to Ethel, age thirty-five, and Aaron Nunnery, age fifty-five, in Holland, Missouri, about eighty miles from Cape Girardeau. It was Dad's second marriage, so I had two grown half-sisters. I also had a brother, Ronald, age five, and a sister, Nancy, age three. My dad was a sharecropper on forty acres of land, and although we were poor, we had a good name. It was always said "Mr. Nunnery doesn't have to sign anything; his name is good enough."

The house we lived in had four rooms—a front room, a kitchen, and two bedrooms. The yard where we played had no grass, just dirt which we swept clean every day. There were three big cottonwood trees which provided shade and tons of white fuzzy stuff in the fall which made me scratch until I drew blood at times. There was a black coal stove in the front room and a kerosene heater in one bedroom for heat. When it got very cold, we all slept in the bedroom with the heater. We had no electricity until I was five and no indoor plumbing ever. There was an outhouse, and we pumped water from a well in the backyard into a lime-treated barrel for all our water needs.

My parents were strict, but I never remember feeling abused by them. If Momma disciplined us, she used a switch on our legs and we had to cut the switch for her. If Daddy disciplined us, which was rare, he gave us a couple of swats on the bottom with a belt. In total, I recall being spanked only three or four times—and each time, I deserved it.

My parents had an old-fashioned marriage; that is, Momma pretty well did what Daddy told her, and he made all the big decisions. If they disagreed with each other, Momma usually just got quiet. In a lot of ways, their relationship resembled that of Archie and Edith Bunker except that Daddy was constantly hugging and kissing Momma. I'm told that before my brother was born, Daddy was a heavy drinker, but he quit when my brother was born, so I never saw any of that.

All in all, we were a close, loving family. I was especially spoiled by Daddy because I was the baby. I was a tomboy and followed Daddy around as much as I could. By the time I could toddle, it was my job to take him a jug of water, morning and afternoon, out in the fields where he was working.

From the time I can remember, we grew cotton, soybeans, wheat, corn (enough to feed the animals), plus a vegetable garden large enough for us to can food for the winters. Until I was about six years old, we had two mules to do the field work—no tractor and no car. Then we got a tractor, and it was used for field work and as transportation anywhere we went. We also had a cow, a few pigs, and some chickens. We started to work early on the farm and were usually in bed by 8:30 p.m.

School was let out in the fall so we could pick cotton full time. The going wage for cotton was three cents a pound. We worked for Daddy, and he paid us two cents a pound. When we were waiting for the second opening of the fields, we worked for neighboring farmers; then we got three cents a pound. Cotton picking was hard for us kids. The cotton burrs broke off in our hands, and the morning dew on the cotton, called poisoning, got into these scratches so that our hands were always infected. At times, we picked barefoot with our pant legs rolled up, standing in water up to our knees. The black edges of the cotton bolls stayed in our hands like splinters for years.

Sitting around trying to pick these out of our hands was a common evening pastime. Cotton picking makes you old before your time. I watched my daddy become on old man with skin cancer on his hands, face, and ears. I remember wishing my momma didn't have to pick because she still had to come in and cook and clean after a full day in the fields. I knew how weary she must have felt because often we were too tired even to eat.

Momma held each child's money and kept records for us. She gave us a small amount each week to spend for candy or junk, but we used most of the money to buy our clothes and school supplies. On Saturdays, we went to Holland or Steele to buy groceries, clothes, or other necessities.

Across three fields from our house stood the Samford Church of Christ. It was named for Boss Samford, a big land holder and store owner, noted for being honest and a very good man. The church was built on his land, and it was comforting to be able to see it from home. We belonged to this church and attended regularly. I never remember a time during my growing-up years without the church.

When I was about twelve years old, we moved to Steele, Missouri, because our farm was rented to someone else. That first summer and fall we worked on other farms, chopping and picking cotton. Then I found a job in a small ice cream stand, making fifty cents an hour.

Living in town meant hard times for us because we had to buy all the things we had previously supplied for ourselves on the farm. We all had to pitch in and work at whatever we could find. Once I turned thirteen, I began working in a restaurant and tried to continue school. I finished grade school in Steele. Then the junior highs of Holland and Steele were combined to form South Pemiscot, so we were bused to Holland every day. I always liked school and made good grades, but the working and going to school got to be too much for me, and I dropped out in the tenth grade.

Growing up was no bed of roses, but I think working hard and being raised this way taught all of us some good values. Mainly, work for what you get, do the best you can at your job, and don't be ashamed to sign your name to your work if you've done the best job you can do.

While I never fancied myself beautiful, I knew the boys liked me. When I finished growing, I stood five feet four inches and weighed about a hundred pounds. I had long honey-colored hair and big blue-green eyes. Everyone said I had a beautiful smile and a low, sexy voice. Although I had plenty of chances, I never dated much because I didn't have time.

In January 1968, I visited my sister, Nancy, who had moved to Memphis. I was seventeen and felt quite grown-up. While there, I found a job as a coupon clipper for a gas station. On the job, I met and soon married John Theodore Walker, the station manager. Terry, as he liked to be called, was older, twenty-four, and I was impressed by his air of confidence. I guess you could say we had a whirlwind romance. We married on May 4, 1968, but I only lived with him a couple of months. He got drunk and hit me one time. That was it for me; I left immediately and went back home to my parents even though I was pregnant. I was hurt and scared, but as time passed without a hassle from Terry, I was relieved that my marriage had ended.

Back in Steele, I found work right away, keeping house and baby-sitting three children, ages six, five, and two, for a recently widowed neighbor man. His wife had broken her leg and died of tetanus. I stayed with my parents and worked during the days until one month after the birth of my first son, Roland Matthew Walker, on February 8, 1969. I only missed five days of work when I had Matt.

Matt's birth was an ordeal for me at eighteen with no husband. The doctor had planned to do a caesarean if the baby was larger than five pounds, but the doctor was not available when I checked into the hospital. I was alone in hard labor for eighteen and a half hours, and since I refused any drugs out of concern for possible damage to the baby, I felt every pain. Only when the baby's hand and arm were hanging out did someone begin to pay attention. I heard them whispering, "We can't get the baby back in or out." So when they strapped me down—my wrists, my elbows, my ankles, even my thighs—I knew I was in for something bad. I kept praying they wouldn't kill the baby as they delivered him with forceps. Matt was blue, not breathing when he was born, and it took several minutes for them to get him started. Then I could relax. Although the doctor had told me I couldn't deliver a baby larger than five pounds, Matt was seven pounds three ounces at birth.

I lost my job when our neighbor remarried. I had always been interested in nursing, so I took the training for Nurse's Aide in the spring of 1969 and began work for Pemiscot Memorial Hospital. I worked there for about a year, but I was barely getting by, and my parents' two-bedroom house was overcrowded with Matt and me staying with them.

I had heard there was a lot of work in Chicago, so in May 1970, I decided to make a new start there on my own. Right away, I got a job as a waitress and found housing in a condemned building. Matt and I had a three-room apartment on the third floor, and we were allowed to keep my dog, BoBo.

Conditions were so bad there that one morning I found a rat in bed with me and the baby. Of course, everybody else in the building was more or less in the same boat, so we tried to help each other. One of the welfare mothers baby-sat for me while I worked.

After a few weeks, I found a job in a jukebox factory and did some part-time modeling for the Patricia Stevens Modeling Agency. We walked to the nearby grocery where everything cost twice as much, but since we had no vehicle, there was no other choice. We all shared one ancient washer and hung our clothes in our apartments. I saw no one outside work except the other people in my building. On my off time, I baby-sat for others.

My parents were constantly asking me to bring Matt back home. Mom especially missed him. I found myself getting homesick and increasingly concerned about the city's bad influence on Matt.

I decided to return home after a neighbor, pouring coffee into a cracked cup, scalded my thigh. I couldn't work, I was broke, so I had to go home. Within two weeks, my leg was better, and I was back working as a waitress at the Drumstick, a small restaurant in town. I had the early-morning day shift and walked back and forth to work. My mom baby-sat Matt along with several other children.

After about a month, the manager of the truck stop out on the highway hired me and arranged for my rides to and from work. This was a big boost for me because I made more than twice as much money, and by the first of 1971, I was able to rent a one-bedroom house on Main Street for Matt and me. I had the night shift at the truck stop, which allowed me to spend more time with Matt during the days. Soon I was made Assistant Manager on the night shift.

I felt great, finally making it on my own, reunited with my family and friends. Occasionally, I went out on my nights off with my friends, Marilyn and Susan, and my sister, Nancy. My life was peaceful; everything seemed in order.

This was my life when Sam came into it. As I said, at first I wasn't interested in him at all. Over the next few months, I seemed to run into him every time I went out with my girlfriends. But we were always in a group, and I really didn't notice Sam that much.

About mid-April, Susan planned a Sunday excursion to Crowley Ridge, a state recreation park with a natural swimming lake, sixty miles from Steele. I thought this outing was just a random group of friends, but Susan pulled a fast one on me. Only after I was in the car and we were on our way did I learn it was just two couples—Susan with her date and me with Sam. This was my first date with Sam.

During the ride to Crowley Ridge, I felt resentful and sat quietly as far away from Sam as I could get. Even after we got there, I kept my distance. I remember trying to sleep on a blanket under a tree, while Sam kept putting ants on me. He made me laugh, and I began to like him a little. We kissed for the first time on the way back from our third outing to Crowley Ridge, about a month later. Sam was so sweet, so romantic about it. We were holding hands in the back seat when I felt a slight flutter on my cheek. As I turned to look at Sam, he grinned and said, "That's a butterfly kiss." I giggled and he did it again, blinking his eyelashes against my cheek. To me, it was a beautiful gesture, reminding me of all the times I had held a butterfly in my hand. I hadn't seriously thought of dating him until that time, because I knew he was seeing other girls. But from the first kiss, I was hooked.

Then Sam became a regular at the restaurant where I worked. Often he would come in with Susan and her guy, leave to take them home, then come back to the restaurant, staying to give me a ride home after I finished work. He was so thoughtful and caring, talking, laughing, joking. Soon he told me he loved me, and although I wouldn't say that to him, my spirits were higher than the clouds. He gave me lots of romantic cards, usually with a poem he'd written for me. In one card, he wrote:

I love you because it's so easy to do
There's no one for me that's more natural than you
To me you're so real, yet in only a dream
Could exist one so perfect as you, it would seem
I think you are real, but if you're a dream it's OK
'Cause then my mind is a friend to deceive me this way
But it really doesn't matter if you're a dream or for real
'Cause you're mine and I love you as I always will.

No one had ever written poetry for me, and his words touched me in a way nothing and no one else had. I was totally in love although I wasn't ready to admit it to him.

In May, when Matt got sick with anemia and had to be hospitalized in Hayti, Missouri (a small town sixteen miles north of Steele), Sam drove me to the hospital every day for five days. He was so good with Matt, he really won me over. When Matt came home from the hospital, I left him with my folks quite a bit while I worked, so of course, the family met Sam. My dad told me, "I don't like that guy, there's something phony about him. It's so obvious—you go after the calf to get the cow." My sister,

Nancy, called him a "cocky little bastard." I could see my mom didn't like Sam either, but she didn't have much to say about him.

I began to feel that no one understood Sam but me. He talked about how lonely and discriminated against he had felt during his first weeks in Blytheville. The more he talked, the more I could sense him letting his barriers down with me.

I had told him many times, "I'm not interested in sex," and his reply always was, "You've never slept with the right man yet." It was after another outing at Crowley Ridge that Sam and I made love for the first time. The day was magical, filled with laughing, swimming, and picnicking. By that point, I was enchanted by everything he said and did. When he pulled into a motel on the way back from our outing at Crowley Ridge, I was shaky with fear and desire all mixed together. But I didn't say no. I had never enjoyed sex before Sam, but with him, the earth moved and bells rang. More than anything, he was gentle and patient and seemed concerned only with satisfying me. I began to see him as my one true love.

I was excited but scared by the strong feelings he brought out in me. So at breakfast the morning after our first night together, I told him I was getting too involved, that he would be around only a short time, and that was just about as long as I wanted the relationship to last. "I'm not going to see you every day," I said. He just said, "We'll see." I had a strong premonition not to get too involved with him and refused to go out with him for several days.

Sam's reaction to this was to show up at my job every night; there he was, right under my nose, hanging around during most of my shifts. The song, "Let the Devil Take Tomorrow" was popular then, and I heard it played so often, I began to think like the song. After almost a week, I broke down and went out with him again.

We talked a lot about the Vietnam war. One of my friends from school had died in Vietnam, and two others had returned home severely wounded. I had tried to organize a welcome-home party for one of them, but the reaction I got from other people was, "You want to give a party for a baby killer?" It bothered me deeply to see these Vietnam vets treated as if they were traitors. Sam had already done a tour of duty in Vietnam and had put in a request to be reassigned there. I cringed every time I thought of him going back to such a hellhole. While we agreed that the military was necessary to protect our country, we questioned the handling of U.S. troops sent to Vietnam—as if they were disposable. Our views on this became a strong bond between us.

As time went on, I began to see Sam's cockiness as confidence and charm. He could be the life of the party, making everybody laugh, including me. He could also be very kind, gentle, and loving. He was always coming up behind me, hugging me, and saying, "I could just squeeze you to death." No one had ever been so attentive and affectionate with me before, and I was filled with joy.

Sam occasionally used drugs, mainly marijuana, uppers, or downers, when we were together. I didn't like it and told him as much, but he said he only used them once in awhile and that it was no problem for him to control his usage. He drank heavily almost daily, but I didn't pay much attention to that. After all, his buddies drank, and they were young and away from home, plus they were stressed about Vietnam. At Susan's house, Sam and his buddies turned one wall into a pyramid of empty beer cans. At the time, I didn't see this as a problem; I guess I thought Sam would outgrow his drinking habit.

The one thing we disagreed most about was his belief in free love—that it was OK to have sex with anyone anytime, married or single. He had different rules for me, though; he said that if I were ever unfaithful to him, it would be wrong because of my own rule not to have sex unless I loved the man. This riled me in one way, but in another way, I saw it as a sign that he didn't really believe in free love.

I guess I should have believed him, because I soon developed a vaginal infection which my doctor could not diagnose. Much later, I learned that Sam was being treated for chlamydia and venereal warts at this time. But it would be years before I received the treatment I needed.

Some time in June, I gave him a key to my house, and he came and went as he pleased. Often he watched Matt while I worked, and Matt became very attached to Sam. At times, Sam took Matt with him to his barracks. I never expected a man to do anything for me, and I didn't really notice that Sam didn't bring food or contribute to any of my household expenses. I did notice that he seemed to like all my cooking; he wasn't hard to please at all. Often he sat on the couch watching television while I cleaned up the dinner mess. Once I asked him if he would buy my cigarettes at the commissary if I gave him the money to pay for them; he refused, saying, "That's illegal and I won't do it." I was too much in love to notice the discrepancy—he could do drugs, which were illegal, but he couldn't buy my cigarettes. He began to open and read all my mail. At the time, I looked at this as another sign that he preached free love but really did not want to practice it.

In June, we went with another couple to Reelfoot Lake, a resort area in northwestern Tennessee sixty miles north of Steele. Sam canoed me across the lake, and when we got to the other side, he told me how much he loved me. He held up the palms of his hands and said, "See, I've got the blisters to prove it." He started talking about marriage that day. "I didn't plan to marry until age twenty-four; I'm only twenty-two now, but I'm beginning to change my mind," he told me. I reminded him of his own belief that marriage wasn't necessary, but he said, "I've changed my mind about that." I told him, "I haven't changed mine; I don't want to get married. Living together is enough of a commitment." Throughout that summer, I felt wonderful. Sam spent his free time with me, as much as my schedule allowed.

In July, I ran out of my birth control pills for one weekend. It hardly seemed important at the time; the doctor just said, "Double up for a couple of days." I did as the doctor told me and thought I was safe.

But by August 1, I knew I was pregnant. I had decided to tell no one, absolutely no one. I knew Sam's request for Vietnam duty was in the works, and I planned to let him go without telling him about our baby. I figured if he came back to me, then I would know he really loved me, and we could decide about marriage at that time. One day my friend Susan caught me throwing up and questioned me until I admitted that I was pregnant. I swore her to secrecy and trusted her not to tell anyone.

That same night, Sam came storming into my house and grabbed me by the shoulders, shaking me and yelling, "What the hell's going on? Why do I have to find out you're pregnant from someone else?" I was already sick, throwing up, when he walked in, and at first, I just stared at him, speechless, in shock. I wasn't sure if he was concerned about me or the baby or both.

I felt scared and disappointed; it kept running through my mind, "he's not the person I thought he was." I started throwing up again and told him to get out.

He calmed down then, started telling me how much he loved me, how much he wanted to marry me, how much he wanted the baby and for us to be a family. All the while, he was taking care of me, putting a cold towel on my head, holding me, trying to make me feel better. I let him stay, but I was firm about not marrying him. Even so, he phoned his family in Nevada and told them that I was pregnant and that he was planning to get married. After he got off the phone, I said, "Why don't you talk to me about it? I am not marrying you." He started to threaten me with his family, saying they would take me to court and get my baby. "After all," he said, "you're very poor and you already have one child to raise." When I still didn't say yes, he changed his tactics. "How can you face staying here? Everyone will talk," he said. I just said, "So what? All they can say is that I'm pregnant and I'm not married. That's true and I'm not ashamed of it." He also argued that I would get no benefits or status for me or the baby if we didn't get married. But I still was not willing to marry him. I felt he was the only man I had ever loved, but I didn't want to marry him with a cloud over my head.

Throughout the next month and a half, Sam was very nice to me, no more threats. But I got all kinds of pressure from several of my friends. They said what a good guy he was and that he really loved me, that it wasn't fair to anyone if I didn't marry him.

In September, Sam had to spend a week in Little Rock, Arkansas, on a work assignment. I really missed him during that time. He returned on September 19, and after that night together, I agreed to marry him. We drove to Memphis, Tennessee, and got married at the courthouse September 20, 1971. My friend Marilyn went with us as a witness.

It was definitely not formal; I wore a lilac pantsuit, and Sam wore dress slacks with a green shirt. Sam was so romantic in those days. He said, "One day we'll marry each other again—in a mountain meadow. Very simple, no minister, just exchange the vows we've written to each other. You'll wear flowers in your beautiful hair and a long white dress, not a wedding gown. We can't do all that right now; the most important thing is for us to be legally married so that I can take care of you and our baby." Of course, I lapped this up, glowing in the warmth of his love. Sam really loved me—I could feel it. I knew everything would work out right for us.

We planned to have dinner at a nice restaurant before driving home. I had lived in Memphis, and I knew the way to the restaurant. But when I tried to tell Sam where to turn, he flew into a rage. He screamed and cursed me all the way to the restaurant. "Shut up, stupid!" he yelled at me, and I did. I was hurt and humiliated that he would treat me this way, especially in front of my friend. It made me so sick I threw up my dinner. To myself, I thought, "This is why I didn't want to get married again. Men think they own you and don't have to be nice to you anymore once you're married." Sam hadn't wasted any time letting me know that as a female from the South, I wasn't on his level.

After we got back to Steele and picked up Matt from my parents, Sam pouted, wouldn't say a word to me. I had chilled champagne to celebrate, but he sat in front of the TV and refused to drink any of it. I had told him when we first became intimate that I never wanted to go to bed angry, but that night we went to bed silently with Matt between us. I always remember my wedding night as being alone with my angry husband, both of us frozen in silence.

Sam's pout lasted about two weeks, with him staying at the barracks more than half the nights. I didn't know what he wanted, but I finally told him, "If you're going to act like this, you can just go to Vietnam and I will divorce you."

He never apologized, but suddenly, he turned back into a sweet, loving person—the Sam that I loved so much.

Toward the end of October, Sam flew out with his best friend for a month's training in Florida. They left about 9 a.m. in a rented Cessna. Everything was good between us, so I wasn't worried, just sad with missing him. About 2 p.m., an hour before they were due to arrive in Florida, I was suddenly filled with panic and I began pacing the floor. I just knew something was wrong. Momma said, "If you feel that strongly, there must be something to it." A few minutes later, the phone rang. It was Sam telling me they had made a forced landing in a Mississippi bean field. To me, this was a symbol of our closeness and how right our marriage was—that I could know beyond a doubt that

Sam was in danger although hundreds of miles separated us. A few months later, that same plane lost power and crashed, killing everyone on board.

Matt and I joined Sam for the final two weeks of his training. We stayed in a small motel, and I remember it as a very pleasant time, even though my pregnancy was troubled, and I was sick all the time. Sam was loving, concerned, and attentive toward me, Matt, and our unborn baby.

From there, we flew to Nevada to visit his family in Mina, a rural town of 400 about 175 miles southeast of Reno. Although Sam was nice to me in front of his family, they seemed rather cool and disapproving to me. We got there a few days before Thanksgiving, and Sam flew out of Reno a few days afterward for Vietnam. Overall, it was a peaceful visit, and I felt very sad and lonely as I flew back to Missouri. I already missed him and he'd only been gone one day.

2

And Baby Makes Four

Before leaving Steele, I had arranged for a teenage girl to take care of my cats. When Matt and I got home, I found that she had stolen all my food and run up a big long-distance phone bill. Having been off work for three weeks, I was broke. When Sam left for Vietnam, he didn't offer me any money, and I was too emotionally torn up to think to ask. Except for the fact that Sam had drawn a $2,000 advance to pay for his flights, I knew nothing about his finances. Before he left, he told me not to worry about money, that he had filled out allotment papers for me.

I started back to work at the truck stop immediately, and I expected that the $100-a-month allotment would start any day. I knew it should be retroactive to our wedding date in September, so I wasn't worried at first. Several times, I borrowed a few dollars from my parents, who were living on minimum Social Security, but I felt terrible about that, as if I were taking advantage of them.

During the four and a half months until James was born, I wrote Sam daily telling him the news, how much I loved him and missed him, even though he only wrote me every two to three weeks. With him so far away and in constant danger, it was easy for me to forget the "few little" hurtful things he had said and done to me. Although I could barely make my expenses, I didn't worry because Sam repeatedly said, "the allotment's on the way." Meanwhile, I sent Sam brownies, cookies, Hershey bars, chewing gum, Kool-aid—whatever he asked for. During this time, I began to get bills from his credit cards and calls from bill collectors. I felt it was my duty to make payments on his bills, but the money situation got so desperate for me that I took an extra job selling Avon in addition to my full-time job at the truck stop.

Somehow I managed to feed Matt and me and pay the rent. But I was sick all winter. Several times I started spotting and my blood pressure went up. Although I worried about losing the baby, basically I was happy. I really believed that Sam loved me, and I knew I loved him. When he said he was too busy to write as often as I did, I accepted it. Later, I learned that he had gone R & R (rest and recuperation leave)—once to Saigon and once to the Philippines during this time. When he said the allotment money was on the way, I accepted that, too. By February, money had become a severe problem for me. My family said, "Either he hasn't filled out the papers or somebody needs to trace it; either way the Red Cross is there to help you." In a letter to Sam I wrote,

> Still waiting for a letter. I'm sure you must be real busy or sick. I sure hope you're feeling better if you have been sick. I did something today, I hope it doesn't make you mad. I went to the base to buy groceries and went to family services. They sent me to the Red Cross on base. I told them the fault wasn't yours and not to contact your commander since I didn't want you to get in any trouble.
>
> Anyway, they're sending a letter to find out why we can't get the allotment checks started. All they'll do is ask your permission to check the records. Please don't get mad. I told them the whole story, that you were trying to get them started. They understood and said they could speed it up a little. Most of all try and write. We miss you so very much.

The Red Cross reported, after a thorough check, that there was no record of Sam's ever applying for my allotment. I felt like I had just plunged to the bottom of a roller-coaster ride. But immediately I began to talk myself out of it, telling myself, "No, he loves me; he'd never lie to me or deprive me of my benefits." That same day, I received a card from Sam with this poem:

I could write you words of love
From a poet's verse of rhyme
To let you know how much I care
That I miss you all the time
I could say that you're my world
Or you're my only one
Or you're my life, my everything
And you're my morning sun.
And though they express the way I feel
And would be so very true
I'd rather write words from my heart
And say to you "I love you."

Then I was overcome with guilt. "How can I think such awful thoughts when he writes me such beautiful poems?" I asked myself. I told myself I was being selfish and uncaring to question Sam. Whatever was holding up the money, I convinced myself it couldn't be Sam's fault.

Within a few days, Sam called. At first I was thrilled to hear his voice. But he was fighting mad. He told me I had gotten him in trouble for no reason, that the chaplain and his commander had called him in and reprimanded him for failure to support his family. He yelled, "Why the hell can't you take my word for anything; just keep your nose out of my military life!" He slammed the phone down, and the monitor said, "Miss, he's hung up." After I put the phone down, I cried for hours. At that point, I gave up trying to get my allotment.

The next week I got a tape from him, saying,

> I didn't get mad, just disappointed [that] you didn't talk to me first. I expect you to talk to me first. It [my going to the Red Cross] caused quite a ruckus between us, but it's no biggee. Next time, write to me first. It only takes

> two or three weeks to get a letter to me and if it's something important, I can always make time to write you back.
>
> When we get this pay thing straightened out, we can save some money because I have to have a new car when I get home. . . . You know how I feel about you working—If your working caused us to lose the baby, in all honesty, I'd probably hold it against you. Because in certain situations, I don't have any control over myself. I can't picture you going through anything so rough that you have to work. If you are, just try and bear with it until you get your allotment checks. You should get your check for back pay at the end of February or first of March. March should be the magic month.

That tape did nothing to ease my financial worries, but I couldn't bear his anger. So I sent him a card with a note saying, "I am sorry. I won't do anything like that again. I just didn't want to be a burden, but you can be the head of the house. . . . P.S. Please don't be mad." In a way, I felt relieved, but I was disappointed that he did not apologize or explain about the money. I silenced the alarm I felt about his mention of buying a new car when we didn't have rent or food money. And I didn't allow myself to register his implied threat that he would never forgive me if I worked and lost the baby. I see now this was the beginning of my hopelessness and despair. I knew if I lost our baby, Sam would blame me, but at the same time, I had to work two jobs just to survive. I was in a no-win position with Sam—don't work versus work; pay the bills versus stay at home to be a "good wife and mother."

Toward the end of March, I was admitted to Chickasawba Hospital in Blytheville, Arkansas, having regular but weak contractions. They kept me for two days. The contractions never stopped; they just didn't get strong enough to have the baby.

I went back home and back to work. By that time, I had stopped waitressing and was cooking at the restaurant. I continued to have difficulties with my pregnancy, including premature water leakage. Sam wrote letters and sent tapes, pushing me to get him home to stay. He had already gotten his tax-free reenlistment money, but he didn't want to stay in 'Nam. He said

I was having a hard time and that if I told the doctor I needed Sam home, maybe the doctor could fix it.

I went into labor on April 12, but the doctor told me I couldn't have the baby yet because my hormones weren't right. The doctor sent for Sam, and two days later Sam came into my hospital room. My doctor made an appointment for X rays the next day and sent me home. Within minutes after getting home, Sam insisted on sex. Loving him as I did, I submitted. When I was x-rayed the next day, my doctor decided to induce labor for the sake of the baby because my blood pressure had skyrocketed. I gave birth to James at 1:46 p.m. on April 14, 1972. Sam's face was filled with joy, and I was proud to have given him a son. Of course, we had Matt, but James looked like Sam and even had a headful of red hair. I heard him in the hall, calling his family; he sounded thrilled.

The baby and I were in the hospital two days. On the third, Sam picked us up about 1 p.m. We were to go to my parents' house directly from the hospital. Instead Sam took us to the base exchange to shop for baby clothes and then to his friend's house, where Sam and the other guy proceeded to drink for four hours. I was in pain, just aching all over. I told Sam several times I wanted to leave, but he just ignored me. Naturally, my family was worried and upset because we only visited with them about fifteen minutes that day. When we finally got to our place about 6 p.m., Sam said, "I'm starved. What's for dinner?" So I cooked him a big dinner—fried chicken, mashed potatoes, and gravy. When he didn't help clean up the mess, it was clear to me that in Sam's mind, having just delivered a baby didn't excuse me from any of my duties. Later that night, he insisted on sex, even though I begged him not to. He just said, "I love you; you have to let me." I tried pushing him off, then flailing with my hands against his arms, but he clamped down on my wrists and pressed on. I just lay there and cried. He tore out half my stitches, causing damage I still have. That night, I couldn't admit to myself that I had just been raped.

Afterward I showered and sat up the rest of the night, rocking and feeding James. I worried about the fact that Sam had left Vietnam on short notice and hadn't been checked for disease. He had told me in letters and tapes that he had had sex with other women because to him, sex and love weren't the same, and he saw no reason to do without sex when he could get it. I thought of things my mother had told me about men and their "rutting around." I told myself he really couldn't stop once he got so excited. I wanted to hold on to the feeling that he loved me; I didn't want to believe he would hurt me.

Sam was home about nine days and forced sex every day. I couldn't even start to heal. After he left, I saw the doctor for my checkup; not only did I have bruises on my arms, legs, and abdomen, I also had vaginal, bladder, and uterine infections. The doctor seemed not to notice the bruises, made no comment about the infections, and asked no questions about the torn stitches. Of course, I was much too embarrassed to question or explain. Since I couldn't take antibiotics because of breast-feeding, it took me a month to heal after Sam left.

During this visit, Sam had also begun flying off the handle with Matt. He screamed at him constantly and spanked him several times. I wondered if now that he had his own son, he didn't love Matt any more. Sam wouldn't even let me hold Matt while I held James. Sam didn't give me a penny while he was home, but he did buy food. He continued to tell me he just didn't know where my allotment money could be, but to be patient. As for his reenlistment bonus, Sam told me he needed all of it for his overseas expenses and that I was too dumb to understand his situation over there.

His whole time at home was a drunken blur. His friends came over every day to drink. I was sorry he had to go back to 'Nam, but I was relieved when he was gone. As soon as I got back from the airport, I lay down with the children and slept for twenty-four hours, only feeding the children when they woke.

Two days later, I started back to work at the truck stop. I worked nights and continued to sell Avon during the days while my mother kept the kids. This worried me because James had colic and frequently choked on his own vomit. I knew Momma couldn't keep him much longer, and I didn't trust anyone else with James.

Once Sam got back to 'Nam, he began pressuring me to "get him home" with his letters, tapes, and telephone calls. "I know something bad is going to happen to me," he said. "You've got to do everything you can do to get me back home. I don't want you to be a widow with two little kids. I have nothing to leave you now." I began to have terrible nightmares; in the worst one, a mortician beckoned to me, saying, "Do you want to see your husband?" and when I followed him, I found a casket filled with butchered meat wrapped in plastic.

One day I answered a knock at my door to see two Air Force men standing there—an officer with stars on his hat and another with chaplain's crosses. I was in shock until I realized they were talking about someone else, not Sipe. I was so relieved I almost fainted.

At first, Sam instructed me to write to our congressmen and senators, saying he should be home with me and the kids. Then he extended it to anyone political—the police chief, the mayor, whoever. He knew I was against the war anyway and had put a big peace sign on my car; so this was no problem for me. But I didn't get anywhere with my letters, not even a response.

Then Sam told me to tell my doctor I could not survive without him. My doctor sympathized but said he could do nothing. As Sam increased his pressure, I became a nervous wreck. The doctor prescribed tranquilizers, but I didn't take them because I was breast-feeding. When Sam found out about this, he instructed me to empty all the capsules except maybe two, then swallow all of them. He said they would send him home for sure if they thought I attempted suicide. The idea disgusted me and I told him no. But with every call, he told me "my death will be on your head."

My nightmares grew worse, and I finally agreed to do as Sam told me. My friend Marilyn helped me prepare the capsules, and I swallowed them all. That's how strong Sam's influence was on me; I faked an overdose even though I was terrified and I didn't want that on my medical records.

Marilyn drove me to the hospital, saying she had found me asleep when she dropped by for a visit and was concerned. They hospitalized me, made me drink a lot of water, and woke me every hour. The next day a doctor and chaplain talked to me and persuaded me to admit myself to a mental hospital in Memphis. It felt like sleepwalking to me—I'm sitting there listening to people talk to me about killing myself when I wasn't suicidal at all, but had to pretend that I was.

My sister drove me to Gartley Ramsey Mental Hospital in Memphis. They gave me a hypodermic of vitamins every four hours and something that made me sleepy for the first two days. I remember being hungry every time I woke, but I don't remember talking to a doctor. I sneaked a peek at my chart, which said I was suffering from exhaustion and malnutrition, and later a doctor told me, "your condition is like a bucket of water filled so full, the water just keeps running over the top."

On the third day, they let me get up, take a shower, put on clean pajamas, and go into the recreation room. Suddenly, I looked up to see Sam walking in. I recall crying and running to him. He was laughing and hugging me. I was overjoyed to see him, to be with him.

When I was released, Sam and I went back to Steele. We were both happy to see the kids, and everything was fine for a few days. I began to notice that Sam was spending money as if there were no tomorrow. I said, "It's not fair for you to have all this money to spend when we don't even have enough for food." He just hollered at me, "You're so goddamn selfish, you're rotten; just shut up and trust me, I'm your husband and I'm in charge of the money." I didn't know how to answer him.

Then I discovered that Sam had almost $1,500. When I asked him about it, he told me it was the allotment money. I asked him how he got it—did a check come to my apartment or was it mistakenly sent directly to him? He just told me, "Shut your stupid mouth. If the military had wanted me to have a wife, they would have issued me one. You're just excess baggage."

I couldn't bear his anger, so I left it alone. I was learning to appease him. At least he was buying food and was kind and loving to me and the kids if I didn't question him.

During his leave, he went to the base almost daily, trying to get reassigned to the states. I remember saying to him, "Why did you cook up this awful scheme? All it's done is make things worse." He just said, "All I get from you is bitching. If you really loved me, you'd do anything. A good wife doesn't question her husband." When word came that he would not be reassigned to the states, he asked for more leave to move his family to Nevada. I really didn't want to move away from my family, but he wouldn't let up on his pressure. He said he wanted me near his family because they would be more supportive than mine. My protests only made Sam angry. Then he'd yell or pout, or do both. Finally, I gave in to him.

I hadn't worked since my hospitalization and was dependent on Sam to take care of us. One day when Sam was gone, the landlady came, demanding the rent money. I had to make excuses and felt very embarrassed. When Sam got home, I asked him for the rent money. His only answer was, "We're leaving before the end of the month and I'll pay her when we leave." A few days later when we came home from some errands, there was a padlock on the door. Again, I felt humiliated, but Sam simply cut the lock off, and we continued to live there. It was very uncomfortable for me because paying my bills had always come first with me. I was relieved that he at least paid a prorated amount of rent before we moved out.

During the last week of June, we set off for Nevada, pulling a U-Haul. My friend Marilyn went with us because she was pregnant and didn't want her family to know. We were on the road for three long, unpleasant days. Besides Sam, me, the kids, and Marilyn, we traveled with my dog, BoBo, and two cats. Every time we stopped to eat, Sam jumped out and left me to take care of the kids and the animals. He was ordering by the time I could get the kids cleaned up to go inside. Once Sam made a quick turn off the freeway without a signal and a semi truck hit the back of the U-Haul. It really jarred us all, and the truck driver yelled, "Hey! Son of a bitch, what the hell ya' doing?" He acted fighting mad, and Sam turned meek. Once we got to Mina, Nevada, my furniture was put in storage while my clothes ended up at Sam's sister's place in Carson City. Sam moved us into an old twenty-five-foot trailer, parked by his parents' house. It was hooked up for electricity but not for water. Although Sam had to leave in a couple of days (around July 4), he treated me awful in front of his family, constantly criticizing me. According to him, I couldn't do one thing right. Once again, I was relieved to see him return to 'Nam.

Living in that trailer, I felt so scared, dumped, and cut off from my family. If it hadn't been for Marilyn, I would have been totally alone. Since I couldn't take the birth control pills while nursing James, I lived through the first month terrified I might be pregnant again. When I got my period and was sure I wasn't pregnant, I had a Dalkon Shield inserted. Sam had refused to take any responsibility for birth control, and an IUD seemed my only choice. This time, Sam had given me $200 in traveler's checks when he left, but he did not sign them. Without his father's help, I couldn't even cash them. "Will he always be so flaky with us?" I wondered. A fear began to grow inside me, one I didn't want to admit even to myself, that I would have to do it all on my own. Clearly, it was up to me to find a place to live, find a job, and take care of my kids.

3

No White Picket Fence

For almost two weeks, Marilyn and I searched for a place to live. Every place we checked in Carson City was too costly. Finally, we rented a small condemned house at the Babbitt Army Depot about 35 miles north of Mina. It hadn't been occupied for seven years. The dirt had blown in and piled up in the corners a foot deep; the windows were sandblasted so badly we could hardly see through them; the house was overrun with lizards and field mice. We spent four days cleaning just to get it up to livable standards.

As always, a big part of my life was writing to Sam. With him in Vietnam, it was easy to push his abuse to the back of my mind and allow the love I felt for him to rise to the surface. On April 23, I wrote,

> "Hi Daddy," I miss you so very much. I want you to know I'll be OK and I won't let anything happen to the kids. . . . We'll be together soon and make a real home for our boys. Words can never tell you how very much you mean to me or the love I feel for you, so all I can say is, You're my world.

I wrote Sam almost every day and lived for his calls, tapes, and letters.

Once we were settled in the house, I looked for work. Marilyn had planned to get a job, but she was really too sick with her pregnancy. She signed up for welfare and I began to receive my allotment checks. Also, we both applied for and received government surplus food.

But I knew this wouldn't be enough. I put in applications everywhere and within a week, I started to work at a casino, the El Capitan, as a change girl. My problem was I couldn't stand the casinos; I lasted one night on that job. Soon I began to baby-sit. I took care of six different kids, but none of them were full-time. Somehow we got along. We weren't cold or hungry. I told myself, "This won't be forever; it's just until Sam gets home." In my mind, my life was on hold until then.

One thing that kept me going was Sam's promise that I could meet him in Hawaii when he went on R & R in September. We had discussed it and agreed that I would use our income tax refund of $327 to pay for my plane ticket and a few new clothes. When the check came, his dad signed it and cashed it for me. I didn't have a second thought about mentioning it to Sam in one of my letters—after all, I shared every detail of my life with him.

In the meantime, Sam had some things in storage at his parents' house and told me to get them out and use them. The main item he encouraged me to use was a stereo system. Marilyn and I had records we wanted to play and looked forward to using the stereo. It was a luxury we couldn't afford otherwise. Marilyn had begun dating an electronics specialist from the base who came and set up the stereo for us. In my letter of August 8, I told Sam, "It only took him about an hour to get it put up, and he didn't have to do anything over so I could tell he didn't hurt it."

Also among the stored items was a hand-carved wooden crucifix about four feet tall from the Philippines. When I unpacked it, I saw that it was too large for a home and that it was badly cracked and split from the desert heat. I repaired it and gave it to Sam's mother, thinking she might want to donate it to the church. I was so proud of being able to repair it that I wrote Sam and told him all about it. All of this "news" about the income tax check, the stereo, and the cross was in my letter of August 8.

About this time, Marilyn, her boyfriend, and I were planning a two-day trip to Disneyland. I checked the mail as we were leaving and was thrilled to receive a new tape from Sam. I took my portable cassette player with earphones so I could listen to Sam's tape in the car without disturbing anyone. It was ninety minutes of viciousness. I sat there crying silently as I heard Sam saying,

> You really blew it this time. Don't never have Dad do something like that again. It really burned me. I'm talking about you having Dad forge my income tax check. . . . How goddamn stupid can you be—you took a piece of religious art and defiled it with man-made glue. It's sacrilege; you contaminated a holy cross. . . . I know I said you could use the stereo, but I wanted to set it up myself. The damage is already done. I never dreamed you'd do something so stupid.

On and on he raved, berating me. I was so crushed that I cried for days. Of course, the trip to Disneyland was ruined for me.

On August 28, I answered his tape by writing this letter:

> It seems I can't talk to you, but one thing I want to tell you. You're wrong, I do love you, I love you so very much that all of this is hurting me. But I won't, I mean it, I won't live with someone who finds fault with every little thing I do. I can live with your faults, but if you can't live with mine, then you'd better grow up. After all the trouble I've had with marriage I know more than you do, you can't expect someone to live their life the way you want them to. I can manage better than you think. I seemed to have done alright finding us a place to live. . . . Sometimes I feel like just picking up and leaving, but I do love you and if there's a chance, I'll try it, but only if you'll try. You're not perfect either.

Early in September, Sam answered this with a phone call in which he ranted and raved again about the cross and the stereo. Then he said I had no right to cash the IRS check, threatening to report me for it. I told him, "Go ahead; your dad cashed it." Worst of all, he told me he had already gone R & R to the

Philippines so "forget about Hawaii." I was so hurt I just knew I couldn't take any more. "We're separated," I told him. "You can't expect to run every detail of my life from where you are."

I stopped corresponding with Sam but decided to stay in Nevada until December, when Marilyn's baby was due. Overall, life was peaceful. I was still fighting female infections, and James's digestive system was super-sensitive. No matter what I fed him, he frequently threw up or had diarrhea. I took him to the base hospital time after time, only to be told he was a colicky baby.

Around the first of October, my doctor decided I had to have a D & C (dilation and curettage) to remove the Dalkon Shield which had embedded itself in the wall of my uterus. On the day of surgery, Sam's mother ran a red light while driving my car, crashing into another car. My car was totaled. When I got out of the hospital, I had no car, no transportation.

At the same time, my milk had almost dried up, and I had started James on formula. James got sicker, with continuous liquid diarrhea. I took him back to the base clinic several times, walking and carrying him because I no longer had a car. The doctors didn't seem to know what to do. Finally, I asked my neighbors for help, and we took James to the emergency room at a hospital in Hawthorne, a town of 4,000 about three miles from Babbitt. He had such a bad ear infection that the doctor punctured both eardrums to keep them from bursting. The doctor said he was dehydrated and had started passing the linings of his intestines. I literally moved into the hospital, staying with James day and night.

After a few days, I received notification from the Red Cross that Sam was on his way home. This was a shock to me because I had told Sam I was separating from him and I meant it. I didn't want him home. I had enough to deal with—recovering from my surgery and taking care of James. I dreaded seeing Sam and immediately felt an added strain. Always an animal lover, I was also grieving over my new puppy, which had to be put to sleep due to distemper.

The next day, I was rocking James when Sam walked into the hospital room. He was icy cold to me and didn't seem at all concerned about James. He simply demanded that I leave with him and go home. As exhausted as I was, I went. I hoped we could talk about our problems. On the way home, I attempted to explain to him how hurt I was about his decision to take R & R in the Philippines when we had planned to be together in Hawaii. He told me it was my own fault, that I had no right to feel that way and no right to cash the income tax check. I ended up apologizing. As far as discussing our other problems, he said we'd talk about that when he came home to stay.

As soon as we hit the door to my house, Sam demanded we go straight to bed. I refused, saying, "I'm not one of your Vietnam whores," but once again he forced himself on me. Almost immediately, I fell into a deep sleep. I woke up at daylight, totally shocked and panicked at James spending the night alone in the hospital. I tried to wake Sam, but he would not get up, so I went to the hospital alone. I prayed things would work out; despite how roughly he had treated me, I clung to the idea that I loved him and he loved me.

I stayed at the hospital that night. James seemed a little better. The doctor had started him on a meat-base formula with no milk. Sam didn't show up at the hospital until the next day. He seemed very happy as he told me he had orders to Hill Air Force Base in Utah. His remaining time was too short to go back to Vietnam. As soon as James was out of danger, I had another type of IUD inserted.

James was barely home from the hospital when the van arrived to move us to Utah. A few times, I tried to talk to Sam about our problems, but he just shouted, "Shut your mouth about it; why do you always have to pick a fight?" Day after day, Sam acted like nothing had ever happened. He never said, "I'm sorry," never mentioned the separation. And I didn't push it. He treated me a bit better, so I held to my pattern of doing anything rather than upset him.

As we started the drive to Utah, I had high hopes for our future one minute and paralyzing fear the next. On the way, one of my cats had diarrhea all over my lap as I was giving James a bottle. Sam went crazy. "You and your stupid fucking animals!" he screamed. We stopped, I changed my clothes, and Sam was silent until we stopped to eat at Windover. Matt didn't want to eat, and Sam made an issue of that. "You're going to eat or else," he yelled. I tried to make peace by saying, "He doesn't feel like eating—it's the middle of the night and he doesn't feel good anyway." Sam just said, "I don't give a damn; he'll eat anyway." Matt whimpered and tried to eat, but he couldn't. As

I felt every eye in the restaurant turn toward us, I was sick with humiliation.

It was hard to keep my hopes up, but I kept thinking I could do something to calm Sam down. It became a twenty-four hour a day job just trying to satisfy him. It didn't matter any more whether I was right or wrong, just as long as I could pacify him.

4

Lord and Master of the House

After a ten-hour drive, we reached the base in Utah, about sixty miles west of Salt Lake City. The weather was cool with a wet, fluttery snow. We checked into temporary living quarters, a house up on a hill overlooking the whole valley. Sam went to check in with his squadron; he was raving mad when he came back because he was told we would have to board the animals.

Once the animals had been boarded, Sam decided it was lunchtime and pulled into an Asian restaurant. He knew Matt didn't like that kind of food, but Sam picked on him, trying to force him to eat throughout the meal. I pleaded with him, "Sam, he's only a kid; it doesn't matter if he eats this food." But he told me straight out, "I'm home now and I'm going to straighten his little ass up; you've got him spoiled rotten." Matt sat there crying quietly, and I shut up. "Just don't make matters worse," I told myself. I tried to believe that Sam was just tense and tired, that somehow everything would work out right. Marilyn seemed very uncomfortable but remained silent. Back in the car, Sam went into his silent "don't talk to me" shell.

All afternoon we looked for housing, but everything was either too expensive (over the limit Sam had set) or Sam didn't like the place. Sam still had all the money and controlled all purchases, including groceries. I felt helpless to do anything other than go along with him. We stopped house hunting that day about six o'clock, but I still had to take care of the kids, cook a big dinner, clean up that mess, and unpack the car. By the time I had finished, it was midnight. But Sam insisted on making love before I could sleep. Since he wasn't abusive about it, I tried real hard to please him.

Sam had to report to his shop for work the next day, and I was totally occupied with caring for the kids and housework. Life settled into a comfortable routine for a few days. Things seemed better between Sam and me, but I had a feeling of walking on eggshells.

The next day, Sam chose an apartment way out in the country near Syracuse, a small town about thirty miles north of Salt Lake City. I didn't want to live out there with two babies and my friend Marilyn almost due to have her baby. We had only one car, which Sam drove, and no bus service. I couldn't get my Utah driver's license because I hadn't had driver's education. Stuck out there, I couldn't even get to school to take the course. So, although the area was beautiful, I felt stranded and isolated. I desperately wanted to work, because I had no access to our money. For most of my life, I had been used to working and the freedom of having my own money. But living out there, my working was out of the question. I couldn't even get baby-sitting jobs. I worried all the time but felt helpless to change anything. During the six months we lived there, I felt like a prisoner. Sam was working a 3 to 11 p.m. shift. Usually he was grumpy if I asked him to drive me anywhere, so gradually, I gave up on any outings except for necessities.

One morning I awakened him at 10 a.m. as we had agreed the night before, to take me for groceries. I was brushing my hair at the dresser when he started screaming and cursing me, grabbed me by the shoulder, spun me around, and slapped me hard across the face. It ran through my mind, "Now he's going to start beating on me as Matt's father did." My feelings were so hurt I didn't feel the pain in my face. I couldn't stop crying, thinking, "How can he do that when I love him so much?"

When I finally stopped crying, I told him, "You better not touch me again; I won't be here if you do." "Well, I won't have to if you just shut your face," was all he said. Before this time, Sam had a habit of hitting me in his sleep. He had explained it as a battle-ready reaction from Vietnam. I had accepted that, but now I began to wonder. Although we were in our bedroom, Marilyn heard all this. Thank God she was there; she was the only comfort and support I had.

Sam was very moody and private. I wasn't allowed to know about our finances or where the money went. I tried to ask him about his work and the people he worked with, but he said he didn't like to discuss work at home. I wanted to meet the other wives, but Sam just blew that idea off. Almost every night after work Sam went drinking with his buddies until 3 or 4 a.m. He always woke up in a foul mood and, after the first time he hit me, he would find some reason to slap me about once a week. It was usually over getting ready to go on an errand; he simply refused to get up and get dressed until he had to go to work. With me totally dependent on him, there was no place I could even get milk without him. I kept telling him I was leaving, but we both knew I didn't mean it. One Saturday as we sat watching one football game after another, I began hemorrhaging. Sam refused to move and I ended up passing my IUD. Even then, he refused to take me in for medical attention. That left me with no birth control protection.

Shortly after Thanksgiving, Marilyn went into labor. We were in the middle of a snowstorm and Sam was at work with the car. After calling him several times, telling him she was in hard labor, I began to feel anxious and angry. When he finally arrived, Marilyn's water had broken, and we got her to the hospital just minutes before her baby boy was born. I was so relieved and happy I couldn't stay mad at Sam.

After Christmas, Marilyn began talking about moving back with her family. Little by little during the months of her pregnancy, she had worked things out with them. She was homesick and wanted to take her baby home. She was also tired of hearing us argue so much. After her baby came, she began staying in her bedroom most of the time when Sam was home. Marilyn and I cried together about her leaving, for we were as close as sisters. With her gone, I knew I'd be totally alone.

In early January, Marilyn's grandparents, who were retired and who traveled a lot, decided to drive out to get her and the baby. Since they were driving directly back to Missouri, they invited me and my boys to ride along with them so we could visit my family. I tried to talk about our situation with Sam—that I was considering leaving him and that my visit to my family would give us a break from each other to help us decide what to do about our marriage. Sam didn't seem upset when we left, so I assumed we were in agreement.

After four days on the road, we arrived in Steele, and I called Sam to check in with him. He didn't even wait to hear about the trip or the boys, but told me he had filed for a divorce in Utah and since I was in Missouri, I'd have to come to Utah to answer or he'd get full custody of James by default. I was stunned. I hadn't decided to leave him; I just wanted a cooling-off period for both of us. In my heart, I had hoped Sam would miss us enough to realize he needed to change.

After this call, I talked to my parents about the way Sam had been slapping me around, but they didn't have much to say, except, "You married him, and your kids need a father, so you live with him." I also called two lawyers in the area and was told I couldn't fight Sam's divorce action from Missouri because I'd resided outside the state too long.

During my week's visit with my family, Sam called every day. Sometimes he threatened me about the divorce, and other times he said how much he loved us and missed us. When he said, "How can you take my baby away from me?" he really got to me. I began to feel guilty, confused, helplessly trapped. Finally, I told Sam I would come back if he would promise to see a marriage counselor with me. He agreed and even promised he would be nicer to me. Most important, he promised never to hit me again. "I realize I have to learn how to be married," he said.

We flew back on a Friday. Sam met us at the plane and he seemed happy to see us, showing affection to me and the kids. He took us straight home and me straight to bed. I felt wonderful, hopeful. But later that day, Sam got irritated and was picking on both the boys. "Can't you do something with that damn kid?" he yelled. His griping increased throughout the weekend and he started slapping me again.

On Monday, I made an appointment to see a marriage counselor over Sam's protest that "we don't need outsiders; that's just a bunch of bull." But I insisted we go because I was constantly fighting a sinking feeling of "here we go again."

Again, I was stuck—no driver's license, no access to a car or other transportation. The only hope I had was that marriage counseling would make a difference.

About a week later, we saw a male counselor. Sam complained that "we can't go anyplace because by the time she gets the kids ready, the baby craps his pants again while she's trying to get ready." The counselor said to him, "Did it ever occur to you that you could change a diaper while she's getting ready?" The counselor also suggested that Sam either allow me to work or give me a household budget. On the way home, Sam ranted and raved about the counselor—"He's no damn good; where did he get a license?" Sam refused ever to go back to that counselor.

I insisted that he keep his promise to go for counseling, so I found another, this time a woman. She made similar suggestions. "Go straight home after work at night and stop putting pressure on your family to be quiet while you sleep all day," she said. She also suggested that Sam cooperate with baby-sitting, scheduling, and transportation so that I could take some classes and get my driver's license. She said that I needed some freedom and some companionship other than the kids and pets. We saw her twice before Sam refused to go back. "Counselors are all full of crap," he said. "Besides, we shouldn't involve other people in our problems."

Without Marilyn there, the abuse got worse. Sam developed the habit of throwing me on the bed and sitting across me while he held my jaws in a viselike grip. Then he'd tell me that he was in complete control of everything, that I had no rights because he worked and I didn't, and that I was nobody. He screamed at me, gritting his teeth with spit flying. He always ended by saying, "Got that." The physical pain was bad, but the mental anguish was worse. I tried and tried to figure out why he treated me that way.

About this time, Sam announced one day that he had accepted an invitation from another couple for an evening out. I was thrilled. We hadn't been out or socialized with anyone for a long time. I gladly arranged for a baby-sitter and we went. I had an odd feeling as soon as I walked into their house. When they offered drinks, I asked for iced tea, which was what they were drinking, but they pressured me to have a "real" drink. I held out for iced tea anyway. They sat and stared at us. Meanwhile, Sam proceeded to get drunk. I felt more and more uneasy and when they began hinting about wife swapping, I asked to leave. When we did leave, Sam confirmed that they had the reputation of "swinging." I was very disappointed; I had hoped to find a friend. Sam was disappointed that I would not cooperate. "What kind of man am I married to," was a thought I couldn't get out of my mind. I felt crushed, dead inside. If I could have gotten away from Sam financially, I would have gone.

Soon after that, Cindy, the wife of another man who worked with Sam, called me saying she wanted to get acquainted, and within two hours, she came out to the apartment. I couldn't believe it because it was about twenty-five miles each way from her house to mine. I was very impressed with Cindy. She wore blue jeans, a sweater, and boots, and she had long straight hair. I felt ridiculous in my polyester double-knit pantsuit, but Cindy didn't seem to notice. She brought her two children, who were about the same ages as mine, so my kids were happy to have someone to play with.

The first words out of Cindy's mouth were, "What the fuck is Sam doing, sticking you out here in the country?" She obviously already knew about my problem with getting a driver's license. She told me about the night school program at Davis Adult High School in Farmington, and she encouraged me to sign up. She said if I would do it, she would take me four nights a week. She had even arranged for a baby-sitter, who she volunteered to pick up and take home. After we talked for awhile, we got in her vehicle and drove uptown. It was my first time to see uptown Ogden, a city of 65,000 about ten miles from Syracuse.

At last I had a friend, and she had opened up a whole new world to me. I was so excited I couldn't wait to tell Sam. His reaction was, "No, you belong at home with the kids; you don't need a driver's license and you don't need to go out."

But I persisted and he seemed to lighten up, mainly to avoid embarrassment with coworkers in his shop. Within days, I was registered for English, science, math, and driver's education.

The first night Cindy came to pick me up, I was wearing a tweed suit and heels. She laughed and said, "They don't dress like that at school," so I changed. Even after I changed, I didn't match Cindy because I didn't own a pair of jeans anymore. Sam had told me so often, "you're too skinny to look decent in jeans" that I got rid of mine.

Going back to school gave me a tremendous boost, and it was challenging. I soon found that I had to study when Sam wasn't around, because he constantly complained and demanded my attention if he thought I was studying. But I was determined he would not stop me this time.

One Saturday, Cindy and I had planned to take the kids to a matinee in Ogden to see *Alice in Wonderland.* Sam was still in bed when we left at noon. I went in, gave him a kiss, and told him we were leaving. He grunted, then yelled, "How dare you take the kids and go off and leave me on a weekend!" Since I had told him about the plan earlier in the week, I was shocked by his reaction. I didn't want to make a big scene in front of Cindy, so I gathered up the kids and we left. We all had a good time; it was nothing fancy, hot dogs, sodas, popcorn.

When we got home about 4 p.m., Sam had the car packed up with his belongings. He announced he was moving into an apartment with a single guy in Ogden. "You've got a lot of nerve running around with that whore," he said, "and I'm not coming back until you straighten up your act." Later I learned that Sam was so determined to end this friendship that he told Cindy's husband "to keep his wife away from me." I didn't say anything, but I resented his double standard. He could go out drinking all night with anybody, but he didn't want me to improve myself or even have a friend. I was apprehensive about how I would pay the bills and buy food for me and the kids but relieved that he was gone.

Sam stayed away for two weeks. He didn't visit me or the kids once during that time. Then one day, he just appeared back at home with his things. "I'm moving back in," he said. I replied, "It's your house." That was the total discussion about that separation. At least, I didn't have to worry so much about the bills with him there.

Throughout it all, Cindy continued to give me encouragement and support. When Sam was gone, I had to depend on her to take me to the commissary to buy food, and she never let me down. Thanks to her, I continued with school and finished up the semester with all As.

At the end of winter semester, Sam went TDY (on temporary duty) to Maine as part of the backup for the space lab. By then, I had my driver's permit, but I still couldn't drive alone. While he was gone, the base called with available base housing. Someone had to come in and sign up for it immediately. I went door-to-door until I found a girl with a driver's license, then went to the base and signed for the housing. Although the housing area was condemned, the apartment was very nice, a two-story with hardwood floors. Our cost was $80 per month. Within a week, we were moved onto the base, about one block from Cindy.

Of course, Sam was furious. He wanted me to refuse the housing, because he didn't want me near other military wives. But I had had enough of isolation and being stranded. Besides, we just weren't making it on his income. Living in base housing was the same as getting a raise, the rent was so much cheaper. Also, at a level I could barely admit to myself, I felt much safer living on base.

My life was definitely improving. I bought a used sewing machine from a neighbor and taught myself to sew. As soon as spring semester started, I went back to school. I bought myself some jeans and started wearing them. After all, I had always worn jeans and enjoyed them before I married Sam. Cindy and I took our kids on more outings—to movies, to parks for picnics, on shopping trips at Goodwill and Salvation Army stores. Sometimes after classes, we stopped by Sam's shop, just to visit with our husbands.

On Valentine's night, Sam and I went out with Cindy and her husband. After dinner, Sam began drinking doubles and his mood turned nasty, mean. He was bitching at everything. I told him, "I'm not riding home with you if you don't stop drinking; you're getting drunk." He slapped me hard across the face in front of everyone. I left the table crying, called a cab, got home, paid the baby-sitter, checked on the kids, and went to bed.

Much later, Sam came in and went directly to the bathroom where he violently threw up until he passed out. I lay in bed wondering what he would do next. When he finally woke up the next morning, he told me I'd better never go off and leave him again. "You spent my hard-earned money on a cab when you could have come home with me," he said. "You had no business telling me to quit drinking, so you got what you deserved. If you have the right to tell me to quit drinking in public, then I have the right to slap you in public." I began to think maybe I was wrong, maybe I should go along more with him. When Cindy called, worried that Sam might have beaten me again, I shared these thoughts with her. She told me I was full of crap, but I still wondered. I resolved to try harder to please Sam, to make our marriage work.

From the night of that incident, Sam's after-work drinking increased. I never knew when he'd come home. Then he'd sleep until it was time to go to work; at times he was late for work. Almost every night, he'd wake me with whiskey on his breath and want to make love. Most of the time, he couldn't. So he began to demand oral sex. This was very difficult for me because I have an easily triggered gag reflex. He seemed to delight in pushing my head down hard and holding it down until I vomited. Then he'd yell, "You goddamn bitch, can't you do anything right? Clean me up." Several times on the weekends, I saw him masturbating in the shower right before coming to bed with me. I just didn't know what to think.

In spite of everything, I finished my spring semester classes with all As again, passed my driver's test, and got my license. Sam was not too pleased with that, and he was even less pleased when I told him I had put in some job applications. He made such a fuss, I gave up on that for the time being.

Sam complained frequently about my best friend, Cindy. We took our kids out almost every day. But Sam wouldn't take us anywhere, and he spent all "his" extra money at the NCO (noncommissioned officers) club. So in spite of his complaints, I would not give up Cindy. Our friendship provided the greatest enjoyment in my life. She had helped me turn my life around.

One afternoon, Cindy and I decided to take the kids to family night at the NCO club. When we walked in, our husbands were there drinking and watching a belly dancer. We walked over to them and they were startled. "What are you doing here?" they asked us. Before I could say a word, Cindy said, "We brought the kids to you; we're going out." Then we left for a couple of hours. When we got home, they were there with the kids—mad and snockered. Sam slapped me around some that night, but by this time, I thought this was normal, not a real beating.

Toward the end of summer, I learned of an Air Force resort area in northern Utah and asked Sam if we could go there as a family for a weekend. He agreed and was even enthusiastic about going. We stayed in a condemned trailer, and there was an outdoor chuck wagon for meals. We fished and hiked around the area, which was awesome. We saw some bear and deer and sheepherders. Sam was loving and fun throughout the weekend. Even the trip back was fun and pleasant. I fell in love again. I told myself Sam had been going through a bad time, adjusting after Vietnam, and that now everything would be fine.

A couple of weeks later, I was cooking supper and pushing potato peelings down the garbage disposal. Sam was standing behind me, ranting and raving about the kids. Suddenly, he grabbed my elbow and shoved my hand down into the running disposal. He held it there as I struggled to get free. I felt all the blood drain from my face and knew I was close to blacking out. When he let go, my hand flopped around a few more times before I got it out. It had cuts all over and the tendon to my elbow was torn.

I had to beg him to take me to the hospital. On the way, Sam told me, "You get me in trouble and I'll fix your face. You get me kicked out of the military and I'll kill you." When we got there, I didn't dare cross him. I told them I had had the water running as I used the disposal and couldn't see what I was doing, that I had gotten my hand too close and the disposal grabbed my hand and pulled it in, that it was accidental. They seemed to believe me; I guess they thought I was stupid. They outfitted my arm with an aluminum brace, then wrapped my hand and arm with ace bandages. The pain was terrible, especially when I had to remove the brace the next day because I was allergic to the aluminum.

I couldn't use my right hand and arm for several weeks, which made my regular tasks very difficult. But my emotional pain was even greater than the physical pain. Cindy was the only one I could tell the truth. She said she knew it anyway and that I had to leave him. How to do that neither of us could figure.

Armed with my driver's license and living on base, I decided in September it was time for me to get a job. When Sam objected, I told him I was just trying to help out and soon got a job at Denny's, working the early morning shift. I had to schedule my working around school four nights a week from 6 to 9 p.m. One of the first things the manager said to me was, "Girl, where did you pick cotton?" He was from Arkansas too and recognized the signs of cotton picking in my hands immediately.

Within a few weeks, I was called to work at a nursing home where I worked with long-term care patients. This job was from 5 a.m. to 3 p.m. four days a week, so Sam took the kids to the nursery each morning that I worked. I picked up the boys each afternoon, fed them, and then was off to school at 6 p.m. When I got home from school, I studied. That semester, I was taking math, psychology, science, and American literature.

Although it was a tight schedule, I enjoyed it, and Sam seemed to drink less. I bought bunk beds for the boys. Until then, James had been sleeping in his playpen and Matt in a double bed. I made fitted bedspreads and curtains for their room, my first big sewing project. I used most of my paychecks to buy these extras, plus all the kids' clothes and most of the groceries. I felt almost reborn during this time.

It was near the end of October when I realized I was pregnant again. I hadn't been to the doctor to confirm it but figured I was about four months along. Sam pushed me to have an abortion, but I felt it would be committing murder and I knew I couldn't live with that. Finally, I went to the free clinic in town to get the pregnancy test. I wasn't surprised when the test was positive. About two nights later, Sam came home drunk and mean. For over an hour, he beat me in the chest, the stomach, and the kidneys. The next morning, I started bleeding and asked him to take me to the hospital. But he took the car and went to work.

I tried to lay still, but I was cramping violently. I crawled to the bathroom and James followed me, patting me on the leg while I sat on the commode. I lost the baby sitting there with blood spattering everywhere. I pushed James out of the bathroom and stood up, my knees shaking so badly I could hardly stand. I looked and saw the baby was formed. Although I'd always wanted a girl, part of me was afraid to see if it was a girl. Quickly, I flushed the toilet before my curiosity got too strong. But I guess I'll always wonder if it was a girl.

When Sam came home that night, I told him I had lost the baby. He just said, "I wanted you to have an abortion anyway." Since I am Rh negative, I needed a RhoGAM shot within seventy-two hours after any miscarriage or delivery to protect any future child. But Sam would not take me, and I was too weak to try to go by myself. I just let it go.

For months, I was so down, depressed, but I had to grieve alone and in secret. Sam refused to discuss it, and I didn't want to make him mad. A few times, I talked about the miscarriage with Cindy, and she was furious. Again, she warned me, "You've got to leave him."

Sam chose this time to move out again, but it was just an excuse for him to party and avoid facing what he had done. He took the car so I had to depend on others for transportation. After about a week, he just appeared at home. I asked if he was home to stay. His reply was, "Shut up. It's my house and I'll do what I please." I shut up because I didn't want to get hit. I tried to hope things would get better. At least, I had my job and school to give me hope.

It was the end of November 1973 that Sam got mad and threw me and the boys out of the house into a heavy snowstorm. I started walking with the kids, and some people gave us a ride to the Clairemont Truck Stop. I called a friend who came and picked us up. Sam didn't know or care whether or not we froze to death. I had no money, but I called my family and they wired me money to fly home. The flight was very scary because the planes had been grounded for twelve hours due to the storm. We watched as they de-iced the plane, and I could see ice hanging from the wings when we landed. All I could think about was where do I start, where do I turn now, how can I get out of this?

I saw my dad's lawyer almost immediately, and he said I had to reside in the state for six months before I could file for divorce. Dad said he would pay for the divorce, so that's what I planned to do. Everything hinged on my getting a job immediately within walking distance of my parents' house since I had no car. The only clothing and possessions I had were what I could pack for myself and the kids in one suitcase.

Sam started calling almost as soon as I got home, telling me he would file for divorce in Utah and get custody of both kids. This time, I thought I could fly back to answer the divorce action if I could get a job quickly. Sometimes Sam would say that he loved me and missed me but that if I didn't come back, he would take the kids away from me. I believed he could do it. I kept looking for a job and stayed with my parents until a few days before Christmas. But I never found a job, and every day, my hopes of freedom from Sam dwindled.

Once again, I gave up and returned to Sam. I got back just in time to put up the Christmas tree and fix a nice dinner. I felt hollow, totally beaten down. There was nothing I could do to get free. Once back, I had no job, no money, and no school; my best friend, Cindy, had moved to Salt Lake City. She too was having marital problems. Sam sat me down and told me, "You will not go back to work, you will not see your friends, and you can't go home again. Now you're going to do what I tell you. Got that."

Then he proceeded to beat the hell out of me. He began punching me in the face and broke out two of my teeth, which I was forced to swallow because he stuffed a towel in my mouth so that I couldn't scream. He punched my face until he busted my lip and broke my nose. Blood drained down the back of my throat causing me to gag and choke. His punches landed on my arms and chest as I tried to hold my arms up to protect my face. He just kept punching away at my head, face, and chest. When I fell, he kicked me in the ribs. When he grabbed a metal lamp and hit me over the head with it, I passed out.

I came to in the bathroom. The door was shut and Sam was sitting there watching me. He said, "I'm going to kill you, bitch," and started punching and kicking me again. I tried to get away from him by climbing into the bathtub, but nothing helped. The kids came to the door, calling out to me, and he told them to go back to bed. This beating went on for more than an hour. At times, he'd stop, lean against the sink, and smoke a cigarette. Finally, he stopped, left the bathroom, and stomped through the house and out the back door.

For about half an hour, I sat there in a stupor, hurting all over and looking at blood splattered everywhere. As I pulled myself up off the floor, I caught a glimpse of myself in the mirror. I couldn't believe what I saw. I washed my face and mouth, then took off my clothes and threw them in the garbage, put on clean clothes, and tried to stop shaking. I had to get cleaned up before I could go in to take care of the boys. They were in bed together, crying as quietly as they could. Matt asked, "Did Daddy do that to you?" I answered, "Yes and we're leaving." I went downstairs, saw the car was there, and knew I'd better hurry. I grabbed some blankets and pillows, a few clothes, and toys for the kids, and we took off.

We drove around all night. There was no place we could go, and no one to call. I couldn't report the beating because if Sam got in trouble with the military, he'd really kill me. I felt I had to stay hidden, afraid that someone might notice how bad I looked and call the police. I tried to keep a scarf wrapped around my face and head.

We lived in the car for three days, buying food and diapers at 7-Eleven stores, using service station rest rooms, and moving the car from parking lot to parking lot, mostly in the bad part of Ogden. We were like fugitives, scared of being found and scared of possible carbon monoxide poisoning from running the car. Of course, the kids were hyper from being cooped up in the car, so a few times, I ventured into parks where they played on the swings and fed the geese.

I kept calling home at times I thought Sam would be there, but there was never an answer. So after three days, I thought it was safe to go home. One neighbor lady saw me coming in with the kids and came over to me. "My God, what happened to you?" she asked. For the first time, I told a stranger the truth about what happened. She went back to her house and got her camera.

As we went into the house, I could smell the soured blood. My neighbor started looking around and taking pictures of the mess. There was some blood in the kitchen, the living room was completely torn up, and blood was splattered everywhere in the bathroom. The metal lamp Sam had used to bludgeon my head was the only thing missing. My neighbor took pictures of me, too, because, she said, "There may come a time when you need these."

This lady stayed with me while I cleaned up the bathroom, urging me to call and report this to the police. "Calling the police will only make it worse," I told her. It was crystal clear to me that I now had no choice, that the only way I would ever be free of Sam was for him to kill me. And it was always in the back of my mind that he would do exactly that. At that moment, I would gladly have killed myself just to get out of the mess, but I still had two kids to raise.

After my neighbor left, I cleaned up the kids and took a shower. Then I lay down with the children and we slept. While it was good to feel warm and comfortable, I was anxious about when or if Sam was coming back. Our dog and cat had been there for the three days, and I could see they had been fed and watered. I knew he'd be back—just not when or in what mood.

Sure enough, Sam came in late that night and acted as if nothing had happened. Neither of us said anything. I was so nervous, I twitched all over. I felt very close to the edge. He gave me a disgusted look, ate his dinner, took a shower, and went to bed. After I was sure he was asleep, I went to bed on the couch.

Next morning, Sam told me the whole incident was my fault, that he wouldn't have to do that if I'd just mind him. What could I say or do? He had all the power.

It was two weeks before my face healed enough for me to leave the house. Sam demanded sex the second night. I didn't fight him, but I didn't help him either, so he started calling me gutter names. For several days, I went around the house in my robe without bathing, hoping I could turn him off that way. It didn't work. Once I told him there was a name for having sex with a dead body. Another time, I asked him, "How can you beat me up one day and expect me to make love to you the next?" Nothing stopped him; he simply called me more nasty names and slapped me. He bruised me by pushing his knees into my groin as hard as he could.

That summer of 1974, I was called home to Missouri because my dad was critically ill. Sam said we couldn't afford for me to fly back with the kids, so he let me drive back. That was a big surprise to me. It was the first time I had ever tried to drive that far on my own. By then, I understood that Sam had to be in control of me and the kids. I also knew that he liked to get rid of us at times so that he could really party.

I stayed with my parents for three weeks. My dad survived, but he was never right again. When it was time to return to

Utah, Sam flew out to St. Louis to drive back with us. He did nothing but complain from the time he landed until we got back. First, he was mad because I hadn't brought the kids to St. Louis so that we could leave directly from there. He kept up his tirade in front of my family. I was completely humiliated that he could be so mean to me in front of others, especially when my dad was so sick. We were on the road for thirty-six hours with no sleep, and he was angry every time we had to stop at restaurants and restrooms. The kids became cranky and nervous from him slapping at them.

For the rest of the time in Utah, Sam's violence was not extreme, just what I had come to accept as normal. Cindy had gotten her divorce and moved away, so I had no close friends left on base. Sam seemed more contented when I had no friends and stayed at home, so I didn't try to make any new friends. In September, Sam got orders for Blytheville, Arkansas. That was my only ray of hope, because I knew I would be near my family again.

5

Going Home Again

It was early November as we left Utah and headed for Blytheville, Arkansas. Already the snow and sleet had started, and miserable weather followed us all the way. At that time, our animal menagerie included one turtle, one rabbit, two gerbils, two finches, two dogs, and one cat. This drive was like most other trips with Sam; he was angry, complaining all the way. But I clung to the hope that things would be better once we got to Blytheville. At least, I'd be near my family.

At first, we stayed with my parents in Steele, Missouri, and I insisted we pay expenses while we lived there. Sam didn't want to live in base housing, but as hard as I searched, day after day, I could not find a house to rent or buy within the first two weeks.

My feelings of anxiety and guilt about crowding my parents were growing when I found a trailer for rent which seemed livable. I called Sam at work to arrange a time for him to look at it that evening. But like most other nights, Sam didn't come home until 11 p.m. He was drunk and in a fighting mood when he staggered into my parents' house. Almost immediately, we began arguing. Then he began choking me. I was gasping for air when my mother opened the bedroom door and saw him. Mom told him, "You'd better get your hands off of her and get out of here." He let me go, grabbed James, and took off in spite of a heavy sleet storm. "Does he act like that all the time?" my mother asked me, and I told her, "At times, worse." We notified the police, who caught him at the state border and escorted him back. James was hysterical when Sam brought him back into my parents' house. Sam just threw James at me and took off again. The next day when I picked up the car, I found an empty wine bottle under the seat, so I knew he had been drinking and driving.

Of course, we missed our appointment to inspect the trailer. When I called the next day, the trailer had been rented. By the time the Air Force called a few days later to say they had base housing for us, I had mixed feelings about leaving my parents' house. On the one hand, Sam didn't demand sex or abuse me as much at my parents' house. But on the other hand, four extra people plus our whole menagerie of animals made it very crowded, messy, and cluttered for my parents. Finally, I decided to take the base housing for my parents' sake.

Once we moved into base housing, Sam let up on the violence, but he still went out drinking with his buddies at least a couple of times a week.

On the days when my dad had bad spells, I went to help my mother as soon as Matt left for school. I also spent most weekends with my family and usually Sam came along. In the spring, I helped put in a large vegetable garden at my parents' house. This boosted my spirits because I've always enjoyed gardening. Just from my share of the crops, I canned 500 quarts of vegetables that year. I look back at this period as one happy time in my marriage.

About once a month, my dad had to be hospitalized for catheterization and at those times, my mother stayed with us. During one of these visits, my mother said to me, "I don't know what he's doing, unless he's trying to drive you crazy. I just saw him put your wrought iron skillet in the linen closet." When I asked Sam about it, of course he denied it. But I tucked this away in the back of my mind. Was he trying to drive me crazy or make me think that I was? It was a very scary thought.

Later in 1975, I had hemorrhoid surgery. My hospital roommate said something about wanting a dog and the next thing I knew, Sam had given her James's dog. When they came to visit me, James was crying his eyes out, heartbroken. Sam had been taking care of the animals while I was in the hospital. It was wet and muddy, and he didn't want to clean up after them. We argued about it, but he couldn't get violent with me right there in the hospital.

When I got home from the hospital, we got into an argument over my friendship with Marilyn. She had developed a drinking problem, and Sam insisted I shouldn't associate with people like that. We went to see a priest for marriage counseling. During the session, the priest told me I couldn't expect to get my marriage together until I quit associating with people like Marilyn. I reminded him of Christ and the prostitute, but he didn't seem to know what I was talking about. This was a recurrent sermon in my church, that as a Christian, you're supposed to help people less fortunate than you and spread the gospel to them. When the priest did not acknowledge my point, I left the session. For months afterward, Sam used that against me; "You don't care about our marriage or you'd do what the priest said. That just proves that all our problems are your fault."

In September 1975, my daddy died. I helped with the funeral arrangements, but I took Daddy's death real hard. Sam called me stupid for carrying on so. About twenty out-of-town relatives came into town, and two of my cousins stayed with us. Sam was at his worst during this time. The night before the funeral, I promised to fix my mother's hair early the next day. The morning of the funeral, I got up early, cooked breakfast, cleaned up the kitchen, and got myself and the kids all ready, but Sam refused to get out of bed. I told him, "I'm taking the car; I have to fix Mom's hair." In front of my cousins, he said, "You take that car and I'll beat the hell out of you." It crushed me to let my mother down, to have to call her and say I couldn't do one simple little thing that would have meant so much to her.

Sam lay in bed all morning, while the rest of us grew more and more frantic. By the time he finally got moving, it was too late to make it to the funeral home so I could see my daddy one last time to say good-bye. We barely made it to the church for the funeral. The music had already started and the church was full as we walked down front to sit with the family.

Everyone went to my mother's house after the funeral. There was lots of food brought in by friends and neighbors. One by one, the out-of-town family left. Matt and his cousin were in the kitchen and spilled something. Sam grabbed Matt and threw him from the kitchen into the bedroom. Matt hit the wall and just sort of slid down onto the floor; he seemed stunned. Sam was yelling and swearing all the while. I was scared that Matt's neck was broken. We told Sam to leave, but he refused until we threatened to call the police. Then he left and this began another separation.

For two weeks, I stayed with my mother. This meant that I had to drive Matt back and forth to school, a fifteen-mile trip each way, every day. Sam kept calling, begging me to come back. But he never apologized. Just the opposite, everything was my fault—I shouldn't have tried to get him up and I should have kept "those goddamn kids quiet." Lord knows, I did everything in my power to keep the kids quiet. If they cried during the night, I'd put my hand over their mouths until we could get to another room, then walk the floor with them until they went back to sleep. It was better than seeing him shake them until their heads snapped or hit the wall. Anyway, Sam kept calling until I gave in and went back again.

In October, during a routine physical at the base, I had a positive result on the tuberculosis test. The base clinic refused to give me a second test, so I went to the public health department; their test brought a negative result. In the South, a test for histoplasmolysis is also given, because that virus is prevalent and damages the lungs. The base had given both tests, one in each arm; then they read the TB results from the wrong arm. They had already started me on some sort of medicine which causes liver damage and made me very nauseous. To my horror, Sam immediately began looking for a TB sanitarium to put me in; he was very disappointed when he found out I didn't have to go. He got so mad that he told me he had put in for a transfer "anywhere away from your fucking family."

In November, the kids got chicken pox, and I was quarantined to the house with the kids for six weeks. Sam moved into the barracks and came by to throw food at us once a week. By the end of the quarantine, the kids had pneumonia and had to have medication about every thirty minutes. Then I came down with pneumonia myself. I called Sam and told him, "You've got to come home and take care of the kids." He came, but he bitched and moaned about it. For two weeks, I was too sick to care.

As I got better, Sam began coming home at bedtime, then leaving to sleep in the barracks. We were supposed to go to a Christmas party, but Sam picked a fight about my dress and went without me. That really hurt me. Still, I pulled myself together and cooked a big Christmas dinner, and we had my whole family over. It turned out to be a very pleasant day, mostly because Sam was so nice to me. After my family left, we made love and I felt like a bride again.

In January 1976, I signed up for two classes at the local junior college. Attending classes gave my spirits a boost. At last, I was working toward a goal, improving myself. But by February, I had another problem to deal with. My Mom looked at me one day and said, "You're pregnant." I was shocked because I didn't think I could get pregnant. At first, I was very upset. I had just had a bone scan for arthritis and had been taking the steroids prescribed for me. The doctors could not tell me whether or not the fetus would be damaged by this. After a lot of investigation, I learned that the damage could be anything from minor to Down Syndrome. I was also concerned about the Rh blood factor and the fact I hadn't had the recommended shot of RhoGAM after the miscarriage.

Sam moved back from the barracks early in February. He was still waiting for word about his transfer. Very shortly after that, he was sent TDY to Denver to cross-train for his transfer. When he left, we still did not know what to do about the baby. I talked to a doctor at the base about my fears. I was shocked by his response. "Your husband ought to kick your ass for asking about an abortion," he said, "and I never said that. This child is yours, whatever it is." I never went back to him, but within days I started to feel the baby move, and I knew I couldn't have an abortion.

Sam was sweet and supportive during this time, but some parts of his letters bothered me a little.

> Dearest Beth & Boys,
> We went downtown Saturday and looked a small portion of Denver over. They [sic] got a bunch of "X" rated movie houses and topless and bottomless clubs. We went to see *Deep Throat* and *The Devil in Miss Jones*. It would have been nice to have had you go with me to see

> it. Who knows, you might even have let me sneak my hand in your blouse or drawers or something. After the movie we went and watched the naked ladies dance. Anyway between the movie and the price of drinks in that club, we spent our weekend allowance.
>
> I miss you so much. It's kinda strange, when we're together, we fight like cats and dogs, but whenever you're not with me, just missing you makes me want to crawl up the walls. I remember when the plane pulled away from the terminal in Memphis, I could see you at the window and my stomach got all tight and I think that if I could have, I would have gotten back off the plane. I didn't like leaving you at all.
>
> So how you been feeling? Are you taking good care of my baby? I think you having the baby is pretty nice. I know that at times you think I'm just another male chauvinist, but I really do appreciate that you are willing to go through everything you do to give me another child. Anyway thank you. I love you very much, and I really do need you to be with me and to love me.

I held onto the loving things his letters said and tried to forget about the porno movies he seemed so interested in. After all, I already had two boys and was pregnant and sick again. I focused on staying healthy myself and hoped everything would work out OK when Sam returned.

Sam got back in early May 1976, with news of reassignment to Langley Air Force Base in Virginia. So almost immediately, I had to start packing. It was very difficult for me to leave my family again. I had hoped the reassignment wouldn't come through until after the baby. I tried to console myself with the thought that Virginia wasn't so terribly far away from my family, that we could have gotten a much more distant assignment. And I tried to believe the violence was over, that our love for each other was worth any sacrifice I had to make.

6

And Baby Makes Five

During the move to Langley Air Force Base in Virginia (May 1976), I had terrible uterine cramps with spotting. Sam had found a place off base in Hampton, a few miles from Norfolk. It was miserable. No air conditioning, high humidity, and constant salt spray from a polluted inland bay. Once there, Sam ignored my physical condition and insisted I help him unload the U-Haul. It was also up to me to unpack everything and maintain the usual routine for the family. Several times I asked Sam to carry in some boxes from the garage so I could unpack, but it was always, "in a minute, in a minute, in a minute." If I pressed him, he'd get very nasty, so I ended up hauling in all the boxes myself.

Sam also put off taking me to a doctor. "Just don't press; wait till I'm ready," he said. It was two weeks after the move before he was ready. The doctor said that my uterus wasn't growing to accommodate the baby and that was causing the cramps and spotting. The doctor was very concerned that I hadn't had proper care after the miscarriage and that just before our move, I had been given a shot of Cafergot for a migraine and high blood pressure. He sent me to the lab for blood work immediately.

The results indicated anemia, low blood pressure, and restricted fetal development. The doctor ordered me to bed to stay, but there was no way I could do that. I was very scared for the health of my unborn baby, but I was more scared of Sam.

During this period, Sam's violence wasn't as severe, but he was cruel and indifferent to me and the boys. He said he wanted the baby, but he acted unconcerned about the physical problems I was having. In fact, if I found a minute to lie down, Sam acted like it was a major inconvenience to him. I painted every room in the house, made new curtains for every window, got the house fixed up real nice, plus made baby clothes and my hospital gowns during this time. Once again, Sam controlled all the money. He even insisted on doing all the grocery shopping, deliberately refusing to buy foods I liked. We lived on beans, potatoes, and hamburger meat. Soon I was diagnosed as having malnutrition to the point that my liver was dissolving to feed the baby. That was just one more concern to add to those I already had about this pregnancy; I could never stop worrying.

Another worry I had about the health of the baby I was carrying is embarrassing for me to tell even now. Although Sam wasn't beating me, he was sexually violent. He was at me constantly, forcefully. I knew I was being raped, but because he was my husband, I thought he had the legal right. During this time, he frequently forced anal sex. "Is this hurting the baby?" I wondered. As a woman, I felt so degraded that I wasn't good enough to have normal sex with him. Inside I was crying, wondering how I could hold back all the pain. Sam saw nothing wrong, so he never said he was sorry for anything. I couldn't think about the future because I knew I was trapped. I looked at the kids I had: one in first grade, one almost ready for kindergarten, and one about to be born. I used all my strength just to meet their daily needs. I just tried to hold on, get through one day at a time, and believe that everything would turn out alright in the end.

In July, Sam surprised me by agreeing we could take Lamaze classes together. This made me feel closer to him, even though he said he would not be in the delivery room. My mom came to be with me about two weeks before my due date, and that was very comforting for me. It was about then that Sam changed his mind and decided to be my coach during delivery. He even arranged to make a movie of the birth. This meant everything to me, sort of muting my memories of his violent and emotional attacks in the past. I went into labor about 5 p.m., September 29, 1976. I had been cleaning house and had a show of bright red blood. I called Sam immediately, but he didn't come home to take me to the hospital until about 10 p.m. My mom and I were getting frantic. By the time Daniel was born the following day at 4:29 p.m., I was exhausted. For awhile, the doctor thought I would have to have a caesarean. For a few hours, Sam left my side to take Matt to a doctor's appointment. When he got back, the baby's head was in position for birth, but the doctor didn't arrive for another forty-five minutes. Sam kept telling me, "Don't push, wait for the doctor, you don't want to tear." Sam was very attentive and I felt closer and more in love with him than ever.

Daniel was a month early and only weighed six pounds. After three days in the hospital, Sam brought us home and I went right back to all my duties. That same day, Sam took my mom and the boys down to see the Freedom Train, while I stayed at home catching up on all the laundry. Mom was supposed to stay on another week, but she said to me, "Sam doesn't like me and doesn't want me here, so I'm leaving." I couldn't deny it, but I felt sad to see her go.

As soon as Mom left, Sam went back to his same old hateful self. He forced sex the night she left and ripped out two stitches. But I had my hands and mind full of taking care of the kids, myself, and the house. It seemed someone was always sick. No matter how hard I tried, I was always treating a fever, an ear infection, vomiting, dehydration, diarrhea, and so on, with one of the kids.

In October, we got word that Sam's brother had died after falling 500 feet in a mine shaft. Sam sat at the kitchen table and proceeded to get drunk while I made arrangements for us to drive back for the funeral. I did all the packing, even strapping the luggage on the luggage rack. Sam wasn't himself and I was scared to death. Looking back now, I wonder where I got the strength to function.

We had to take the longer southern route to Nevada, because of snow and ice in the mountain passes. After we hit St. Louis, I drove the rest of the way, breast-feeding three-week-old Daniel as I drove. It took us four days to get to Mina, and we were there almost a month. During this visit with his family, Sam was verbally abusive and began to slap me around in front of his family. He continued to rape me nightly, knowing that I was not physically recovered enough for intercourse, but also knowing I wouldn't scream. I was still bleeding and had not been checked by the doctor since Daniel's birth. The rapes grew weirder. He seemed angry, slapping and hitting me constantly. Although Sam was more violent during sex, he seemed to finish quicker and I was thankful for that.

When we got back to Virginia, the kids and I had a very bad winter—sick constantly. The house we lived in was cold and drafty. Because of a gas shortage, the gas lines were shut off at night, leaving us without heat. One night, I saw a rat as big as a cat in our bedroom. When the landlord finally got around to this problem, I was horrified to learn from the exterminators that these were wharf rats, carrying deadly diseases. About this time, I had a third IUD inserted. So many things in my life were so wrong, I just couldn't chance another pregnancy.

In early December, I contracted pneumonia again. It was then the doctors discovered that my liver and spleen were enlarged, and they did extensive testing, including a liver scan. They finally decided I had had mononucleosis and hepatitis at some time, which had led to spleenomeglia. I was jaundiced, so they took blood tests every two weeks for a few months. I was never contagious, but I was throwing up bitter bile and was too weak to do anything.

In January, Daniel became so congested he couldn't breathe. He was hospitalized on base and placed in a croup tent. He stopped breathing altogether once. At first, the doctors diagnosed him as having bronchitis, then they changed it to asthma. I was still very ill, and the doctors were considering hospitalizing me for more tests. So when Sam suggested inviting his sister to come and help out, I agreed. Up to this point, there had been no serious incident since we moved to Virginia. Sam would slap or push me occasionally, and the verbal and sexual violence were constant, but I had become numb to that treatment. Health problems—my own and the kids'—took most of my energy and attention.

Sam's sister arrived sometime in March with her two-year-old son. Almost simultaneously, we got notification of available base housing. Right away, I saw that Sam's sister would be no help to me. Her presence just meant I had two more people to wait on. She sat up all night watching TV or reading and then slept all day. During the move, she was just in the way. In fact, she was worse than in the way. Sam took me into our bedroom and beat me one morning because I hadn't fixed his sister what she wanted for breakfast. My kids told me later they could hear me screaming while Sam's sister stood in the hallway with her ear to our door.

One day soon after the move, Sam and I went to pick up a second car he had bought and left his sister to take care of the kids. When we got back, James, then age five, was missing and Sam's sister was asleep on the couch. We looked everywhere for him before calling the base police. We grew more and more worried because we lived near a large reservoir. The police searched unsuccessfully for two hours. When they asked for a piece of James's clothing, I fainted.

With the use of two bloodhounds, they found James asleep in some bushes beside the reservoir. I was furious and screamed at Sam, "Get her out of my house." He refused, saying, "This is my house and I'll do whatever I want. I will not tell my sister to leave." I couldn't believe it.

Again, I took the kids and went to my mom's. By this time, it was May. I put in job applications everywhere, but I could not find a job. More and more, Daniel seemed to have difficulty with his breathing. Of course, this made my mom very nervous about watching him.

Sam kept calling, alternately begging me to come back and threatening me if I didn't. So after the kids' school was out, I drove back to Virginia to find Sam's sister still there and the house in chaos.

I had started hemorrhaging vaginally during the drive back and was too sick to care what was going on around me. When I went to the emergency room, X rays showed that my third IUD had punctured my uterus and a peritoneal infection had developed. With me flat on my back in bed, Sam expected his sister to pitch in and take care of our three boys. Oddly enough, she flew home the next day.

As soon as I was on my feet again, Sam went back to his same old abusive pattern. I didn't even mind being pushed around or slapped anymore, as long as he didn't hurt me too badly.

In July 1977, Sam went TDY for a month to Denver. I was thankful for the peace and quiet I had with him gone. The kids and I went to the base daily to tend our garden. That was one nice thing about Langley; they had garden plots and I had planted my favorite vegetables.

The tough part of Sam's absence was no money. After I brought the kids back from Missouri, Sam didn't allow my name on the checking account. He had supposedly provided for us by signing a few checks before he left, but his checks bounced. It got so bad I had to use rolls of pennies to buy milk and bread. When I told him the checks were bouncing, he said there was some mistake and that he'd take care of it. On top of that, I constantly got notices and calls from Sam's bill collectors. He never paid the bills when he went TDY. Still, he wrote me loving letters that kept me going.

> Dearest Beth: Hi! I've been sitting here for about 3 hrs trying to write you this letter. All I can think of is how much I love you and how much I wish I were with you now instead of trying to write you a letter. I miss you very much. I think I'm becoming more and more aware of how much I really do love you.

At times, I was overwhelmed with a bittersweet feeling—torn between wanting to believe that he loved me and the kids, but at the same time, doing without the bare necessities and remembering the beatings. It was particularly hard for me to see the kids do without food and clothes.

After Sam's TDY was done in Denver, he announced he was going to visit his folks in Mina, Nevada. I accepted that, even though it was difficult to understand. Later on, I found receipts from his vacation trip to Las Vegas during that time, including several nights at an X-rated motel. How it hurt me to see that Sam felt free to party while his family almost starved.

Usually when Sam came home from a TDY, we had a honeymoon period, but this time he couldn't stop talking about the sex shows he had seen on Colfax Avenue while in Denver. He seemed even more obsessed with oral sex, constantly nagging me, "If you loved me, you'd go down on me every day." I pleaded with him, but he was much more aggressive after this trip. He would force me in the mornings, then go back to sleep while I took care of the kids, getting the two older boys off to school, feeding and bathing Daniel.

Soon after Sam got back, I started working, cleaning people's houses and baby-sitting. Sam made me feel it was some kind of privilege for me to work, so I gladly juggled my schedule to accommodate him. I breast-fed Daniel when I was home and pumped out milk into bottles so that Sam could feed him when I was at work. I also prepared baby food from scratch so that Daniel's allergies wouldn't be aggravated by salt, sugar, or additives. I'd get home from work about 2:30 p.m., thinking Sam would be ready for work and Daniel cared for, only to find Daniel wet and dirty and Sam still in bed with the drapes drawn. More times than not, Sam gave Daniel regular milk or formula, ignoring the special bottles and food I had prepared for him. This really hurt me because I was trying to give my baby something of me. Instead, both Daniel and I missed out on the benefits of breast-feeding, physically and emotionally.

One afternoon, I got home to find Daniel sick on the floor beside our bed, nearly unconscious. He had thrown up and his face was laying in the vomit. Looking closer, I saw that he had eaten several unfiltered cigarettes. For once, Sam got up when I asked him, and we took off for the emergency room. On the way there, Daniel quit breathing. I started CPR on him, and he threw up in my mouth. His heart didn't stop, but I had to start his breathing several times. Daniel was placed in intensive care immediately. He was given a charcoal treatment and put in an oxygen tent to counteract the tobacco poisoning. It was such a relief to know Daniel would be OK. But imagine my shock when, in front of the doctors, Sam said, "If you'd been home where you belong, this would never have happened. You don't have to work and I've never wanted you to work." I was furious and for once, I talked back. "I do have to work; God knows, I don't enjoy scrubbing other peoples' toilets. But you're not making a living. What you do make, you don't share with us." I was dressed in old jeans, a loose shirt, and a bandanna on my head since I had come to the hospital directly from work. I stayed there all night and went to work again the next day in the same clothes. The day after that, Daniel was given oxygen and transported by ambulance with full sirens and lights to King's Daughter Hospital in Virginia Beach. A female doctor rode with us and radioed ahead to the hospital to arrange a life support system for Daniel.

After this incident, I began taking Daniel to work with me. But it wasn't a week later before Daniel was sick again. This was his first major asthma attack. He was in intensive care with his own private nurse, and we could only see him fifteen minutes of each hour. His breathing and his heart stopped several times the first night. The doctors told us they had never seen asthma this bad in a child so young. During the fall and winter of 1977, Daniel had to be hospitalized so many times I lost count. Once I hadn't even taken off his hospital identification bracelet before he had to be hospitalized again.

In March 1978, my brother's wife told me about LaBoners Children's Hospital in Memphis, Tennessee, for acutely ill children. Their son had been treated there. It took all my money to pay for the flight, but I've never regretted taking Daniel. We were there one week. During that time, I was hungry because I had no money to buy food, and I slept sitting up in a chair. The important thing was that at last Daniel was getting proper treatment. Daniel was put on Crawford's Solution and maxi-mist treatments every four hours. They taught me how to administer these treatments and how to drain his lungs by cupping him on the back. Once he was on this program, he began to improve dramatically.

I took Daniel to my mom's in Missouri until Sam could get there to pick us up. When Sam arrived with Matt and James, he was already fighting mad. He complained about Daniel's treatment plan and all the attention I had to devote to him. Mom told him he should be glad we had found an effective treatment for Daniel, but Sam didn't listen.

The drive back to Virginia was hell. Sam was ranting and raving all the way. We drove straight through, taking about twenty-four hours. April 6 was my birthday, but I got no card, no gift, not even "Happy Birthday, Hon." Even worse, Sam didn't take the boys to buy cards or gifts for me either. I really missed that.

Sam was up for reenlistment and as usual snubbed me about going with him to the base. All the other wives attended reenlistment with their husbands. The military made a big deal of it, recognizing that the whole family was reenlisting. They even took pictures and published them in the base papers with stories about the families. Sam didn't behave like the other men. Instead he cut us out of his life. I was terribly hurt; after all, I had contributed a lot of time, energy, and sacrifice into supporting his Air Force career. I remember sitting in the bathroom, hugging myself, rocking back and forth, patting my own head, just trying to comfort myself from the pain of his total disrespect. About a week later, we took Daniel for a checkup with the nurse practitioner on base. Sam was holding Daniel and when Daniel reached up and pulled his glasses off, Sam slapped him hard. When I protested, he called me a vicious little bitch, yelling so loud that the spit was flying. Not one person on the hospital staff moved to intervene. While Sam went to get a prescription filled, I got the kids together and took them home, leaving him there. About an hour later, he came home and started knocking me around and pulling my hair out by the handfuls, but he couldn't do it very long because he had to go to work.

I knew Sam would continue the fight when he got back, but I had no place to go. I put special effort into cleaning up the house and cooking a big dinner so at least he wouldn't get mad about that. I might as well have saved my energy. Sam came in from work about midnight and started all over again. I asked him why he was doing this when he knew how tired and run down I was. He said, "Because I caught you at your lowest point; I can beat, defeat you now." The hair pulling hurt me terribly because I had kept my hair long for him all the years of our marriage. It was a lot of work to take care of, and I had asked him about getting it cut. He always threw such a fit that I never did. That night, when I thought he was finished, I went into the bathroom and started cutting my hair off. He opened the bathroom door, saw what I was doing, grabbed me by the hair, and dragged me into the kitchen. He threw me on my back on the floor, straddled and pinned me, and continued to punch and slap me. Matt, then age eight, woke up and came into the kitchen, begging Sam to stop. It distracted Sam long enough for me to reach the phone to try to call the police. But Sam knocked Matt away, pinned me again, and pulled the cord out of the wall. Then he proceeded to beat me in the head with the receiver and choke me with the phone cord, all the while sitting on me.

Somewhere in this fight, he grabbed the middle finger of my left hand and bent it back until I heard it crack. The pain made me so sick, I threw up.

I knew I was in for a long siege when Sam ordered Matt to get him an ashtray and a pack of cigarettes. He had done the same thing in Utah. Matt obeyed, but he kept hollering at Sam to get off me until Sam got up, grabbed Matt by the shoulders and took him off into the boys' bedroom. I was terrified that he would hurt Matt, so I went into our bedroom, got the pistol, came back, and pointed the gun at Sam, telling him to let Matt go. Sam let Matt go, then walked over to me, laughing as he came, and grabbed the gun away from me. Sam took the gun, went back into our bedroom, and I didn't see it when he came back out.

By this time, James had awakened and I was trying to comfort him and Matt. Sam didn't say a word, just grabbed a pack of cigarettes and left the house. Once the kids had quieted down, I fixed up a bandage for my broken finger with Popsicle sticks and masking tape.

About two hours later, Sam came back, bringing two military police with him. They came in with their guns pointed at me. I didn't know what to think. From their questioning of me, I learned that Sam claimed he had left the house under direct threat. When I told them what had happened, they didn't believe me. They called for reinforcements to conduct a search of the house for the gun. With a whispered clue from Sam, they found the gun in our bedroom. Then they informed me I was under arrest. They refused to allow me medical attention but did call the nurse practitioner when I told them I was afraid to leave the kids with Sam. They not only wouldn't let me press charges against Sam for battery, they didn't even write down what I said. The nurse practitioner ordered the MPs to bring me to the hospital. They ignored that order. She also ordered them not to leave the kids with Sam, so they called social services. Daniel had awakened during this commotion, and I had started to give him a maxi-mist treatment when the MPs jerked him from my arms and double-locked handcuffs on me with my arms behind my back. I tried to grab my purse, but they jerked me away, refusing me that small dignity. Matt and James were screaming, "my Momma, my Momma," as they threw me into the police car. The MPs seemed to take great pleasure in telling me my kids were going to a foster home, and of course this made me frantic. I was forced to sit on my hands, broken finger and all, throughout the seventy-mile ride to Richmond State Mental Hospital.

All I could think about was, "What's going to happen to my kids?" I couldn't comprehend how the MPs could do this to me. Sam's vicious words kept ringing in my ears, "I've got you now, you bitch; I'll get you put away real good." I was crushed that someone I loved, the father of two of my children, could treat me like this, and I was scared to death.

When we got to the hospital, I was forced to sit in the waiting room for what seemed like hours. Then I had to go through a physical exam, including a pelvic and rectal. I asked for medical attention for my broken finger and was refused. I asked for something to ease the pain and was refused.

After the exam, they walked me outside to another building. I had on house slippers and lightweight clothes, no jacket. The weather had turned cold, and it was drizzling rain. My feet were soaked, and they put me in a dank, drafty cell which had nothing but a dirty, bare mattress on the floor. It was freezing cold, and I never got warm the whole time I was in that hospital. The smell was so bad, I looked around and could see feces on the floor. I stood until they let me out the next morning. I was then taken to a dormitory with about twenty other women. I was bewildered by the screaming, crying, and hollering which surrounded me. When they marched us down to breakfast, I couldn't eat. I asked for a cigarette but was told I had to provide my own. Since the MPs had not allowed me to bring any personal belongings, not even my purse, I had no money. I felt totally alone—helpless and hopeless.

After breakfast, I watched the others fighting themselves and talking to people who weren't there. I just got more frightened by the minute. Then I noticed a black lady who kept looking at me. When we made eye contact, it was as if we each understood the other and the nightmare we were living. Finally, she came over to me and said, "You're not crazy and neither am I, but I am scared of these other loonies." As it turned out, she had been severely abused by her husband, and she had five children who had been taken to her in-laws. It was soothing, comforting to talk with her.

The psychiatrist who did mental status exams only made rounds there one day a week. Lucky for me, he came the next day. He saw me, recognized the abuse, told me that I wasn't crazy and that abusive men frequently try to get rid of their wives by having them committed.

The following day, I had to go before a review board for a mental status hearing. Sam showed up for that, and when they brought me in, he began raging. They asked me a few questions and told me I was released. Sam protested that I needed to be checked further, but the psychiatrist told him he needed to be checked and dismissed him. Sam stormed out of the hospital, and I had to call the young couple for whom I baby-sat to bring me home. The nurses were much nicer to me after the hearing and actually gave me some Tylenol while I waited for my ride.

In spite of hurricane warnings, these almost-strangers drove seventy miles each way through the storm to pick me up. We got to my house only to find the electricity was out, so I had no lights or heat. As soon as they left, I got out some candles and started cleaning up the mess from our three dogs, which Sam had locked in the house. I put some paper down for them in the bathroom because they were too frightened to go out in the storm. Then I started making calls, trying to get my kids back. Since it was after 5 p.m., I was told nothing could be done until morning. I was worried about Daniel getting the medication he needed but could do nothing about that either.

At first, I was scared to death that Sam would come back, but when I called the military police to try to press charges, I was informed that Sam's commander had ordered him to stay in the barracks and away from me. That eased my mind a little, and I had the dogs in the house with me, but still I could not sleep that night.

The next day, the electricity was still out, the phones were out, and the streets were flooded. I had no car and was so anxious—wanting to get the kids home, but knowing I had to wait until phone service was restored. So I got busy, going through everything that the kids and I possessed. I put together five or six bags of clothing and blankets as donations and left them on the side of the porch. Late that night, a man called me anonymously. He told me that he knew Sam, he knew what I was going through, and the best thing I could do was to get my kids and get out. I was sitting there in the dark, still no electricity or heat. His call chilled me to the bone. One part of me believed I could get away. The other part knew there was no way. At least I knew the phones were working, so I didn't feel quite so alone. The following day at 8 a.m., I started calling again, making arrangements to get the kids home. I answered a knock at the door to find an MP. He told me my neighbor had complained about my dogs messing on her lawn, and he asked to see my ID. I looked for it in my purse, but Sam had taken it. The MP tried to arrest me for being on base without authorization. I kicked the door shut and locked it, then called the social worker. She told me to stay inside and not to open the door until she got there. When she arrived, she and the MP came in together, and in the face of her authority, he backed down. That afternoon, the York County police arrested Sam, and he was in jail two hours until his commander got him out and confined him to the barracks.

I picked up the car while Sam was in jail, and it was arranged for me to meet the social worker at a mall the next morning to get the kids back. Daniel was in the middle of a full-fledged asthma attack, so I had to take him straight to the hospital. While there, I had my finger x-rayed. It was broken and the knuckle was pulled out of its socket. As soon as we finished at the hospital, we went home, packed up the car and left. We spent the night somewhere in Tennessee, but I didn't sleep all night because Daniel needed so many treatments.

Once again, I sought refuge with my family. From the beginning, I had a problem because of Daniel and his need for a sterile environment. The Jaycees provided an air purifier for him but he still had severe attacks.

For a few days, I thought Sam was going to leave me alone, that I had finally gotten free. I was able to get a job at the nursing home, and I planned to work nights. But the day before I was to start work, Momma panicked and said she was too scared to watch Daniel because of his attacks. Then Sam started a barrage of calls—one minute begging me to come back and the next minute threatening me—the same old pattern once again. He said he had gotten orders to Denver, and we could start all over. I didn't realize it at the time, but he didn't want me to come back to Virginia because of the pending charges against him. Without me there, they couldn't prosecute him. He did get a subpoena addressed to me, but I never knew it until ten years later.

It was then I gave up hope I could ever get away from Sam. There was nothing to do but go back to him. He packed up our belongings in a U-Haul and drove from Virginia to St. Louis. He called me from a motel and I met him with the kids.

On the way to meet him, I tried to prepare myself to avoid any confrontation, to swallow my questions, to shut off my wounded feelings. He seemed glad to see us, and once I got the kids settled down, he demanded sex. I felt disgusted, but I submitted. Evidently, he sensed my distance and asked me about it. I told him, "I don't think things will ever be right between us again unless we resolve what you did to me." He refused to discuss it. After that, I didn't believe anything he said. I felt doomed as we started off for Denver. I just prayed I could hang on long enough to get my kids raised.

7

Rocky Mountain Lows

The drive to Denver was not pleasant. At one point in Kansas, Daniel got so sick we had to take him to an emergency room. At least when we arrived in Denver, base housing had an air conditioner which helped filter the air, and Daniel improved right away.

As soon as we had settled in, we went to visit Sam's family for a few days. Then Sam and I went to Las Vegas for four days. I tried my best to enjoy it, but I had to go to an emergency room with a migraine. They gave me a shot of Demoral, which made it difficult to stay awake. Sam was acting very loving, and I soon found out why. He insisted on checking us into an adult motel. He kept waking me up, wanting me to watch *Deep Throat.* I had already told him that if he wanted that kind of sex, he should do it with someone else. Those kind of movies just turned my stomach. I remember this as the last time Sam was nice to me, even if he was fooling me.

After we returned to Denver, things got back to normal. With the move to Denver, Sam was promoted to an instructor position and acted even more like a dictator at home. He controlled the family and the money. We opened a checking account together, but true to his pattern, after a couple of months, he closed it. I couldn't buy groceries at the commissary without him to sign a check.

That winter of 1978, I worked for the Denver Personnel Services as a nurse's aide. Although we had two cars, I was not allowed to drive, so my schedule had to revolve around Sam's taking me to work. It was very difficult, because again Sam refused to help with anything at home. I'd try to sleep off and on during the day, but Daniel was so active that was almost impossible. When I mentioned this to my mom, she suggested I pin him to me while I slept. I'll never forget waking one day to find that Daniel had unpinned himself and pinned me to the bed. He had climbed up on the dresser and was throwing my glass whatnots onto the bed. What a picture! I couldn't help laughing.

Matt and James came in from school at 3 every day, so I had to be up by then. I always cooked a big dinner for the family, and Sam would say, "Lie down for a couple of hours; I'll do the dishes and put the food away." It sounded nice, but he never did it, so I just stopped trying to get a nap before work. There were times when I'd stay up two or three days without sleep.

One night in the fall, I fled with Daniel to a women's crisis shelter in Aurora, Colorado. Sam had been hitting me pretty hard. I left Matt and James with him because of his threats. I had to take Daniel because he was still breast-feeding. After two nights, I went back and got Matt and James. Matt had a black eye, and the shelter reported Sam for child abuse. I was terrified when they filed the report because they could not give me any assurance of protection or of even being allowed to stay in the shelter more than a couple of weeks. An investigator went out with the police to question Sam and bought his story that Matt got hit in the eye with a softball.

Of course, I caught hell when my time at the shelter ran out and I had no place to go except back to Sam. He told everyone that I had tried to ruin his career. I found that ironic, considering all the lying I'd done to cover for him throughout our marriage. Sam started in on me as soon as he got home from work, grabbing me, hitting me in the head, and pushing me down on the floor, swearing and calling me vile names all the while.

Around the first of December, I got so worn out I quit my job and stayed home. The rest of that winter, I stayed at home, doing alterations and ironing clothes for other people. I also made some dough art and Christmas ornaments that were sold in a gift shop on consignment. In the spring of 1979, I started baby-sitting again. Somehow I found ways to make money because I had to.

Sam seemed less violent when I stayed in the house and saw no one outside the family. We still had verbal fights and frequently Sam would move into the barracks. To me, that was a joke, because Sam came back to the house, slept with me, and ate my food whenever he wanted. His absences were pleasant in spite of my suspicion that he was seeing another woman. Later, I found out that he was carrying on with one of his female students during this time.

Sometimes I wonder if there was something bad about the month of April because in April 1979, Sam erupted as he had in April 1978. At one point, he had me in the closet, banging my head on the sliding door frame. Evidently, neighbors called the police, who came and arrested him. They could see that I was injured. I heard the female MP say to Sam, "Shut your mouth; I'd like nothing better than to slap you down on the floor and handcuff you." They took me to the hospital, where I was diagnosed as having massive contusions. The night of his arrest, Sam refused to make a statement to the police. He waited until the next day to think up a good story. In his statement, Sam said that I had gotten tangled up in my clothes while packing, and bruised myself when I fell. The police bought his story, but Matt and James remember Sam dragging me down the hall and beating me as he sat on me in the living room. This was just another instance of Sam getting away with no consequences.

Things settled down again and in July, I took the kids and drove home for a visit with my family. Sam chose not to go, but he did not object to our going. It was wonderful to be free of him for a few weeks and to see my family and friends.

Everything got bad again toward the end of September, and Sam moved into an apartment with another military man. Then in November or December, Sam started divorce proceedings. I was shocked when I was served with divorce papers. I sold just about everything I had to raise $250 to retain a lawyer, but my lawyer did nothing except ask me for more money. Realizing I couldn't count on him, I finally called Sam and told him I wouldn't agree to his terms; he wasn't going to provide for me or the kids. He came over and gave me another beating. For some reason though, he dropped the divorce action and got a legal separation. He also got a restraining order that prevented me from leaving the state with the kids.

Nothing really changed. Sam still came around as he pleased. He seemed to get more and more violent with sex and to need more and more of his "sex toys." He had some stuff he called "rush," which came in capsules. He popped one under my nose one night and I nearly had a heart attack. I didn't know what hit me. He had a key to the house, so I never knew when he would come in, but it was usually in the middle of the night after he was drunk. He would tell me how my body belonged to him, that he could do anything with it any time he wanted, and that I'd better not forget it. He'd pick fights and once rammed his fist through my front door. When he left, he paid the rent, but he gave us no money for food. I tried to get welfare but couldn't because he paid the rent. We were so hungry, and once again, I got government-surplus food—powdered milk, rice, farina, oatmeal, canned luncheon meat, dried beans. Matt and James had free breakfast and lunch at school, which helped. This was all we had for two months until I could get food stamps. The food stamps helped a lot, but I had to sell things out of the house to buy soap, washing powder, toilet paper, and so on. On Thanksgiving morning, a neighbor brought us some real food, then took us to her house for Thanksgiving dinner. Matt and James had been crying because we didn't have a turkey, so the dinner really lifted our spirits.

Again, it was a desperate situation for me. I knew I had to get some kind of work, but I couldn't find a sitter I could trust to take care of Daniel. After a lot of consideration, I decided to run an ad in the base paper for baby-sitting.

Sam found out about it and came storming over, saying he'd report me for baby-sitting on base without a license. Evidently, he did, because suddenly military officials started checking on all of us who were baby-sitting. Before that, there had been no trouble.

It was through this ad, however, that I met a good friend of mine, Esther. She called one day to see if we could trade with each other whenever one of us had an appointment or emergency.

This worked out very well. She had four children she sat for and so did I. Naturally, Sam hated her from the beginning and treated her rudely whenever he ran into her. He didn't carry his constant pressure on me not to see her as far as he had with my other friends, probably because her husband was an officer.

One evening out of the blue, one of Sam's coworkers called me and started pouring out his problems. He asked if he could bring a six-pack of beer and come over. I told him no, in no uncertain terms. To me, it was clear that Sam had put him up to this, because Sam had bragged to me that he'd get me in court. "I've got friends that will testify you've slept with them," he said. I told him, "They would have to be real good friends to lie in court and stupid to boot."

During this time, I had surgery on my nose to correct the sinus problems I was having stemming back to the beating in Utah, when Sam had broken my nose. Surprisingly, Sam agreed to baby-sit during that week, but I had to give him the money I was paid for that week.

I should have known better than to trust him, because he picked an argument a few days after I got home from the hospital. My nose was still packed and had a plaster cast across it. He doubled up his fist and hit me one blow right on the cast. I fell to the floor, crying and vomiting. Later, when I went back to the doctor to have the cast removed, I told him I was climbing up to get a book off a tall shelf and dropped one of the books on my nose. I knew better than to tell the truth. Too many episodes in the past had proven to me that no one could or would stop Sam. It was better for me not to make waves. The doctor said that my nose had slipped off the cartilage as it was healing, so the outcome was that my nose was still broken, only now it was pushed to the left side of my face, and that's where it healed.

At the suggestion of my friend, I began to see a psychiatrist. I was so down on myself, feeling that I was nothing without Sam. Sam kept telling me he had me where he wanted me and that he'd keep it this way, claiming us as dependents so he could get quarters and benefits, but with the freedom to use me and run around all he wanted. He also said that when he got orders out of Denver, I'd have to move with him in order to keep the kids. "I control everything," he'd tell me, "Who would believe you—I'm smarter and better educated. You're nothing, a nobody."

The psychiatrist helped me feel better about myself. He told me that if everyone had an attitude like mine, the prisons would be empty. He suggested that I dress as if I were going to one of the most important meetings of my life and take myself out to dinner. I began to wear makeup and pay more attention to the way I dressed. He assured me that I didn't have to accept Sam's control and criticism.

In June 1980, Sam got his way. The base issued a restraining order against my baby-sitting. This took away our food money, pushing me and the kids to the starvation point. I couldn't pack up and move off base because I had no money to pay for off-base housing. I couldn't take the kids and go to my family because of the restraining order preventing me from taking the kids out of state. When I got the notice that I had to give up base housing because of the legal separation, I decided to leave the kids with him and went to stay with my friend Esther. I talked to the kids every day by phone when Sam was at work. According to them, their dad wasn't handling the situation very well. They told me over and over how afraid they were. I was so torn I didn't know what to do. After a few days, I was so worried and missed the kids so much that I decided to flee the state with them in spite of the restraining order. Esther went with me to pick up the kids, and it turned into another big scene.

Sam called the police and hit me in front of them, but for once, the police supported me, allowing me to take the kids. During the few weeks with my family, I had to hide the kids. I knew there was a warrant for my arrest because my brother, a police officer, saw it, but the local sheriff ignored it. Sam constantly threatened me and my family, but since my mother had moved and he didn't know her new address or phone number, he couldn't get me on the phone. Every few days, I called him from a pay phone, not telling him where I was. Finally, he said he had had the restraining order removed, and he agreed that if I would come back, he would not have me arrested.

Early in July, I brought the kids back by bus. Sam seemed cooperative at first. He allowed us to stay in his apartment while I looked for a place to live. Through friends, I met Mary, a young woman with two small children, and we decided to share a place. We agreed from the beginning that she would not have men spending the night at our house, and in exchange, I agreed to baby-sit for her if she wanted to spend the night away, provided it wouldn't be every night. I found a nice house in Aurora for $400 a month, and the lease was in my name, so for the first time since marrying Sam, I felt I had some control over my living situation.

Mary and I got along fine. I received enough from welfare to pay my part of the rent and utilities. I also got food stamps and Mary got WIC (aid for Women, Infants, and Children), so we had enough to eat. She was studying to be a nurse, so she didn't go out during the week. I took care of all the children during the day, as well as the cooking, laundry, and housework on weekdays. During one two-week period when Sam took our kids to visit his family, I worked at a nursing home, so I made some extra money then. Sam was supposed to pay me $200 a month for child support, but most of the time, he threatened me into signing a receipt stating that I had received it when I hadn't.

In the fall of 1980, things were better between Sam and me because I just went along with whatever he said. If I tried to disagree or protest about anything, he'd tell me he was in charge, that he was head of the house, and this applied whether or not he lived there. Since he wasn't around all the time, it was easier to let things go.

That's the way I handled it when some friends told me Sam had gotten his Tech Sergeant stripe. They knew because they had been at the beer bust celebration. Sam had never mentioned it to me, and I was terribly hurt. In the military, getting the big T sewn on is almost like passing the bar. When I brought it up with Sam, he told me I had no part of his getting the stripe or of his career. I told him if he felt that way, he should let me and the kids go back to my family and have a life of my own. He just repeated his usual threat, "If you want to stay with the kids or even see them, you'll stay wherever I'm stationed." We didn't have a big fight over this. I just let it go.

Early in November 1980, trouble started with Mary, my roommate. Sam and I and all the children were sitting in the living room watching television one evening when Mary came in with a man and took him right upstairs to her room. Immediately, Sam said to me, "You'd better find out what the deal is, her bringing a man in here in front of the kids." I went upstairs and asked her what was going on. She was high on marijuana and told me the guy was spending the night and from now on, she'd have anyone over any time she wanted. "After all," she said, "Sam stays over here almost every night." She was right in a way, but Sam's staying over couldn't be used against me in court, whereas her having guys stay over could and would be used against me. I told her I'd have to call the police if he didn't leave. The guy heard me and promptly left. Mary didn't come out of her room again that night. I left her alone, thinking that we could talk about it the next morning.

Mary was already busy in the kitchen when I awakened the next morning. She was processing a large can of peaches in the blender for her baby. I tried to talk with her, asking for her agreement not to have men over in front of my boys, but she wouldn't agree to anything. I told her she would have to move then. Her only response was to remove the lid from the blender, letting liquid peaches fly all over the kitchen. She took her children and left but came back while I was in the bathroom and poured Daniel's and James's allergy and asthma medications down the sink.

I called the police to find out how to keep her out of the house without any further trouble. I was told to change the locks and to call the police when she came back for the rest of her belongings. About the time the locksmith finished changing the locks, I got an emergency call to pick up James from school.

When we got home, I guess I left the key hanging in the door, because within minutes, Mary stormed in through the front door. She threw Daniel's rocker into the wall and kicked the television set over. I got on the phone to 911 and my kids ran to me. I eased the sliding glass door open about a foot with the curtains still closed, then slipped the kids around me and out the door. By that time, she had grabbed a large steak knife and had it pressed against my throat. Luckily, the police were on their way. She left a red mark on my throat but didn't cut me.

The police made her leave and advised me to pack all her belongings, put them in the garage, and to call them when she came to get them. They also encouraged me to file charges against Mary. I had the locks changed again because Mary claimed she had thrown the key into the snow, but it couldn't be found. A couple of days later, Matt's school notified me that a woman identifying herself as his aunt was coming to pick him up. Sam and I went immediately to the school and signed papers preventing anyone but us from taking our children from school.

On November 20, 1980, I was just about ready to leave the house with Daniel when the doorbell rang. I looked out the peephole and saw a very large man of Spanish descent standing there. I asked him what he wanted, and he said, "Police, Mrs. Sipe, I want to talk to you." It didn't feel right to me, so I called the police and was informed that they had not dispatched anyone to my house. While I was still on the phone with the police, the man started banging loudly on the door, shouting, "Open the door, Beth." I dropped the phone and hid Daniel in a closet. I heard the man break the glass in the window by the front door, and as I went by the kitchen counter, I picked up the first thing I saw, a hatchet. Sam had used it the night before to split firewood. I walked over by the door, shaking with fear. As I started to pull the curtain back, a hand reached through the broken window and grabbed me. I was pushing against the wall with my hand that held the hatchet, then I started to swing the hatchet. I got in a few licks with it, but I think all I hit was the curtain. Anyway, the guy let go of me. The police were still on the phone, and it was only a few minutes until they arrived. I called Sam, and he arrived while I was giving my statement to the police.

Sam was very upset and wanted to protect us. He even said to the police, "A woman alone shouldn't be without a gun, and I'm taking her to get one now." Later that same afternoon, Sam took me to Old West Arms and purchased my gun for $211.08. Sam even taught me how to use the gun and took me target shooting several times.

And it was later that evening that Sam moved back in. He really played up the incident—how dangerous it was and how I couldn't protect the kids. Sam insisted I press on with the charges against Mary and even hired a lawyer. I just wanted to drop the case if Mary would stay away from us.

The man who tried to break in was never caught, but I did have to go to court about Mary. She received a fine and probation. In any case, Sam was back in the house and back in control. He still made me sign a receipt each month for child support. There were times when I wondered if Sam had set up the break-in just to get back home. With him there, I had no more welfare, surplus food, or food stamps, but most of all, I had no money and no freedom. I started cleaning a few houses and taking Daniel with me on the job.

Within a week, we were fighting again, and our situation grew worse with time. More than once, he would grit his teeth and say, "If you ever take my kids or get any part of my retirement pay, you'd better watch every shadow, because I'll see your ass dead." He did exactly what he pleased, showed up whenever he felt like it, and controlled all the money. I began to have unshakable feelings of doom.

In the spring of 1981, I started back to church with the kids, and in April, I was baptized in the Church of Christ. I had a feeling of urgency about being baptized because of the bad vibes from Sam. Sam made all kinds of sarcastic remarks about our attending church even though I didn't try to convert him. I just wanted to live a Christian life as I had been brought up to do. Many times Sam would say, "Oh, screw you and your Christian friends," and once I responded, "Even if we find out when we die that it's been a big joke, living a Christian life makes you a better person."

I began counseling with the pastor at church. He was from southeast Missouri, and I felt comfortable talking with him. I had gotten off track with my beliefs about marriage, thinking that I had to obey Sam to be a good wife and that I had to accept his infidelity which had started in Vietnam. The pastor straightened me out about this. He said I did not have to accept his behavior, particularly the infidelity. It meant a lot to me to have the support of my pastor.

A few times the pastor and another deacon came to the house in the evening to do home study with me and the kids. Sam was always there, and he seemed to enjoy arguing with the churchmen. Sam said things like, "There's no God, or heaven or hell." He would get sarcastic, just playing with the minister. After a few visits, the pastor said he would not come back because "Sam is a heathen."

I continued counseling with the minister and often gave a ride to another military wife who was having similar problems. This pastor was the only preacher who ever told me I certainly had grounds for a divorce. I told him I could forgive Sam for the infidelity, but not for the beatings. And the pastor said, "No man has the right to beat his wife," and that I didn't have to put up with it. It was comforting to hear this, but practically speaking, I still had no way out.

The church had a women's group every Monday and this gave me a chance to get out of the house and make friends. We had cookies and punch, and we all took turns baby-sitting with the small children. We discussed all kinds of topics, subjects to wake up our minds. We had secret sisters each year and disclosed our identities at the end of the year. Sometimes we had sewing circles in support of the scholarship program for training new ministers.

Both Matt and James enjoyed church. They were in instruction classes and expressed the desire to be baptized. Sam had a fit when they were baptized and said right in front of the kids that they had sold their souls to the devil. I could see the hurt and puzzlement on their faces as they looked from me to Sam and back at me. Later, I tried to console them as best I could, but I knew I could never repair the damage.

In July 1981, the man who owned our rental house moved back, and we moved to another house. I started baby-sitting again, because when I worked at home and turned over my money to Sam, we seemed to have fewer problems. In his words, "Just keep your ass at home where you belong." He hated for me to work out in public.

Anyway, we were doing OK for a while. I had my friends at church and the kids liked studying the Bible. I enjoyed the yard work, especially the large garden I had planted. Besides baby-sitting, I began to do volunteer work one day a week with the Colorado Humane Society. They had three nonprofit clinics which took in stray cats and dogs. Of course, I loved the animals, but it was hard work, cleaning cages and litter boxes and feeding all of them.

On September 20, 1981, Sam and I went to a resort for our anniversary. Sam bought new X-rated movies to bring along. We sat in the room and watched these, and all I could feel was disgusted and humiliated. There was a country western band playing in the lodge that I'd rather have seen. But at least we were together and to me, that counted for something.

A flier came in the mail to go for a free day to see some land. They offered $25 in cash and a $50 barbecue. So on October 20, 1981, we went on an outing to look at the undeveloped land in the mountains. When we got there, they were out of barbecues, so they gave all cash, which Sam pocketed. Since Sam wouldn't put me on his checking account, I had opened my own but had put his name on mine since the account was at the credit union. Anyway, Sam decided to buy a parcel of the land and asked me if I could write the down payment check for $900 on my account, and I did so. I didn't know he had transferred $375 from my account to his savings account until a check bounced. We had a major blowup about this, but it didn't do me any good to protest. Sam didn't return my money or cover the check for me.

Shortly after we bought the land, Sam went to San Antonio, Texas, to the Air Force enlisted men's academy. It was a privilege and honor for him to be chosen to go. He was there about six weeks and graduated with top honors. I was supposed to fly down for his graduation, but just before I was to leave, a flight crashed and two wives were killed, so the military canceled my flight. I got a letter of appreciation for supporting my husband in his career, which I still have.

I rented an "adult" motel room on Colfax as Sam had requested to celebrate his homecoming just a few days before Thanksgiving. For the first part of the evening, we went to his awards ceremony. I had made a new dress, but he criticized me and the dress, which quickly dampened my spirits. There was an open bar, and everyone was drunk early. Then they had a strip-o-gram for the wing commander. All the women were embarrassed, but we tried not to show it since we were all sitting at the head table. Sam was drunk when we got to the motel, but he was determined to watch his porno movies. When I opened my eyes the next morning, I jumped because I could see myself reflected in a ceiling mirror. Sam was hungover, which meant, "no talking." After all the planning and anticipation, the whole evening was nothing but a letdown for me.

In March 1982, I applied for a position at St. Joseph's Hospital in Denver to train as an oxygen technician ("O_2 tech"). Since I had been out of the medical field so long, I was thrilled that out of all the applicants, I was accepted. I trained for about two weeks in what was supposed to be a six-week course. They rushed it because the supervisor was leaving to have a baby, and she had to train me and give me the state certification test first. I had to work very hard because I also had to get the equivalent of my high school degree (GED). I started classes at night for the GED, but was running out of time so I took the test without the classes. I can't put into words my delight when I passed the GED and the state certification test. Passing these tests was a major accomplishment and really boosted my self-confidence. Sam didn't have one word of praise or encouragement for me, but he couldn't erase these achievements either.

During the training, I worked the day shift at the hospital, driving eighteen miles each way to the hospital after taking Daniel to the base day care center. Once the training period was over, I worked 11 p.m. to 7 a.m. in order to be with Daniel during the day. I enjoyed my time with him, watching him grow and learn.

I worked at St. Joseph's as an oxygen technician from April until the end of June and began to feel better and better about myself. As an O_2 tech I was on the trauma treatment team which serviced the emergency room and the helicopter pad. We had to be able to respond to any emergency anywhere in the hospital within five minutes. I came in contact with death and near-death constantly. I just did the best I could, even if the situation seemed hopeless. I'll never forget putting the oxygen mask on a six-year-old girl who had lost half her head in an accident. Or administering oxygen to a fourteen-year-old boy who had lost an arm and a leg. It made me value life more, plus I had the feeling I was doing something really worthwhile.

During this time, I was also seeing a chaplain on the base for counseling. I had given up on marriage counseling with Sam. Now I was trying to work on me, to gain back some of my identity, some of the self-respect and confidence I had before I met Sam.

I guess things were going too well or Sam thought I was too happy, because he started demanding that I get off work to go on vacation with him and the kids. I told him he could take the kids to his parents by himself as he had before, but he wouldn't hear of it. He still had the legal separation and held it over my head all the time. I tried to get time off from work, but I hadn't been there long enough to take off two weeks as Sam demanded.

Finally, I gave in again, just quit my job, and went with him to Nevada.

On past vacations with his family, Sam had been critical of me in front of his family, but during this two-week visit, he treated me like a dog. He didn't hit me in front of them, but he was sharp, sarcastic, and demeaning. Everything I did or said was "stupid." I couldn't believe it. Here he had coerced me into quitting a good job only to humiliate me.

We returned to Denver on July 15, 1982, and he moved out again on July 18. I took a job cleaning for an agency until I could get some work on my own by running ads in the paper. For awhile, I worked for two different agencies, as well as for Homewatch. Homewatch involved house and animal sitting, and I loved these assignments because I could work out my own schedule. Soon I built up enough homes to clean on my own and was able to quit the agencies. I also did some work for a small company which renovated old houses—painting, stripping, whatever. It paid well, and I loved the work. Sam didn't seem very upset about this work since I went to work in paint-spattered jeans, sweatshirts, and scarves tied around my head.

When Sam moved out July 18, he reminded me that he was legally separated and wasn't going to help with the rent or any other expense. I told him I'd pay the utilities, but that he could just get sued for the rent since the lease was in his name, and as for the legal separation, it was broken long ago. I was sick of hearing about it. He claimed us as dependents, pocketed all our benefits from the Air Force, filed joint income tax returns and pocketed those refunds, and had insisted on his "husbandly rights" all along. When I talked this over with the legal office on base, the major there said indeed the legal separation was broken because we had lived together and that Sam couldn't use it.

Sam returned around the middle of August. We made big plans to take the kids for a family outing to an amusement park. I got up at 5 a.m. and cooked chicken and potato salad. The kids and I got ready to leave by 8 a.m. as we had planned. We waited and waited and waited until Sam decided to get up at noon. The kids were so disappointed because the park admission covered unlimited rides all day, and they felt cheated.

It was about this time that I had paid for a father-son Boy Scout outing for Sam and James. They were supposed to leave on Friday afternoon to go to the mountains. When Sam didn't show up, I arranged with a friend to watch the other two boys so I could take James myself. But when we showed up, the den leader told me it was fathers only and I couldn't go. Sam showed up at the house Saturday morning after James had already missed half of the campout. I couldn't feel disappointed any more, but it hurt to see the kids struggle with letdown after letdown.

I've mentioned before that Sam was very rough with my breasts. The first time he had beaten me in the breasts was when he raped me right after James's birth. This did not become a constant pattern until after Daniel was born, although he always seemed preoccupied with breasts. Mine were so small that I had no cleavage, so he would grab them and push them together, telling me he wanted to shoot off between them but mine were too small. During my pregnancy with Daniel, my breasts got much larger and Sam seemed pleased with them. Maybe Sam was angry that they shrunk again because he beat on my breasts every time we had sex. Over time, his kissing of my breasts became painful chewing. At times, he made threatening faces at me as he held my nipple between his teeth.

It was not surprising that I began to have problems with my breasts, swelling, pain, and constant discharge from milky to bloody. The doctors did numerous tests and tried different medications, some of which made me sick. Their diagnosis was fibrocystic disease of the breasts with complications. I knew, but never told the doctors, that the complications were caused by the repeated beatings. One of the medications alleviated the pain but reduced my breasts to the size of a half dollar.

When the doctors suggested implants, I was scared, but Sam was ecstatic. After a lot of pressure by Sam, I agreed to go along with getting implants. The base head of plastic surgery was also an elder of my church, and Sam urged me to ask him to do the surgery as a favor. But I was too embarrassed to ask. Ironically, I was referred to that same doctor even though I had requested a different one.

Sam insisted on coming along for the consultation and talked to the doctor like I was a piece of merchandise. Sam kept asking the doctor how large he could make the breasts. I stressed to the doctor that I wanted to look normal, that I didn't want "big boobs." They also discussed the kind of material to be used. I insisted on saline solution because I had heard terrible stories about silicone. After that, I had to have a complete hormone workup and X rays. I remember being at the hospital almost every day for a week. Then they put me on a waiting list because it was elective surgery. In a way I was relieved when they told me it might be a few weeks or a couple of years.

Our lives went on pretty much as usual. All the kids were having trouble at school, so I had appointments with teachers and counselors almost every week. Matt, age thirteen, was in trouble for disrupting classes and food fights; James, age ten, was caught drinking, smoking, doing drugs (marijuana and pills), and skipping school; and Daniel, age six, had temper tantrums and refused to follow the class rules. I reported these meetings to Sam, but he just laughed it off. Never did he back me up in trying to follow through with the school personnel's recommendations. In order for me to keep all these appointments, I had to rearrange my cleaning schedule to the point that I was cleaning houses in the middle of the night at times. Even when James set fire to our kitchen with his smoking, Sam ignored my pleas to help me discipline the boys.

About one week before Christmas, we had another major fight. I remember this because Sam came home drunk after the kids were in bed, and I had on my gown and bathrobe. Sam hit me across the face with his hand, then pulled me up the stairs by my hair from the lower level of the entry hall. I got away from him in the living room, but he grabbed me, threw me to the floor, and sat straddled on me as he cussed and tore at my clothes. He raped me right on the living room floor, with me scared to death the kids would walk in. I tried to be very quiet when he started sex, but I'm sure the kids heard this.

Even so, Sam and I went Christmas shopping together on December 23. One of my church friends was staying in the house temporarily, so she watched the kids for us. After shopping, we went to his barracks to wrap the presents. We got worn out and fell asleep. When we woke up, we were snowed in—that was the big snowstorm of 1982. We were not allowed to leave the barracks. Sam was sort of in charge since he was the top ranking noncom in the building. It was embarrassing for me to have to explain who I was because the other guys thought I was one of Sam's one-nighters. One woman there was TDY and pregnant. I had some apples from shopping and sneaked them to her. Some of the guys there had liquor, and they started drinking early. By afternoon, some of them were getting mean.

Word came from the mess hall that it was snowed in too, but we were promised food sometime during the day or evening. All the females pitched in, setting up tables and putting sheets on them for tablecloths. We occupied ourselves part of the time with a sing-along, but most of the men just got drunker and drunker. The food didn't arrive on the 24th. We talked to the kids on the phone and they were fine. The only way the security police would try to get us out was for us to say the kids were alone. I wouldn't say that because it wasn't true. We heard that one of the high-ranking officers had taken a jeep out and was missing with his aide, so top priority was given to locating them.

The next day, Christmas, we finally got food. About six guys backpacked it in to us. All I can remember is hot chicken and milk. It tasted wonderful, but I threw it up because my low blood sugar went crazy from being without food too long. We got home to the kids about 2:30 p.m. Since it was too late to fix Christmas dinner, we had it the next day. The kids were so excited to get their presents after waiting so long. Watching their happy faces made it all worthwhile. They even seemed to enjoy playing with their new toys more than other Christmases. Denver was shut down for several days, which gave me a chance to clean house and get organized for the new year.

On January 19, 1983, Sam moved out again. I began to have trouble with severe cramps and abnormal periods. I had a pap smear and the results came back abnormal. I had to go in for extensive tests, and I remember being glad Sam wasn't there. They did an upper and lower GI, about four different X rays with dye in the uterus, an EKG, and a pulmonary function test. The worst test was a proctoscopy, which caused such intense cramping that I fainted. Maybe if I had told them the truth about the anal sex, I wouldn't have had to have this test. But I just couldn't.

About March 7, they did a D & C and scope, determining that I had endometriosis. The severe cramps had been caused by the menstrual material escaping into the abdominal cavity and wrapping around my stomach and bowels. Sam was with me during the last consultation and examination. The doctors had noticed damage and heavy scar tissue in the anal area and asked me pointed questions about anal sex. Of course with Sam standing there, I denied it, and I would have denied it anyway because it was so embarrassing. The doctors informed me that if the D & C didn't alleviate my menstrual problems, I would need to have a hysterectomy. From the time Daniel was born, Sam had talked off and on about wanting another child. Now he pressured me to put off the surgery for at least nine months and have another baby. Even though I had always wanted a girl, I wasn't going to have another baby. Sam's lack of emotional, disciplinary, and financial support was too obvious with the three I already had. All three boys had problems at school and at home. No matter how hard I worked, the boys and I just existed at the poverty level. Those realities plus the pain—I couldn't live with the pain—made me decide to do it and get it over with.

On May 20, 1983, I had the hysterectomy at the Air Force Academy Hospital in Colorado Springs. I was only thirty-two and scared of how this might change me, but I was more frightened of the alternative. Sam played the loving husband, bringing the kids to the hospital, sending me flowers, and so on. He called long distance to ask me questions about everything from how to operate the washer to how to prepare Hamburger Helper. To this day, my boys hate Hamburger Helper.

Sam brought me home May 25, and that night, five days after surgery, he raped me again. I didn't beg him to stop. This time, I fought him, pushing on his chest with my arms and bringing my knees up to stop him, but I was never a match for his strength and with incisions, I hardly slowed him down. I stayed in bed two days, not caring about anything, not even whether or not the kids were fed. I just remember laying there sick and sweating.

After a couple of days, I got up, showered, dressed, and went back to cleaning houses. One of the ladies asked me why: "Your husband makes enough money that you shouldn't have to do this." I just smiled at her and said, "It's good for me to stay busy." I was so into the pattern of covering up for Sam and being a good military wife, my words were automatic.

Nothing really changed. Sam continued to storm in and out of the house at will, slapping and pushing me around when he was angry. As long as he didn't injure me or give me a prolonged beating, I hardly noticed the milder abuse. I fixed my attention on one day at a time, one problem at a time. During early July, I took an extra job, cleaning a huge house a family had just bought. I spent four days around the clock, sleeping on the floor for two or three hours at a time, to get it ready for them to move into. This earned me enough extra money to take the kids and go home for a vacation visit with my family. We left on July 11 and returned July 30. We had a nice visit and Sam stayed in the house while we were gone.

On August 1, I was back to work cleaning houses as usual. I had begun to think about attending veterinarian technical school. I wanted to do something besides clean other people's dirty houses, and I wanted a job I could be proud of. I had always loved animals and was good at working with them. Everyone in the animal rescue program encouraged me. I found out that the Bel-Rae school in Aurora, Colorado, had an eighteen-month course with an applied science degree. I applied for and got a $5,000 government loan.

Almost immediately, Sam applied for and received reassignment to Las Vegas, supposedly because of his father's illness. So I had to drop my plans to go to school. I lost the money I had already paid. I couldn't help crying as I put the loan check back in the envelope and returned it.

Neither the kids nor I wanted to leave Denver. During our five years there, we had put down roots, made friends, and begun to feel comfortable. Yet Sam promised me this would be the last stretch in the Air Force, that we'd buy a house and settle in Las Vegas. In his request for transfer, he wrote, "Wife is a Nurse's Aide and O_2 Tech; she can help with my father's O_2 and nursing." My willingness to go along with this helped him get back to Nevada.

During the previous two years or so, I had cleaned house for an older man, about sixty-two, who had become a close friend. He was a retired Air Force major and had worked as a counselor. I could talk to him about some of my problems and had begun opening up to him after he questioned me about some of my bruises. He had taken me and the kids out to Denny's a few times, once for Matt's birthday. One night when Matt suffered with difficult breathing and severe chest pains, he even accompanied us to the emergency room. Matt was diagnosed as having growing pains and released. But while we waited, the police brought in a guy who had blackened his face, beaten his wife, and held her hostage for several hours. I felt shivers run through me as I watched. It reminded me so much of Sam. My friend noticed my reaction and understood. He was part father, part brother to me. He was planning to remarry and shared his feelings about that with me. He and his lady friend planned to travel together after the wedding, and I was very happy for him.

On September 26, my friend had an appointment to have his eyes dilated and examined, and I was going to drive him. I called about 7 a.m. to check with him, but got no answer. I drove by his house on my way to work and got no answer when I knocked. I could see his dog inside the house and this bothered me, so when I got to work, I called the police to check out the house. Later when I called his house, the police answered and said he was dead. I had lost my best friend, and I cried until I couldn't cry any more.

He had told his children about me and my kids, that we had brightened up his life when he was lonesome. His daughter asked me to go to the graveyard a few days later to oversee the removal of his baby, who had died about twenty years before, and its reburial over him. I met his fiancée there and together we watched from a distance as the grave diggers completed his wish. I said my final good-bye and prayed for him that day.

Our lives were on hold as we waited for definite orders to Las Vegas. Sam didn't hurt me too much since I was pretty well minding him. He stayed in the barracks when he wanted and came to the house as he pleased.

In October, my old car totally died, and I bought a new 1984 Toyota Tercel with four-wheel drive. I was approved for the loan with my own credit in my name only. But I allowed Sam to talk me into going to the credit union on base for a cheaper interest rate. I wondered why he was being so nice to me. When the papers came, I saw why. The car title read Sam and Bethel Sipe, not even Sam or Bethel Sipe. By then, it was impossible to change it without his consent and signature. I made all the payments but the car was legally half his.

Nothing else was new or different until February 1984, when I was bitten by a cat at the animal shelter. The bite became infected, and I was sick with a high temperature. I had been working extra hours, saving money to visit my friend Esther in Florida. Her four-year-old son had drowned a few months earlier, and we decided my visit could wait until things calmed down for her. Since I was recuperating and couldn't work right then, it seemed a good time to go. Sam agreed to take care of the kids and I left by Amtrak on February 10, arriving in Florida the 13th. It was great to be out of the snow and free from work and responsibilities, a true vacation for me.

I returned on March 4. We had a warm, happy reunion; the kids especially were thrilled to see me. The next day, it was back to work as usual.

On March 16, 1984, a seventeen-year-old boy crossed two lanes of traffic and hit the side of my car. It wasn't damaged so badly that I couldn't drive it, but it hurt to see my new car dented. The damage was estimated at $2,200, and it took six months to collect the settlement. This is significant to the story after our move to Nevada. At that time, I was annoyed to have to drive a damaged car on which I was making payments and not be able to have it repaired.

In May, I started cleaning three-story condominiums for a construction company. I cleaned them as they were finished, and it was very messy work. I was paid $75, $50, or $40 per unit, depending upon the size. I had to hang out the windows on the upper floors to clean them. It was good money, and I was still doing my regular houses. At times, I'd stay, cleaning as long as I could keep my eyes open, fall asleep on the floor, then wake up and finish the next morning.

By then, Sam had orders to leave Denver at the end of July. I didn't know what was going to happen in Las Vegas, so I was saving all the money I could, sewing it into my padded bras. If Sam treated us as he had in the past, I was going to be prepared. About July 1, I received notice that my breast surgery had been scheduled for July 9. This was minor compared to the other surgeries I had had, and I was allowed to leave the hospital July 10. On July 12, I was back to work, although I recall being very sore, especially when pushing a vacuum or reaching to clean windows. I had stitches under each breast where they slipped in the bags filled with saline solution. The stitches weren't removed until July 20.

They took pictures of the breasts at that time to show the success of the surgery. By this time, I was in the middle of packing for the move to Nevada. We were moving ourselves by U-Haul and that meant that all the packing was my job. I organized a garage sale which lasted two days. Then I took the remaining items to the Salvation Army, getting a receipt for taxes. On July 31, after cleaning the house, we spent the night in a motel. On August 1, we were on our way to Nevada. Matt and Daniel rode in the car with me, while James rode with Sam in the U-Haul.

I don't recall having any special feelings about the move as I drove along with my boys and our pets. I guess I was relieved to have half the job of moving done and sad to leave Denver. I had made a place for myself there; I really belonged, and I had no idea of what to expect in Las Vegas.

8

A House in Glitter Gulch

I don't recall much about the drive from Denver to Vegas, probably because Sam and I weren't driving together. I no longer thought much about our relationship, since I had given up hope that it would ever improve. I just thought about getting to Vegas safely, about the problems of my kids, and about all the work of finding housing and unpacking. I felt an overwhelming sadness at being pulled away from friends and a chance at a real career. I knew that I would be starting all over from scratch in Vegas.

As I started the descent from Mesquite into Vegas, my first impression was "What kind of place is this?" The desert was strewn with debris—couches, mattresses, hot water heaters. Never had I seen so much trash and garbage dumped along a highway.

Sam had received a moving allotment for us, and since we were moving ourselves, we actually made money on the move. But, as usual, Sam pocketed all this money; he shared none of it with me or the kids. He didn't even give me money for food or gas along the way. Of the money I had earned in Denver, I had stashed about $2,000 by sewing it in my bras. So I was prepared to take care of necessities for me and the kids until I could find a job. The two boys and I arrived in Vegas about 8 a.m. on

August 1, 1984, and reported in to Sam's unit at Nellis Air Force Base, a few miles north of Las Vegas. He hadn't given me a copy of his orders, so it was a real mess. The base people said they couldn't figure Sam out, not giving me a copy of the orders. But they went ahead and checked us into temporary living quarters. Throughout that day, I became more and more concerned because Sam didn't get in until 9 p.m. He had stopped to gamble in Mesquite, leaving James alone in the truck for six hours. It upset me to think that anything could have happened to James—he could have been kidnapped or gotten dehydrated from the heat—during those hours, but I knew it was useless to make an issue of it. I concentrated on feeling thankful that we had all arrived safely and put my worry and anger aside.

Before we could begin looking for housing, Sam insisted we go to Mina to visit his family for ten days. This became a pattern, driving back and forth to Mina about every other weekend. The burden of all these trips was on me; I had to pack for everyone, load the car, prepare food, arrange for all the pets. It made a lot of extra work for me and drained away my energy.

Sam decided we should rent the cheapest place we could find until we found an affordable house to buy. The cheapest place to rent turned out to be a dilapidated two-bedroom trailer in an unkempt trailer park. We moved in August 17. All three of the boys had to share one bedroom, and we had the other. We all shared one bathroom. The trailer had no cooling, so until November, the 110°+ heat was unbearable. Then, as the winter began, we froze because Sam refused to have the gas connected. I had to turn on the electric oven each morning to knock off the chill in the air. I did our laundry at a Laundromat because there was no room for a washer or dryer in the trailer. In no way was the trailer comfortable or homelike.

We put all our furniture and most of our belongings into a storage shed, hoping we would find a house to buy within a few weeks. This was a worry to me, because on several occasions, I had to go into storage to find things we needed. It was so hot in there that the pitch from the roof melted and dripped in sticky black puddles onto the furniture and storage boxes.

Toward the end of August, we made a bid on a house. We were able to do this because I had received $2,200 to cover the damages to my car just before we left Denver. Sam pressured me to use this money as the down payment for our house. It had always been my dream to have my own home, so I guess I wasn't that hard to convince.

At the same time, we had to enter the boys in school. We enrolled Daniel in Redrock Elementary because it was near the house we had bid on. This meant I had to drive him thirteen miles each way every day. By the second week of school, we got the word that our bid on that particular house was not accepted, but I didn't want to disrupt Daniel's school year unless we had something definite.

I began looking for a job without much success. Either I was overqualified, I was underqualified, or the jobs paid only minimum wages. It was discouraging, but I didn't stop filling out applications. I even checked into starting my own cleaning business but found I had to get separate business licenses for every area of town, plus several other complications involving phone, mailing address, and taxes. Sam refused to back me on this, so I gave up the idea. At least this time I was prepared. Dollar by dollar, I used my money for gas, school clothes, and supplies, all the "little" extras of daily life. Sam wasn't extreme with his violence at this time, just the usual knocking me around. He had always used my hands to hurt me, knowing I had arthritis in them. At that time, he seemed to twist and wrench my hands even more. Sam had total control at home. He purchased the groceries, and I cooked whatever he brought home. He paid the trailer rent and electric bills, but he gave me no money for daily expenses. To handle these, I kept dipping into my stash saved from working so hard in Denver.

On November 21, we were getting ready to go to Mina for Thanksgiving. Sam insisted we take along groceries, so we stopped at the commissary on our way out of town. When we got to the checkstand, Sam asked me to pay, and I wrote the check for $75. I knew we didn't have enough in the account, but Sam said he would cover it as soon as we got back from Mina. No surprise, he didn't deposit the money in the account, so I was the one who had to pay the extra charges and I was the one whose check-writing privileges were suspended on base for sixty days. Then Sam used that as an excuse to take my name off the joint checking account again.

During this trip to Mina for Thanksgiving, Sam was so critical toward me that I stayed to myself as much as I could.

On November 25th, I was in the bathroom when Sam rushed in half-carrying Matt, then age fifteen. Matt was ghostly pale and blood was pouring down his left arm, dripping everywhere. When I asked what happened, Sam grabbed me by the face, leaving bruised prints of his fingers, and pinned me against the wall. "You say one word and you'll be sorry," he told me. I shut my mouth and tried to help Matt.

The rescue squad cleaned up the wound, applied butterfly bandages, and told us to get him to the hospital immediately. It was a seventy-mile drive to the hospital in Tonapah. On the way, Sam told Matt, "You can tell them whatever you want when we get there, but if you tell the truth, they'll arrest your daddy and take him away." At the hospital, Matt lied; "I fell through a window," he said. The artery was visible in the open wound on Matt's arm and required sixteen stitches. After the surface wound healed, Matt had permanent nerve damage in his left thumb.

Later Matt told me the real story. He and James had been roughhousing. Sam was facing Matt, swearing at him in his loudest voice, when James made a face which caused Matt to crack up laughing. Sam kicked him through the window. Today, I'm shocked that I didn't recognize the horror in my son's lie to cover for Sam. At the time, I felt relief that another crisis was past and that Matt was OK.

It was getting close to Christmas, 1984, and Sam said no tree, no decorations, no presents. We had bid on another house, and Sam said we would be moving any day. Boy, was I sick of that trailer. The window over our bed was broken out, and the landlord refused to fix it. We had plastic over it, but the cold air came in anyway. One morning we woke up with the cold rain blowing in our faces.

Late one afternoon, Sam and I came home from a meeting with the real estate lady to find that the kids had picked up a sage brush, sprayed it silver, decorated it, and set it up on the kitchen counter. That did it for me. I still had about $200 left, and I used half of it to buy a tree and a few gifts for the kids. Sam gave us no help or encouragement, but I made a trip out to the storage shed and rummaged through the boxes until I found a few of our decorations. This cheered us up some. To this day, whenever my kids see a sage brush, they say, "There goes a Christmas tree."

In January 1985, we moved into our house. I couldn't wait to get started fixing it up as I had always dreamed. Up to this time, I had always been able to maintain a nice home by painting, wallpapering, making curtains, and so on. But it had always been someone else's house. It didn't take Sam long to dampen my excitement. One day we'd look through samples of paint, wallpaper, tile, and we'd agree. The next day, Sam would deny he ever agreed to anything. So we'd start all over again. Once we got as far as purchasing paint, wallpaper, and tile for one bathroom. But when I got ready to paint, he told me not to do it, that he would destroy anything I did. After a few months of this, I was so discouraged and disappointed that I gave up at home.

I had signed up for Emergency Medical Technician (EMT) classes at Clark County Community College, and I started school right after we moved into the house. Final testing for state certification was to be in May. I found the classes very hard, and I had to study long hours. Sam began beating me again, sitting on me, holding me down for up to an hour at a time. He started telling me, "I've got you now; we're in Nevada, my state. I'm going to get rid of you once and for all." I had asked the kids to call the police when they saw him start this, but they were too scared. They sat like statues and watched television as if nothing was wrong. I had the feeling that Sam wanted me to quit school, because he would wake me in the middle of the night to fight. If I asked him to let me sleep, he'd say, "Hell, no. You're staying up until we fight this out." When I had to go out in public, I used makeup to cover the bruises that my clothes didn't hide. I learned to lie to him and say, "Fine with me if you want to fight all night; I can sleep all day tomorrow." Sometimes this would work, sometimes not.

In February, I began to accept some private duty work for a medical personnel pool. I can see now that I tried to fill up every hour possible with work and school just to be away from Sam. Through my private duty work, I met another military wife who became a good friend. Sam couldn't stand this; he bad-mouthed her all the time. She and I made plans for all of us to get together for an evening at our house, but Sam said he didn't want them over, that he didn't like her husband any more than he liked her. So my friend and I continued the friendship without the men.

In February, I also spent a lot of time and energy cleaning up the backyard to plant a garden of cool-weather crops. I had to dig up huge rocks and rent a tiller. It was hard work, but I enjoyed working with the soil as I had since childhood. I planted onions, radishes, spinach, turnips. My garden did not come to much, because the weather got hot too early. I found out Vegas wasn't the place for cool-weather crops, so eventually I switched to growing roses and other flowers.

By April, I was getting desperate for a full-time job. I had started applying for security guard positions, but my slight build and lack of firearm training got me nowhere with these applications. I had applied at all the hospitals and nursing services, but they required at least one year of the previous three years working in a hospital or nursing home. I didn't meet their requirements. Through another student in my EMT classes, I got a job which did not require firearms with a security company.

I deliberately chose night duty in order to avoid Sam as much as possible. I worked as a guard for a hospital a few days, then I was placed at the gas company. I did two rounds a night, checking the building inside and outside. The job was easy, except for the report writing, about twelve to fifteen pages a night. I was scared many times, out there alone. The few times I called for backup, no one came. I had worked all night before the day of my final exams for my EMT certification.

At the end of May when I finished school, I got a call for a full-time job with UpJohn, and I quit the security job. I worked all private duty. I loved working with patients, one on one, being totally responsible for their care. I've had mostly dear, sweet patients and a few mean old soreheads, but I gave all of them my best. If I really didn't like a patient, I asked to be removed from the case. During those periods when I worked in a hospital, I often felt guilty after finishing a shift because there was no time for individual attention or quality care.

A few times, I was assigned to dying patients who needed hospice care. When they died, I would go home, grieving and crying, unable to sleep at night. Sam would increase his criticism and abuse. According to him, I never did anything right. If I worked most of the time, then I didn't take care of the house right, or cook right, or handle the kids right. But he did nothing to help. When he was home, he lay on the couch and drank until he decided to go to bed. If he thought I needed to sleep, he'd make as much unnecessary noise as possible, noises like slamming the bedroom door over and over again. But no matter what, I always cooked him a full-course dinner, and no matter what, he always ate it.

Working nights not only helped me to avoid conflicts with Sam, it gave me time to take care of other duties Sam refused to do. When the kids had appointments with doctors and dentists, I was free to take them. When the schools called for parent conferences as they frequently did, I was free to go. When Sam forgot to pay the bills, I was free to run all over town, paying them.

Sam's sexual abuse grew worse. He'd wake me out of a deep sleep, beating on my breasts, and force sex. The next morning I'd be sick and sore all over. When I dared to mention it to him, he'd deny he did anything and call me "crazy." At times, I wondered if I was crazy. But there was no denying the agonizing pain in my breasts. I had constant drainage again, sometimes milky, sometimes black tar. Once I told him, "Thank you," because the drainage was very heavy and I thought he had burst a large cyst.

I saw several doctors about this, and their recommendation was to remove both breasts and do breast reconstruction.

This did not appeal to me at all, but according to the doctors, the chances were that this would turn into cancer sooner or later, and this appealed to me even less.

Then in October, I came home from work with such pain in my chest that I couldn't breathe. The doctors found that I had an infection around my heart which resulted in mitrovalve prolapse. This means that for the rest of my life I have to take antibiotics to prevent any infection. Just to have a tooth filled or have my teeth cleaned, I have to go on antibiotics several days beforehand. My breast surgery had to be postponed, but I continued to work seventy-two hours a week. About that, I had no choice.

We stayed in Vegas for Christmas that year because I was working. I started Christmas dinner and we opened presents, then I went to work, came home, and finished our dinner. It didn't feel much like Christmas to me.

On January 13, 1986, Sam drove me to St. George, Utah, to have the breast surgery. I was having the surgery there because it was so much cheaper. Sam came back to Vegas, so I was alone there in Utah. The surgery was done on the fourteenth, and I had drainage tubes running under each arm with a suction device hanging in the middle. The bandages were removed on the seventeenth, and I called Sam to tell him I was being released the next day. He was supposed to pick me up by 10 a.m. on the eighteenth. When he didn't show up, I called home and he answered the phone, saying he'd leave for Utah immediately. The nurses had already stripped my bed, and I was sitting up in a chair. They had to order my lunch and check me back in. One of the nurses said, "Maybe he's not coming because he doesn't want you." I didn't answer, but I was feeling sad and alone already. In my heart, I felt the nurse was right. Sam didn't want me, but he wouldn't let me go.

The first time he saw my chest, he walked in the bedroom when I had on nothing but panties and said, "God, they sure look disgusting." I told him he never had to look at them again, that they pleased me, and that they looked OK in clothes. He told me that no man would ever want me and that he certainly didn't because I looked so ugly. "You're not even a woman any more—no tits and no womb," he said.

That night he forced sex, punching my breasts until he opened the right incision. When I asked him why, he said, "I can't get off with you unless I hurt you." By this time, most of my emotions were numb. I knew what he was doing, but my grief was buried so far beneath my awareness I couldn't reach it. That night I decided I wouldn't go back for the additional surgery required to construct nipples.

I returned to work three weeks after surgery. I was called in to work in the intensive care unit (ICU) at Valley Hospital. I was the only aide they used in ICU because of my EMT training and that made me feel important, that I was really making a contribution. I worked four twelve-hour shifts weekly at that hospital. When I wasn't there, I continued to work with private patients through the medical pool.

After three months of harassment from Sam about my breasts, I finally went in for the nipple construction surgery in April. This turned out to be much more painful than the breast surgery. They took slices of skin from each inner thigh, rolled them up to form nipples and sewed them on. They applied large balls of gauze to each and the gauze had to be moistened constantly with ointment.

The night I got home from the hospital, Sam forced sex and in the process, he cupped both my breasts, squeezing so hard that he tore most of the stitches in the right nipple. Before I returned to the doctor, most of this nipple had fallen off. The fact that I had gone through all that pain meant nothing to Sam. He still said he had to hurt me, that I wasn't even a woman. He seemed to enjoy hurting me and to enjoy hearing me cry afterward even more. At that time, I thought what he had done to my breasts was the ultimate in terror, but later he would teach me the true meaning of terror.

One week after the nipple surgery, I had foot surgery for an ingrown toenail on each foot. So I was off work for about three weeks, mostly because I couldn't wear the regulation closed-in shoes. It was during this time off that I began to get acquainted with our new neighbors, John and Jane Jones.

We had coffee together a few mornings, and at first, Jane seemed pleasant enough. A few times, she asked me to give her children first aid, which I was glad to do. When Jane asked me to assist her daughter, Alice, through the delivery of her baby, I agreed. Alice was young and unmarried. I guess I felt sorry for her, going through childbirth all alone. Jane said she was just too squeamish to do it. I had to wear scrubs to stay with Alice. She was in hard labor for about twelve hours, and she pulled on my hands until they were bruised. When the baby came, the doctors handed him to me, I showed him to Alice, then handed him to the nurses. They checked the baby, then gave it back to me to take to the nursery. The Jones family named me the baby's godmother in appreciation for my help. I mention this incident and others with the Jones family because of their strange behavior later.

One night late in May, the police knocked on our door. A man and woman were with them. When I opened the door and saw them, I didn't know what to think. They said that James and another boy had broken into their house and stolen money and liquor. The people didn't file charges because they had recovered their property from the other boy. They just wanted us to take it seriously. Against my protest, Sam took his belt to James and left welts on his back. I felt sick inside. This was a major area of disagreement between Sam and me. He ignored the kids' behavior 90% of the time; then he'd punish them violently. If I grounded them, he'd unground them, so they didn't mind anything I said. Here was James, only fourteen years old, and already in trouble for stealing. What would become of my kids, I wondered.

Between June 26 and July 22, 1986, I took the kids on a vacation to visit my family in Arkansas. Sam complained about me spending my money for the trip, but we had spent much more visiting his family about twice a month. After we returned from vacation, Sam was really bad, constantly telling me to get out without my kids, always without the kids. I think I became so focused on my work and my boys that I didn't register much else.

In my calendar, I noted that on July 30 I took the kids downtown to watch the filming of *Over the Top.* Several people told me to sign up and get paid for just standing around. I did, and that's how I got started working as an extra. I worked and was paid for four days in *Over the Top.*

When I mentioned this to Jane, she nearly burst with excitement. Who did I meet, who did I talk to, she wanted to know. She told me that her daughter had had an affair with some movie star, but that he was just a "rich asshole." She told me this was my perfect chance to have an affair to hurt Sam. At this point, she didn't really know anything about my marriage except for hearing Sam criticize and berate me. I explained to her that I had no desire to have an affair for any reason, that if I did that, I would only hurt myself, and that I did not want to feel like a whore. She dropped the subject that day.

I continued my work with private patients full-time and worked as an extra every chance I got. In September, I worked a few days on a movie called *Glory Years.* An aunt and uncle of Sam's visited us later in October. Sam was as mean as he could be in front of them. Before they left, his aunt got me alone at the kitchen table and asked me, "Does he treat you like this all the time?" I broke down crying and told her most of the time, it was worse. She told me that Sam "acts just like his father, that's how he treated Sam's mom all these years." She was so kind and understanding and for that moment, I felt comforted.

In an odd way, it gave me hope. After all, if Sam's parents had lived the same pattern and stayed together, maybe things would eventually work out for us.

Right after the aunt and uncle left, I had a crisis with Matt, who was then a senior in high school. Not only was he ditching school and getting failing notices, but he was staying out past curfew, coming in drunk, and punching the younger boys with his fists. Then he started copying Sam's treatment of me; he told me he'd knock me across the room and actually tried to punch me. I ordered him out of the house, and he left for a few days. Matt calmed down for a few weeks after he returned home, but I didn't expect it to last. I felt he should have some rules in his life and face some responsibilities, but since Sam refused to back me, I knew there would be more problems with Matt.

About this time, Production Services started getting extras lined up to work in *Crime Story*. Jane typed up a resumé for me and took pictures for my portfolio. I was lucky enough to work steadily in *Crime Story* as a result.

One night in November, I was lying on the couch while Sam sat in a chair at the end of the couch. Matt came in very late. He hadn't asked to go out or told anyone where he was going. I said something to him about it, and like a whirlwind, Sam jumped up and punched at me, going for my face. I had an interview for extra work on *Crime Story* the next day, which he knew, and I threw my hands up covering my face. He hit my hands with a hardcover book he was reading, then grabbed me, beating and cussing me as he pulled me into the bedroom. He threw me on the floor, sat on me, and beat me in the face and head until I blacked out. I remember tasting blood and choking on it as I went in and out of consciousness. He told me no one in the house had to tell me or ask me a damn thing, that it was none of my business, and that I had no say about anything in the house. "Just keep your mouth shut and stay in your place," he yelled. After he left the bedroom, I came out intending to call the police. Sam was sitting there holding the only phone in the house. He smirked and said, "Not from my phone, bitch."

I grabbed my purse and ran out of the house to Jane's. The only person at home was Jane's son, who let me in to use the phone. When I called the police, they said I had left the house, and therefore they couldn't respond. I went back to my house, got into my car, and drove myself to the base hospital. After medical treatment, they gave me the phone number for the domestic crisis center and I called. The people there were sympathetic, and I talked to them for a long time, but unfortunately, the center was full. So I drove back home and slept in the car, parked in the driveway.

The next day, Jane and her whole family saw me, and I told them Sam did it without going into detail. Jane even asked Sam about it, and he said, "I gave her what she deserved." Jane called him a "son of a bitch," and told him what she'd do if any man ever hit her.

Later when Jane and I talked alone, she asked me why I stayed with Sam. I told her about his threats to take the kids and never leave me alone. I explained to her that I'd left before and he wouldn't leave me alone, that I'd talked to lawyers but they had no answers for me. I also told her that I still loved Sam, but I just couldn't live with him. She asked me about the house and furniture, and I told her, "I don't give a damn about any of that; in fact, I hate the house. We were going to do so much to fix it up, but Sam won't let me do anything. According to him, everything is his—his money, his house, his food, his kids. He tells me all the time that if it wasn't for him, I'd be out in the street, begging for my meals." I told her that at times I felt like taking the kids and torching the house just so Sam would shut up about it. Jane told me I was stupid to leave my house, that she'd never do that, that she and John had wanted to buy our house but couldn't afford it.

Back in Denver, some of my friends had thought I was so funny that they encouraged me to use some of my stories in a stand-up comedy routine. So I tried a couple of times at Davy's Comedy Palace. Women seemed to like my stories and people in the audience sometimes sent over drinks. It was all volunteer; that is, I did not get paid for it. It made me so nervous that I threw up before I went on every time. It just wasn't worth it to me to continue.

Then several people from Production Services began encouraging me to enter Sandy Hackett's Talent Showcase at The Mint in Las Vegas. So on November 16, 1986, I went on at The Mint for the first time. Jane went with me that Sunday night and several times after that. I continued every Sunday night for almost three months. But again, it made me a nervous wreck, and I never went on without vomiting first. Then I started working a lot in *Crime Story,* so I didn't have the time or energy for the Showcase any more. In *Crime Story,* I was always an extra, but I made up to look different each time. What was consistent was my "big hair" and "sleazy dresses."

On Christmas Day, we were back and forth to the Joneses all day and evening. Nobody seemed very happy though. About 2 a.m. on December 26th, we got word that Sam's dad had been hospitalized in critical condition. Sam was so drunk he could hardly talk on the phone. I did laundry and packed for everyone, secured the animals, loaded the car, and left a key with Jane so she could feed the animals, but I couldn't get Sam up until noon. Even then, I had to yell at him; "Get up," I said, "your father's dying. Don't you want to be there to see him before he goes, to say goodbye, to help your mother?"

We arrived at the Reno hospital about 9 a.m. on the 27th. His father was in ICU on a respirator, but he was fighting the machine. I'd seen so much of this when I was working in ICU. It was obvious that he didn't want the machine to keep him alive, and I didn't blame him. He'd write us notes and tears would stream from his eyes. It was rough for all of us. I tried to comfort Sam, but he rejected me. After that, I stayed out of his way, helping any way I could. On January 1, Sam's father passed away. It was a few days until the funeral, so I started cleaning the house. People came and went in a steady stream. Sam and I and the kids were the only ones staying at the house with his mother, and I kept busy cooking and cleaning.

The night after the funeral, Sam came to bed after me, grabbed me, and started mauling my breasts. He put his hand over my mouth and told me not to make a sound. I panicked because I didn't want his mother to know this went on, so I punched at him enough to get loose. I ran out of the house, barefoot in the snow, to the trailer. I slept out there by myself for the remainder of our visit.

A couple of days later, I was in the kitchen washing dishes when Sam came in and began searching through cookbooks. From the binding of one of them, he pulled out six $100 bills. He said his dad had told him where to find them before he died. Sam smirked as he put the money in his wallet. I told him he should be ashamed of himself and that if he didn't give that money to his mother, I would tell her about it myself. He then gave the money to his mother, and I hadn't thought about it again until now. Looking back, I see more clearly who Sam was—a person willing to steal from his own mother; a person who had no concern for the suffering or needs of anyone other than himself.

Just as we were preparing to return to Vegas, my car overheated, the heat light didn't work, and so the engine block cracked. We had to stay there two more weeks while Sam and his friends tried to fix my car. Since school was starting right after the Christmas break, we sent Matt and James back on a bus. If there had been enough money, I would have taken Daniel and accompanied the older boys back to Vegas. Because of previous trouble with Matt and James, I worried about them being home alone, but at the time, I didn't see any other way to handle the situation.

A few days after Sam and I got home, the police called to say they had arrested James, then fourteen, for breaking into and vandalizing a public grade school. He and another boy had destroyed files and painted HELTER SKELTER on the walls. This really scared me, especially the HELTER SKELTER part. I wondered what could be going on in James's mind to do this. Nothing was stolen, so it wasn't for money. To me, it showed such anger toward himself and others, anger at the world. James was so closed off. All he would say was that he didn't know why he had done it. I knew our home was the cause of James's problems, but I still felt helpless to change anything. All three of the boys talked back to me. Whatever I asked them to do, they replied, "Don't have to—Dad said I don't have to listen to you." I had hoped that the court's involvement would make a difference, but James was given six months' probation. Since I couldn't enforce the rules of James's probation and Sam just laughed them off, nothing changed. I tried to "give up"—just not worry about kids or the future. But even when I didn't voice my worries, they nagged at me. I could see myself developing Sam's pattern: ignoring the kids one day, yelling the next.

On January 16, 1987, almost coincidental with James's trouble, Sam came in drunk from the Joneses, acting mad, edgy. In front of the kids, Sam jumped on me, beating me in the face and head. Then he grabbed me by the hair and dragged me, kicking and screaming, into our bedroom. He threw me on the bed, sat on me, and held a pillow over my face until I blacked out. When I came to, I felt fuzzy headed, my ears were ringing, my fingers and toes were cold, tingling. Sam was screaming and throwing things at me. At first, I could only crawl on the floor, then I pulled myself up against a wall. My jewelry box hit the wall by my head, and I heard Sam yell, "There, bitch, throw something else!" My head was too fuzzy to fully comprehend what was going on, but I tried to get out of the room. Sam grabbed me again, threw me on the bed, and pounded on me—my face, my chest, my stomach, everywhere. Then he stood up, grabbed one of my crystal pigs that the kids had bought me for my pig collection, and threw it into the mirror. Glass shattered everywhere. I remember covering my eyes an instant before he grabbed me again, threw me on the floor, and tried to grind my face in the broken glass. I put both hands up over my face when I saw all that glass coming toward me. God, I was so scared as I felt the glass like hundreds of needles sticking in my hands. Then I felt something like fire burning my left hand.

When he finally let me go and left the room, I crawled into the bathroom. I had a two-inch cut in my left hand and lots of little pieces of glass stuck in my hands. As I tried to pick them out with tweezers, blood began gushing from the large cut. I could see it was too deep to heal without stitches, something I hate and fear greatly. I grabbed my white ski jacket, wrapped a washcloth around my left hand, and put my left hand in the jacket pocket so the kids wouldn't see it. In my right hand, I carried a piece of the glass as a weapon in case Sam wouldn't let me leave the house. I walked through the living room and out the front door. At least I was out, but I had no idea what Sam would try next. I saw no lights on at any of the neighboring houses, so I sat on the porch trying to figure out what to do. I was too dizzy to drive myself to the base hospital, and I remembered what the police had told me before, "You left the house so we can't do anything." Finally, I opened the door and asked Matt to drive me to the base hospital. Matt and I waited for more than two hours before I saw a doctor. By that time, I had decided it was too dangerous to report Sam, that he'd maybe go to jail for a few hours, get all boiled up, and come home to beat me again. So I told the doctor I was washing windows and had fallen through one. They sewed up my hand, ten stitches, and Matt and I came home.

I had just laid down in the den when Sam came in, started twisting my wrists, and told me to get into the bedroom. I obeyed; I just felt dead. I thought maybe if I don't fight, he won't hurt me too bad. At first, he tried to have sex with me lying on my back. He hit me a few times, then turned me over onto my stomach, pushed my face in the pillow, and raped me in the rectum. He said, "I can't stand to look at your face, bitch; I'm getting you, bitch. I'll screw your fucking brains out, bitch." I just lay there.

After Sam left, I curled up in a ball with my dog, Skutter Bug, and went to sleep. I had had this dog since 1975. She was just a stray that someone threw from a moving car. Sam hated her, hit her, kicked her, but she was a major comfort to me. The next day, I had to call in sick for work. Then I called the base Mental Health Clinic and tried to report Sam. The person I talked with couldn't focus on anything except telling me I should have reported it the previous night, so I dropped it—again.

For three days, I stayed in bed and told everyone to take care of themselves. I don't think I ate or changed clothes during that time. I think this was the beginning of my half-starving myself, because everything I ate came up, so why bother. I began to be more conscious of my fear of Sam. I couldn't forget how he'd held the pillow over my face, how he'd ground my hands in the broken glass, how he'd punched my head. He'd beaten me so viciously, he could get carried away and kill me. How did he know when to stop, I asked myself.

These thoughts were tied in with the weird movies he'd been watching. He had started talking about "snuff" movies. "That has to be the ultimate orgasm, get the last dying quiver," he said. Then I'd tell myself, "He's just trying to scare you, hold onto reality; Sam couldn't do anything like that." The thought was growing in my mind, "I have to get out, with or without the kids."

As 1987 moved into February and March, I drifted into working longer and longer hours. I recall several times, leaving my twelve-hour shift at the hospital or with a private patient and going to work eighteen more hours on *Crime Story*. Jane seemed fascinated with how much "fun" this was. I'd tell her,

"Why don't you try working, walking, running, being pushed or knocked down?" We worked out on the streets in every kind of sleeveless, backless dress and toe-pinching spike-heeled shoes. In the big, final shoot-out scene, we worked out in drizzling rain and sleet. We were supposed to be having fun, but we were all turning blue from the cold.

About this time, I began to cut down my contacts with Jane. Several times when she had accompanied me to The Mint for the talent showcase, she had gotten drunk and made a scene which embarrassed me. I was also uncomfortable with the way she yelled and swore at her children, calling them bastards, sons of bitches, assholes, or fuckers. I told Sam I didn't want to encourage any more "get-togethers," and he agreed. As time went on though, I noticed Sam spent a great deal of time at the Joneses. Then I noticed he was buying a lot of things for them at the commissary—coffee, cigarettes, meat, milk. At the time, I thought that they were reimbursing Sam for all those things. Later, I would learn differently. It bothered me because back when I had first met Sam and asked him to buy cigarettes for me, he had made such an issue about that being illegal. It didn't make sense that he would do this for neighbors he said he didn't like.

There hadn't been a severe beating for a few weeks, just the usual slapping, knocking me around. But now Sam never had a kind word for me. Just as *Crime Story* ended, I flew to Canada with a lady patient who had had a heart attack, stayed overnight, and flew back. Sam was supposed to pick me up at the airport. He left me waiting at the airport for four hours. I called his shop about four times. Each time, I was told he was on his way. This is just one example of how deliberately mean Sam could be. Matt moved in and out of the house every couple of weeks, so I began sleeping in his room when he was gone. When Matt was home, I slept in the den.

It became increasingly clear to me that Sam was trying to drive me crazy. He'd tell the kids I was crazy, then deny that he ever said such a thing in front of them. I'd beg him to tell me why he was doing this. He'd just smile like a possum and say, "to drive you crazy. I'm going to take everything from you, I'm going to make you nothing, I'll see you in the gutter; I'll take your life." I thought he meant he'd take my kids away, and for so long, my kids had meant my life. If I tried to confront him in the presence of the boys, he'd say, "I don't know what you're talking about. See kids, your mom is crazy; we've got to get help for her."

Late one night in May, Sam sort of staggered through the front door, coming in from the Joneses. He had that mad, cocky look—sharp hand motions, darting eyes, gritting teeth. He smirked at me and went into his bedroom. I heard him come back into the hall and snap a clip into the gun. I had my head down, and I did not look up until much later. I heard him coming down the hall, and I whispered, "My Father who art in Heaven." He was standing in front of the coffee table and I could see his legs. He stood there, snapping the gun, putting the clip in, taking it out, over and over. Finally, he laid the gun on the coffee table with the barrel pointed at him, then he took one finger and twirled it around so that the barrel pointed at me. Finally, I dared to look up at him. He stood up very straight, pointed a finger at me, and said, "You can take this gun and kill yourself, or you can kill me, or you can kill us both, but you don't have the guts to do either."

Then he turned his back and walked into the kitchen. I could hear him eating, so I took my dog and went to bed, but I made myself stay awake. At that point, I didn't care if he killed me, but I was worried about the gun lying there for the kids to pick up. I heard Sam go to bed, and I waited until I thought he was asleep; then I got up and got the gun. I saw that there was a bullet in the chamber and that both safeties were off. I took the clip and all the bullets I could find and I hid them one place; the rest of the gun I hid another place. At that time, doing this made sense to me. I thought I was protecting myself and the kids. I knew then Sam was playing a very dangerous game and I was terrified. Still, I was stuck, thinking I had no choice but to stay.

Matt graduated from high school on June 1, 1987. I paid all his expenses to graduate—cards, gown, pictures. I told Matt that our vacation trip to visit my family, including spending money for him, would be part of his gift from me. I wanted him to have one last carefree summer, to see his family, and be a "kid" with his cousins. Sam threw a fit about this, saying Matt couldn't go. Yet, Sam made a grand gesture of taking Matt and three tables of his friends out to dinner after the graduation ceremony. Sam acted as if he were paying for the dinner, but in fact, he used my credit card, so I ended up paying for it later. I didn't say a word at the time because I didn't want Matt to know how cheap his daddy was; the dinner was Sam's only graduation "gift" to Matt.

Notes from my calendar indicate another nose surgery in June, 1987. The right side was painful, caving in, I guess. I don't remember too much about it. I was walking around in a daze, just surviving. The surgery to break and reset my nose was done in St. George, Utah. I do recall that as Sam drove me back from Utah, he insisted upon stopping at the casino in Mesquite. He stayed in the casino a couple of hours while I waited in the hot car. My eyes were almost swollen shut, and of course, my face and eyes were black and blue from the surgery. I had asked Sam to bring sunglasses for me, but he forgot. Finally after waiting and waiting in the hot car for Sam, I had to go to the bathroom so badly that I went into the casino. I was in tears from the humiliation of everyone staring at me. Even then, Sam refused to leave his video poker machine. I went back to the car, lay down in the rear seat, and sweated. True to form, Sam showed me that I didn't matter, that only his wishes mattered.

I looked so awful that I didn't work for two weeks. When I had to return to St. George for my checkup, I took Daniel with me. I told Sam I didn't want him to go, that he could find plenty of video poker machines in Las Vegas. Daniel and I had a very nice day. After I saw the doctor, we went to a thrift shop and an antique shop. After lunch, we visited the Mormon Church. On the way back, we stopped to take pictures of bighorn sheep and a camel on display at a gas station.

The contrast between my trip to Utah with Sam and the one with Daniel made a big impression on me, even then. I began to recognize how different my life could be without Sam.

As soon as my nose had healed enough for me to travel, the boys and I left for Arkansas. As always, I was eager to see my family, but I was also eager to get away from Sam. We had a wonderful visit with my family, the best ever. My sister and I grew closer to each other and everybody seemed to enjoy being together again. For me, just being away from the constant threat of attack was like a tonic.

Just before we had to start back to Vegas, my car began to overheat, and I had to pay $150 in cash to have the radiator repaired. Although this exhausted my supply of cash, I wasn't worried. I just figured I'd put motel bills for our return on my credit cards. When we stopped the first night, I tried to use my Mastercard first and then my Visa. Both were shut off. I was furious because I had given Sam the money to write checks to pay these bills, and obviously he never paid them. I also knew "we" had recently gotten a $1,600 income tax refund. Of course, that money was being handled by Sam. When I called Sam, I must have sounded angry and insistent enough that he did wire us $200. But the first night, we slept in the car, waiting for the wire service to open.

We got back on the road again, stopping in Albuquerque, New Mexico, the second night. I was sick with a fever caused by mosquitoes, I think. I called Sam to check in, and right off, he informed me that the car insurance agent had told him that Matt couldn't live with us anymore because we didn't carry insurance on him, and he might drive one of the cars. I said, "Bull. Then we'll just have to find another agent."

Sam said, "No. Matt can't come home." I told him, "Fine, then none of us will come home." I hung up on him and drifted off to sleep. Matt went out, got food, and insisted that I eat. Then he took James and Daniel swimming while I rested. I slept and sweated a lot but woke up hungry and feeling better the next morning. I called Sam again, and he said the same thing—that Matt and I shouldn't come home. I told him, "It's my house too, and we're all coming home."

We got home in the wee hours of the next morning on July 30.

To my amazement, Sam was nice to us when we arrived. He talked nice and touched me with gentleness. When he asked me to come to bed, that's all he had to do. I loved him and his wanting to make love meant a lot to me. I remember lying in bed that morning, rubbing his chest. Lord, how I loved his chest!

The next day, I called and called for Skutter Bug, but she didn't come. Sam had gone to work and I was busy unpacking, doing laundry, and cleaning. In the midst of this confusion, Jane came over to visit. Although I rarely went to her house anymore, I wasn't rude to her. When I mentioned to her that I couldn't find Skutter Bug, she smirked as she said, "Ask Sam about kicking her." I said, "If you know something, tell me." She just said, "I don't want to get involved in this; just ask him." I recalled the hundreds of times Sam had made remarks about me and "my bitch dog." Had he killed her, I wondered. Later when I asked him, he laughed at me but refused to tell me what had happened to my beloved dog. I got the distinct impression that he had killed her. I begged him to tell me if she was dead or alive, but he just laughed again.

There was still the matter of Matt's living with us to deal with, so I called the insurance agent. He didn't know what I was talking about, but as soon as Sam realized what I was doing, he jumped up and jerked the phone out of the wall. I had already heard enough. Matt was standing there watching this, and I turned to Sam and said, "Matt stays." Sam just gave me that smug smile as he walked across the street to the Joneses.

What a surprise! The next day Sam announced he had bought Matt a car from John Jones's ex-son-in-law. Sam had emptied Matt's $300 savings account without Matt's knowledge or permission. He said the car cost $125, plus a $25 finder's fee for John. "I'm keeping the rest," he told Matt. The car had to be towed to our house, never ran, and eventually had to be towed to the junkyard. Matt protested bitterly, but Sam smirked as he said, "You live here. That's the breaks." Matt ended up with no car and no money.

Within the next day or so, I began to notice that all my personal things had been disturbed—my dresser drawers, my closet, my jewelry box, everything. I asked Sam about it, and again he gave me that smug smile as he said, "Well, I gave Jane a key to the house while you were gone so she could get in whenever she wants." I told him I didn't want her in my house when I wasn't home, and he replied, "This is *my* house, and I'll have anyone in that I want."

The idea had been growing in my mind that I had to get out, to get away from Sam. My love for my kids had always stopped me before; they were so little and helpless. Now as I looked at my kids, I realized they were old enough to choose. Matt had decided to join the Army and would be leaving soon anyway. I began to save money to get my own place. I decided that when I had enough money, I would let James and Daniel decide whether to live with Sam or me. If they both chose to live with Sam, I would go back to Arkansas and live near my family, but if either or both decided they wanted to live with me, I would stay at least until they finished school. But no matter what the boys decided, I was determined to divorce Sam, to end the abuse forever.

I worked every extra hour I could get, both in-home nursing and as a movie extra. I was busy, but not too busy to notice that Sam constantly carted groceries over to the Joneses. We ate the cheapest hamburger, while he took them standing rib roasts. I observed Sam giving John cash on many occasions. I didn't know what it meant, but it made me even more determined to get out.

During this period, I became friendly with my new next-door neighbor, Debra. She couldn't understand why I constantly worked so hard. "Your husband makes enough money to take care of you," she said. I confided in her that I was going to leave Sam, that if I didn't, either he would kill me or I would kill myself. She understood because she had previously been married to an abusive man.

Sam continued to come into my bedroom when he pleased, about three or four times a week. He'd tell me, "Go ahead and scream; you'll just wake the kids. I have a right to have you any time I want anyway." He punched me on the head so much he left lumps causing headaches. I was scared all the time, my hands always sweaty. Since I couldn't keep food down, I continued to lose weight. Still I kept going with the knowledge that soon I could leave.

Toward the end of September 1987, I had about $800, enough money to start looking for an apartment. On the night of October 13, I still had not found my own place. Sam had spent several hours over at the Joneses, and I was busy cleaning up the kitchen. At about 11 p.m., I was rinsing the sink, the final step. The rest of the kitchen was sparkling clean. Sam came into the kitchen, humming, acting very cocky. He went to the refrigerator, took out the squirt bottle of mustard, looked me in the eye, grinned like a possum, and proceeded to squirt and smear mustard all over the clean counters. I didn't say a word. I pulled off my rubber gloves, threw them in the sink, and went to bed. That night, October 13, 1987, was the last time Sam raped me.

The next day, I talked with James and Daniel, telling them my plan. Daniel chose to stay with Sam, and James said, "Let's get out; I can't stand it here anymore." It took two days to find an apartment, and on October 16, James and I moved. It was a one-bedroom, upstairs apartment, neat, clean, and peaceful. I slept on the living room couch and gave James the bedroom. Sam didn't seem too upset. In fact, he brought over a carload of our belongings. At the time, I thought he seemed glad to have us out and that gave me hope that I could now have my own life.

9

Rolling the Dice

In searching for an apartment, my two main concerns had been to find a place within James's school district and to find a decent neighborhood, at a rent I could afford. As a nurse's aide, I made about $800 gross per month. I planned to continue working any additional hours or shifts I could get, plus my work as an extra in *Crime Story*. Even though the rent was $325 per month, I was determined to make it on my own this time. In fact, I worked on *Crime Story* from midnight October 18 until 2:30 p.m. on Monday, October 19.

Things were rough money-wise at first. Sam didn't pay a penny for James, but I was so relieved to be away from him that I didn't care. I applied for and received food stamps. I also obtained surplus food—cheese, rice, beans, powdered milk. We ate a lot of red beans and rice, southern style. Once I apologized for this to James, but he just said, "Mom, it's fine. I'd eat dirt to get out of that house."

James really pitched in and helped me with the housework. Often I'd be gone for more than a day, just going from one job to another and back again, once as long as thirty-six hours. Working hard didn't bother me. I was so relieved to be free. James and I got along fine; we savored the peace and quiet of our new home.

During the first couple of months, Sam didn't harass me much except when I picked up Daniel for visits. Then he'd threaten me with "taking everything including your kids." This would upset me to the point of throwing up, but it was worth it to see Daniel. I was trying so hard to keep things peaceful that when Sam asked to use my car to take the kids out shooting in the desert, I traded cars with him for one day. When I got the car back, it was leaking oil five or six places. The repair job cost me over $135, which I couldn't afford; my money situation was tough enough already. But I had a complete check done on the car at that time, and everything else was fine.

Through James, I knew that Sam had deliberately damaged my car. "Dad was really cutting up with your car; he thought it was fun to spin round and round in the desert, throwing up rocks," James said. James also told me that Sam had "accidentally" fired his deer rifle, and the bullet hit the ground between Daniel and James. I thought all this was meant to scare me, and it did. But I didn't say anything to Sam; I just didn't want to make waves. "Please, God, let it be over," I prayed every day.

Matt was still living in the house with Sam and Daniel. From Daniel, I learned that Matt had the house full of his friends, constantly playing Dungeons and Dragons. One night they knocked over a long shelf, breaking most of my crystal collection. When I mentioned this to Sam, he told me it was his house and none of my business. Much later, I found a stack of rental receipts for 150 X-rated movies which Sam had watched with the kids, even Daniel. If I had known that at the time, I don't know what I would have done. Thinking about it now makes me sick, and Daniel is so ashamed, he can hardly admit watching.

One morning as I was leaving for work with a private patient, Daniel called, crying and telling me how sick he was. Sam had gone to work, leaving Daniel sick and alone. Although it tore me up, I couldn't go to him. There was no one to replace me that late, and I had to make a living. I told Daniel to take two Tylenols and lie down with a wet washcloth on his head. When I hung up, Daniel was crying and so was I. Since it was against agency rules for me to receive any phone calls, I called Daniel every hour during the day to check on him. He got better, but I felt his dad should have taken care of him before going to work. I tried to confront Sam about this, but he just laughed it off.

In November, Sam asked me to sign a joint petition for divorce. It stated that we got married September 19, 1972; in fact, we were married September 20, 1971. The petition gave Sam the house, all the furniture and furnishings, and custody of Daniel and James. I got nothing, although Sam said James could go ahead and live with me. James saw the petition and got very upset because he was born April 14, 1972. James thought we had lied to him, so I got out the marriage license and birth certificate, which proved he was not born out of wedlock. James calmed down, but thought it strange that his dad didn't know what day he got married.

Sam's petition also stipulated that I had to keep my married name. He told me he didn't want me, but he wouldn't let me go. I refused to sign Sam's petition and told him, "We can just fight it out in court."

Things got much worse after that. Sam started threatening everything from beating the hell out of me to, "I'll see you dead before I see you get one penny. I'll kill your ass, bitch. You're not getting anything; it's all mine. I'm going to use it to start a new life. And I'm taking your kids too."

Sam had threatened to take the kids and kill me many times before, but now he wasn't screaming it at me. His voice sounded cold, hard, deliberate. Fear and anxiety became my constant companions. I began to keep my loaded gun on my body when I was in the apartment. When I went out anywhere, I removed the clips and carried them with me in my briefcase, along with my marriage license, birth certificates, and other papers for the divorce. I started carrying my briefcase everywhere I went after a large file, containing W-2s, the kids' report cards, medical bills, insurance papers, and so on, disappeared.

One night after working until 2 a.m., I opened the apartment door to find James standing there, pale and shaken, with a knife in his hand ready to attack. He blurted out that someone had tried to get in, that he had watched as the doorknob turned and the door vibrated as someone pushed against it. He asked me to tell him where I kept the gun, but I told him I would not trust him with it. "You'll have to run out on the balcony and climb down if anyone gets in when I'm not here," I said. I knew he could do that, because he and Daniel had gotten in that way once when he had locked himself out of the apartment. On days I was scheduled with a private patient, I began leaving for work at least an hour early, so that I could drive around to make sure I wasn't being followed. Sam had threatened to cause me trouble at work in order to get me fired. "I'll come in there and drag you out by the hair on your head, you bitch," he said. When I was scheduled at the hospital, I didn't worry so much about what Sam would do because there were so many people around.

As Sam's phone calls became more threatening, I began parking my car in out-of-the-way places when I came home from work in the wee hours of the morning. I'd park two or three blocks away, at times in other apartment complexes. Then I'd walk alone to my own apartment—even through dark alleys. I didn't feel afraid of that, and I never carried my gun outside my own apartment. It seems strange now, but in my own apartment, I needed my gun loaded and ready. I was terrified there because that was the one place Sam knew I'd be, the one place he could corner me. Several times, after especially violent calls, I called 911 for help, but the only help I got from them was, "Call after he gets into the house." I was amazed; I thought, "Trying to break in isn't against the law? He has to be inside?" To me, that was no help. How many times had I tried to call for help when Sam was beating me, only to have him jerk the phone out of the wall?

It's so hard to capture my terror in words. I remembered that I had worked at the gas company as a security guard without a gun. There was some trouble about another company trying to steal their company secrets, and a guy who was not from the phone company had been caught working on the phone system. I patrolled the building and grounds at night alone, and I had special instructions to keep my eyes on the main computer and phone system in the subbasement. This required walking into the dark basement and reaching around a wall about four feet to find the light switch. I was scared, but I was never afraid for my life. I never broke the rules and carried a gun, even though I know some other guards did. I'd have quit before breaking the rules. I just never was that scared of anything or anyone until this time of separation from Sam. I had no doubt that he would find a way to kill me.

I began to consider another option, and I discussed it with James. My idea was to leave the country, go to Mexico or Canada, change our names, and just vanish. "James," I said, "if we stay here, things will turn out bad. I have such bad feelings about your dad, of what he might do." James didn't want to leave. "Mom," he said, "Dad owes me something. You've got to stay here and fight. And what about Daniel? I don't think he's going to last over there much longer."

Thanksgiving wasn't much of a holiday with all this going on. I worked all day, then James and I had dinner together, nothing lavish the way it used to be. Christmas was coming up, and I knew Sam had plenty because we had always put away $100 a month for Christmas. But the account was in Sam's name only. Sam showed Daniel $700 that he had drawn out of the account, knowing that Daniel would tell me. Then Sam told me he would give me part of it if I would sign a blank receipt. I told him no and worked every extra hour I could get for Christmas money. James and I managed on what I made for Christmas, although I didn't get enough money together until Christmas Eve day to buy food or gifts.

A few days before Christmas, Sam seemed to calm down. We discussed gifts for the boys and agreed that I would buy the guitar amplifier that James wanted. We also agreed to have Christmas dinner all together at the house. James had skipped several visitations with his dad, and Sam accused me of keeping him away. On Christmas, I insisted that James go, even though he didn't want to. I hoped it would be easier for James to see Sam if I were there also.

James and I went over about noon after I cooked most of the food at my apartment. I had prepared a ham and a hen; I don't recall that Sam bought anything for the dinner. James and I had both been sick with the flu, so we weren't high with the holiday spirit. Sam was already drinking when we arrived, putting whiskey in everything he drank. I tried to be pleasant, to make small talk, but Sam just grunted, watched TV, and went back and forth to the Joneses.

When it came time to open gifts, James was very hurt. Sam had given him another amplifier, one he had gotten on sale and couldn't return. The amplifier I had given James was on sale and couldn't be returned either, so James ended up with a credit at the store, which he never spent—the store just didn't have that much that James wanted. The one thing he asked Sam for, a particular record, Sam said he couldn't find. James had told Sam where to find it and went there himself the next day and bought it. I gave James back his money, but Sam never repaid me. I could see the hurt look on James's face as Daniel and Matt opened all their gifts. Sam really went all out for them. That was the very last time we were all together as a family.

James and I left about mid-afternoon, and Daniel came home with us for a three-day visit. Sam was obviously mad, but as soon as we got to the apartment, we all three relaxed and enjoyed Christmas night. James had given me a guinea pig as my gift. He knew I wanted a pet but couldn't have a dog or cat because that meant a $100 nonrefundable deposit. I couldn't afford that, mainly because of Sam's poor credit history. He paid all the bills late and had such a bad rating with the electric company that I had to pay a $100 deposit to set up an account in my name. They even said that if Sam failed to pay his current bills, they would charge me. The phone company almost charged me a deposit, but a very nice lady who had been in my situation let it go. The fact that I was still legally married to Sam meant extra expense for me, but there were no such consequences for Sam.

One of my private patients was taken to Hawaii for Christmas, which really cut down my income. I started taking two-hour jobs during the day, anything for extra money. After taking care of Christmas, I was worried about paying my regular bills in January. "What if I get really sick," I'd think, "then I'd have no income." I knew that one reason Sam kept up the nerve-racking phone calls was to keep me upset enough that I couldn't eat or sleep. He'd always known that my stomach was super sensitive, that I'd throw up if I got too upset. The day after Christmas, I was back at work and the same old routine. I cried a lot at night, missing Daniel so much. He came over for visits at least once a week, but Sam was so nasty to me about each visit, I was usually nervous and upset during the visits. Daniel would tell us about expensive outings with Sam, and he had started wearing designer clothes. James looked hurt and showed his bitterness in statements like, "My dad's possessed by the devil." I tried to discuss this with Sam by phone, telling him, "It isn't right for Daniel to have so much and James so little." Sam just said, "His choice. He'll find out that he either lives with me or he gets nothing." I wound up crying, begging him to stop doing this to his children. His response was, "How do you like it now, bitch? I'm getting you."

Shortly after the new year (1988), I was caring for a hospice patient who was dying of lung cancer. I received a phone call at work through call forwarding from a process server. His voice sounded loud and agitated as he told me, "I have divorce papers to serve you; I know you're in there—I can see your car." I had walked to work that day, about six blocks, so I was not in my apartment. I was trying to order more oxygen for my patient, and I finally told the man, "Fine, throw them at the door for all I care," and hung up on him. After that call, I stopped using call forwarding and began wearing a beeper. When I got home that afternoon, I found the divorce papers in the bushes downstairs. The process server didn't even attach them to my door.

It was obvious from those papers I had to get my own lawyer. This was just more money I didn't have and another expense I couldn't afford. My sister loaned me some money, and on my next Saturday off, James went with me as I retained the services of Connie Thompson, a female attorney. I paid $100 to get started, and her secretary gave me a receipt. This secretary, Louise, seemed very friendly and sympathetic. In fact, she gave me her home phone number and encouraged me to call her anytime. My attorney read the papers Sam had served on me and said they were "bullshit." "What about the house?" she asked. I told her from the start I didn't care about the house, Sam could have it. But she encouraged me to fight for my half of everything, plus child support and joint custody of the boys. She prepared a response to Sam's attorney.

About the time Sam received this response, he began taping some of our phone arguments without my knowledge. First, he'd call me, threatening everything—from court action, to tearing up my car, to killing me. Then he'd hang up on me and call me right back. I'd be so mad, I'd start telling him off, and once I remember telling him, "You take my kids and it will be the last thing you ever do." I'm not sure whether I meant it or not, but at any rate, he had me on tape threatening him. It did not occur to me to tape him or that he was taping me. He told me, "You better look over your shoulder, bitch. Sometime, some place, you'll never know when—I'll be there. Don't forget, bitch, you'd better look over your shoulder all the time. I'll see you dead before I give you a penny."

I began sleeping with my gun. I was always battle ready. I'd start out the night, fully clothed, sitting up with the TV on and the gun in my hand. By morning, I'd find myself slumped over on the bed, the gun still in my hand and the TV still running. A few times, I woke up scratching my head with the gun, my right hand stiff and sore from holding it. At times, there were red imprints on my hand and face from lying on the gun. I stopped taking showers because I couldn't hear with the water running. Baths seemed a little safer because I could stay by the door while the water filled the tub, then turn it off and fly in and out of the tub.

I would leave the bathroom door ajar while I washed my face and brushed my teeth, keeping my ears open for any sound from the hall or balcony. My gun was ready and with me. I'd lay it on the floor to use the commode and on the sink while I washed. I'm surprised it didn't rust.

Several times, I tried to call my attorney, but Louise always told me Connie was busy or Connie was out. When I tried to make appointments, there was never an open hour when I was free from work. In the middle of this divorce mess, I received a $700 check from the military insurance company. It was reimbursement for my medical bills, which I had already paid. I tried to call Connie to see if it was legal for me to cash it since Sam was giving me no support money. I didn't get to talk with Connie, but Louise relayed Connie's message: "Go ahead and cash it, in lieu of child support." I finally questioned Louise about no contact with Connie, and she said, "Beth, you don't talk with Connie. I'm a paralegal; you talk with me. I'm the one that handles the cases; Connie just shows up in court. Do you want her to continue the case or not?" At that time, I didn't know this was unusual, and I didn't see that I had a choice.

One Saturday, Daniel was at the apartment for a visit when Sam called to say he was on his way over, that he was going to beat the hell out of me. I called 911; they said, "Call after he gets in." I tried to call my attorney. When I couldn't reach her, I called Louise. I was crying, begging for help. I told Louise I needed a restraining order or something to keep Sam away from me. Louise said she'd get word to Connie as soon as she could, but she was sure she couldn't reach her until Monday. I called Sam's first sergeant asking for help. I had spoken to him once before, trying to get some child support for James. At that time, he told me Sam was under no obligation to pay child support unless the court had ordered it. This time I told him how scared I was of Sam, and his reply was, "From what Sam's told me about you, I don't blame him for beating the hell out of you." I ended the conversation by saying, "Your good little GI is going to jail if he touches me once more. I won't back down again; I will press charges." There was no help anywhere for me and the kids that night. We were so terrified, we pushed all the furniture against the door. All our belongings were piled to the ceiling. We had to climb and crawl over it to get to the bathroom or kitchen. I sat with my back against a wall all night, my gun in hand, ready to defend myself. Sam never showed up that night.

The next night, Sunday, Daniel called Sam, asking to stay with me one more night. He seemed afraid to go back to his dad's house, and both he and James were running temperatures. I couldn't afford to take them to a private clinic and wait for reimbursement, so I planned to take them to the base clinic on Monday. Daniel talked to Sam a couple of minutes, then got upset and passed the phone to me. Sam was shrieking in a high-pitched voice about how he was going to "get me." I told him to shut up, that he had Daniel most of the time and that this was Daniel's decision. "If Daniel wants to stay tonight," I told Sam, "he damn sure will." I tried to tell him that Daniel was sick, but Sam hung up in my ear. I tried to call him back several times, but it was the same thing—he slammed the phone down.

The next morning I tried again to tell Sam that Daniel was too sick to go to school, that I was taking him to the clinic, and that I would bring him home afterward. Sam hung up the minute he heard my voice. After hours of waiting at the clinic, James was given an allergy shot, and Daniel, who was diagnosed with an ear infection and ruptured ear drum, was given a prescription for antibiotics. It took another hour to get the prescription filled.

It was almost 5 p.m. as I pulled into the cul-de-sac to drop Daniel at Sam's. I told Daniel, "Just give me a kiss now. I'm not getting out because I don't want a run-in with your dad." Before Daniel was out of the car, Sam was running across the street from the Joneses, arms waving, screaming, "I'm going to take your kids; I'm going to take your car; I'm going to take everything you've got." He grabbed Daniel by the neck, his fingers digging into the boy's neck as he'd done to me so many times, waving his free arm with a fist at me. He was half pushing, half dragging Daniel up the driveway toward the house.

A hundred fears ran through my mind—was he going to force Daniel down on his hands and knees, was he going to beat Daniel because he couldn't get to me, was he going to make Daniel afraid to come back to visit me? I jumped out of my still-rolling car, asking James to stop it, and ran toward the house. I beat on the door and rang the doorbell, getting no response. I could hear Daniel crying, "Dad, please let me go with Mom; please let me out." I looked in the kitchen window and saw Sam still clutching Daniel by the neck. There was a bottle of whiskey about three-fourths empty on the sink. Daniel was hysterical, but Sam wouldn't let him go, and he wouldn't open the door. I looked around the porch and saw a pair of hedge clippers. I grabbed them and tried to wedge them between the door and the jamb to force the door open. About that time, the door flew open and the clippers fell to the ground as Sam grabbed me by the shoulders and threw me against the wall. He was gritting his teeth and spit was flying, as he yelled, "Now I'll kill your ass!" He slammed the back of my head against the wall several times. I felt explosions of light and dark going off in my head. He was all fists and open palms, hitting and punching me in the face and breasts, coming at me so fast I couldn't do anything. I could feel myself losing consciousness as he twisted my left arm and hand. I barely remember flying through the air and landing in the middle of the front yard. I was lying on my back with blood in my mouth, choking. My chest and ribs hurt so bad when I tried to move, I thought maybe a rib had been broken and punctured a lung.

James had called 911, then ran back to help me up and into my car. Soon the police and ambulance came. By then, Sam had come out of the house and was sitting on the hood of his car.

One of the paramedics was a guy from my EMT class. I was completely humiliated that he saw me like this. They checked me over and wanted to take me to the hospital, but the most important thing to me was to take care of Daniel. The police handcuffed Sam and took him to jail. I refused to go to the hospital because there was no one to take care of the kids. All three of us were so upset we were shaking, in shock. Under police supervision, we went inside to collect the boys' belongings. Daniel said, "Mom, I want to take all my stuff; I'm not coming back here." I told both boys to take whatever they wanted. James looked around his room and said, "I don't see anything I want." I tried to help Daniel get his things together, but I was too dazed to think clearly. We ended up taking only a few of his clothes.

When we got back to the apartment, I tried to call my attorney, but got Louise instead. She told me to go to the police substation and make out a written report. I had just started working for a new family on an eight to four shift, so I had to let them know I'd be late the next morning. With Daniel at my place, which was out of his school district, he had to be driven to school, then take the bus home. The nursing service called me back to say that my hours had been changed to nine to five. With that taken care of, I fed the kids. Then we went to the police substation, and I filed my written report of the incident. Before I went to bed, I checked with the police, who assured me Sam was still locked up; I knew he'd be coming after me as soon as he got out. But that night, I had my first real sleep in a month.

The next morning I could hardly get up. I hurt all over, had a blinding headache, and couldn't focus my eyes. I was sick with the dry heaves until I drank some coffee; then I threw that up. In spite of how I felt, I took Daniel to school and went to work. I was so sick all day that I went to the base hospital that night. I had an open, oozing sore on the back of my head, a concussion, rebroken nose, and sprained fingers on my left hand. The base hospital personnel didn't even know that Sam was in jail. His first sergeant had covered for him by putting him "on leave."

I checked with the jail about a dozen times, making sure Sam was still in there. It had occurred to me that maybe he was just trying to injure me with broken bones, and so on, enough that I could no longer work. Then he would have clear sailing. He could take the kids, push through the divorce, and I'd be a permanent cripple. I told James, "I'd rather he [Sam] just kill me, not leave me all broken and unable to work." I had an image of him sitting back and watching me die slowly. Every time I pulled myself up from one of his attacks, he'd find some other way to get me. He probably thought I'd be laid off from work by this latest attack, but I fooled him. I worked in spite of feeling so sick; I worked every day, even if I had to crawl to do it.

That same day, I called my attorney again, trying to get a restraining order. Louise said Connie was too busy, but that I had to pay another $100 on my bill immediately to get the restraining order. I couldn't leave work to take the money to the office, but I took the money to Louise's apartment that night. When I asked for a receipt, she said, "I can't give you a receipt for money Connie hasn't gotten yet. I'll have to take the money to her and get the receipt. I'll bring it to you next week." I said, "I'll take the cash to a 7-Eleven and get a money order." "No, no," Louise said, "I'm leaving in just a few minutes. I can't wait for you. If you want Connie to continue your case, you have to give me $100 now or she's dropping you." I was desperate; I gave it to her against my better judgment.

Throughout the next week, Louise stalled about giving me a receipt. After I threatened to tell Connie about this, Louise changed her story completely. "Beth," she said, "you must be crazy saying I took money from you. I'd never do that, I could lose my job." Finally, I talked to the head of the nursing service about my situation. She called Connie, told her it was an emergency, and to call me at work. I remember sitting on the floor behind the counter in my patient's kitchen, crying as I told Connie what had happened. She didn't know anything about the attack or my urgent request for a restraining order. I told her I couldn't use her as my attorney if she didn't get this mess with Louise straightened up and that I would press charges against Louise. She arranged for a meeting later that week in her office.

When we met in Connie's office, Louise lied and said she couldn't believe I'd say such a thing. I asked Connie if we took lie detector tests and I passed, would she fire Louise? Connie said she couldn't ask Louise to take the test, but if I took it and passed, she would credit the money to my account. The next week, I took the lie detector test, passed, and went straight to Connie's office with the results. Louise was there, saw me come in, and couldn't look me in the eye. Connie said she would fire her on Friday, but she never got the chance. Louise just left and never came back. Connie credited me with the $100 Louise took, plus the $200 I paid for the lie detector test.

Anyway, I still had a lawyer and I had a restraining order forbidding Sam to come near me or my apartment. Sam was served with the temporary restraining order (TRO) when he was brought before the judge.

Connie told me to pick up a copy of the TRO at her office and take it to police headquarters. "I thought that was part of your job," I told her. She said, "Well, yes. But you could probably handle it faster." I told her I really couldn't take any more time off from work, and she assured me she would handle it.

After twenty-four hours in jail, Sam was released on bail. From then on, I also had Sam's reign of terror on the phone. He hounded me day and night, calling, threatening, hanging up. I thought about killing myself, but always the thought of what that would do to my children stopped me. So I prayed to God to just let me die. If I died and had to leave the kids that way, it wouldn't be my fault, but I'd be out of it, once and forever.

I tried to bargain with Sam; no, I begged him. "Just pay a decent amount of child support until the boys are eighteen," I said, "then no more money. Think of how much you'll save. I won't ask for any of the property or your retirement if you'll just help support the boys." But Sam left no room for bargaining. "I'll kill your ass before I see you get a penny," he said, "it's my money; I worked for it. If the kids don't live with me, they don't get a penny, and you'll never get a penny."

Sam bragged that he had "all the evidence I need, according to my lawyer, to take everything, including the kids." When I asked Connie about this, she said, "Jim Stone [Sam's lawyer] is a decent man; he won't go for all Sam's bullshit. There are laws mandating child support. Sam has to pay it." I began to quote my lawyer to Sam, telling him he couldn't push me any more. "I don't believe your lawyer will risk his career just to please you," I told Sam, "You'll do whatever the law says. You're not above the law. They can lock you up if you don't obey the law, and I'm not going to be afraid of you or your threats any more." This made him even more furious. His calls, hang-ups, and threats grew more frequent and more intense.

Sam played mind games with the boys too, especially Daniel. The week after Daniel moved in with me, he brought home a note announcing that a second set of school pictures would be taken. Daniel had missed out on the first set of pictures, taken in September, because Sam had not given him the money in time. If a child doesn't bring his money on the day pictures are taken, the photographer doesn't even take his picture. I was determined that Daniel should have his school pictures and took him to Albertson's with me to get the $12 money order. The afternoon the pictures were returned, Daniel went from school to Sam's to spend the night. Sam tried to take the pictures away from him, saying that he had paid for them. Daniel told him, "No, I saw Mom get the money order. I know Mom paid for them." Daniel let Sam take one of the five-by-sevens because Sam said it was for his mother, for Grandma. Sam tried everything to get the pictures from Daniel. He told him, "Your mom's a liar," and even brought out a check as proof. Poor Daniel didn't know that checks have to be cashed or that Sam's account did not return canceled checks. Apparently, Sam had written a check but never gave it to Daniel to take to school. There is a letter in Daniel's school file from the school secretary, stating that Daniel came into the office, asking permission to call Sam for the money on the day pictures were made in September. She told him it was already too late. Anyway, Daniel was confused and upset by this. I tried to comfort him, but I could feel the walls closing in around me tighter and tighter. How could this man I had loved so deeply deliberately mess with his own son's mind?

That Saturday night after a dozen of Sam's threatening phone calls, I began sobbing uncontrollably, tearing at my hair until I pulled out several handfuls. I just lost it. As hard as I was trying, I couldn't escape Sam's reign of terror. I wasn't aware of the kids watching, but I guess they saw this.

The next week, on March 7, Daniel went off the deep end. He was getting ready for school, and then suddenly he ran at me and started beating at me with his fists. I wrestled with him until we both wound up on the floor, crying. Daniel said, "Mom, just leave me with him. You and James just leave. He'll never let you go unless you leave me with him. Just leave, Mom, while you can." Then he wrapped his arms around my waist, his head buried against me as he sobbed.

I knew then I had to get help for my kids. As soon as Daniel settled down, I took him to school, came back, and started calling until I had an appointment at a psychiatric hospital for 7 p.m. that evening. The counselor recommended that both boys come into in-patient care for a complete workup. Then we would all get counseling, and the records could be used as evaluations for court. The counselor thought this would help the court reach a fair decision about custody and visitation rights.

The next day I had to take my private patients on an outing to Bonnie Springs, an oasis area about twenty miles outside Las Vegas. Bonnie Springs has a petting zoo, a pond with ducks, a restaurant, and amusement area. So I decided to take Daniel along, too. I asked James, knowing he was a bit old for this sort of outing, and I wasn't surprised or disappointed when he begged off. It was a beautiful sunshiny day, and we had a peaceful, fun time together.

The next day, I went to the school, picked up Daniel's books, then checked him into the hospital. Daniel wanted to go, even though he was scared. He said, "Maybe this will fix it so that I can live with you, Mom." Daniel had been climbing into bed with me, scared to sleep in his own bed. He talked in his sleep and had nightmares every night. He'd fall asleep with his arms wrapped around me, so I didn't sleep much. Daniel was eleven, but he was still my baby, the baby I had fought so hard to save as an infant. I didn't want Sam to know this, even though I slept in my street clothes.

From many past experiences, I knew how Sam could make the most innocent act seem dirty. "Please God, don't let Sam hurt the kids anymore; just let the custody battle and divorce be over."

Looking back at this period of my life, I wonder how I managed to work or function at all. I know I was ready for the funny farm. Every night was filled with terrifying dreams; I'd wake up soaked with sweat, unable to remember for a few minutes *who I was*. I began to pass up my turns when driving. I developed a twitch in my right eye and mouth that I could stop only by holding my hand there. I had severe chest pains and high blood pressure. My heart pounded as if trying to break loose from my body, and my head throbbed as it never had before. The thought of how sweet and restful death would be echoed in my mind. But I just couldn't kill myself, because I didn't want to go to hell. And I couldn't leave my kids to face Sam alone. "This is my fault," I thought to myself. "I should be able to get my kids out of this." In desperation, I called my sister and told her how scared I was that Sam would kill us all. If I were killed, I wanted my family to know that Sam was responsible.

The weekend of March 12 to 13, Sam went to Mina. On Sunday the 13th, James and I went to the house to get more of the boys' clothes and belongings. Daniel particularly wanted his stuffed toys. When we arrived in the cul-de-sac, I went to a friendly neighbor's house to call the police so they could supervise us when we entered the house. Before I could call, the police arrived. Jane had called them and bustled over to involve herself. "Yes sir," she said to the police, "I have the key. I can go in anytime I want, but she can't. Sam had her and her kids locked out." We entered the house with the police, and Jane followed us in. I asked the police to keep her out, but they said, "She has permission to be here." I walked by my refrigerator, and she swung the door open, almost knocking me down as she said, "Let me see; what should we have for supper?" She was rubbing it in, acting as if my house belonged to her. She followed us around from room to room, smirking and twirling the keys. I said, "Get out of my face, bitch." She said, "Oh, it's not me whose own son is going to court against her." "What?" I said. "It's Matt," she said. I was too upset to absorb this information. We had gathered up James's and Daniel's clothes when I noticed my tape recorder sitting by the phone with the listening device still on it. I asked the police if I could take my tape recorder, and they said not unless I could prove it was mine with a bill of sale or something similar. Of course, I couldn't, but it seemed certain to me that Sam was taping telephone conversations, probably mine. Like a bolt of lightning, I understood his pattern of making a dozen threatening calls to me, then saying nothing when I called back screaming at him. As James and I left, Jane stood smugly in the door, twirling the keys and smirking at me. Even now, I feel that same helplessness and humiliation from another woman taking over my house. Sam had given her this power, and the police supported her. I could do nothing about it.

When we got back to my apartment, I called Matt in Fort Benning, Georgia. "What did Jane mean, Matt?" I asked. Matt was evasive at first but finally told me Sam had called him so many times that he (Matt) agreed to make a statement by phone to Sam's attorney. The attorney had questioned him about the November incident in which my hand was badly cut with broken glass. Matt had told him that he did not remember seeing a cut on my hand when I came out of the bedroom. I was crushed; my own son, not even Sam's son, was feeding into Sam's plot to destroy me and his brothers. "Which hand, Matt? Which hand did you see?" I begged him to remember. This was so important to me. "I saw your right hand and it wasn't cut," Matt said. "And where was my left hand, Matt?" I asked. After a long pause, Matt said, "It was in your pocket—God, Mom, I've made a terrible mistake. It's your left hand that bled through your jacket. Now, I remember." That eased my mind somewhat, but what really got me was that no matter how it turned out, Sam had won because he had created a very big wedge between me and Matt.

When Sam returned from Mina that Sunday, I called him and told him I knew about Matt's statement and how I knew. He just laughed and said, "I told you that no matter what it takes in court, I'll get you." He bragged about Jane testifying for him; "she's going to fix your ass." I said, "What can she say to hurt me except a bunch of lies?" Sam said, "Well, most of her testimony is lies. So what." I told him, "Jane must be stupider than I thought to commit perjury." Sam was still laughing as he agreed Jane was stupid, but useful to him because "she is willing to say anything to fix your ass."

After I hung up the phone from this conversation with Sam, the three of us—James, Daniel, and I—sat around, discussing what to do. We talked about the possibilities of going to Canada, Mexico, or even Europe. Forget about trying to settle anything with Sam, just go, use new names, anything to get away from him. All our plans came down to one thing: no money. How could we make it anywhere without money?

A court hearing was scheduled before a referee on March 18, and here it was already March 13. I called Connie the next day to let her know how Sam planned to use Jane as a witness. I knew Jane was into welfare and food-stamp fraud, because she had once asked me to lie for her. Connie told me to report Jane and then evidence of her fraud could be used to destroy her credibility as a witness. But that would be later because in the hearing before the referee, there would be no witnesses.

That afternoon, March 14, James and I went to the legal office on base, trying again to get all our records from the base Mental Health Clinic. I told the lieutenant about Sam's violence and how no one would help me. He asked if I had ever talked to Sam's "first shirt." I told him yes, before the February 8 incident, and I told him what the sergeant had said to me. The lieutenant said that particular officer was "famous for talking to wives like that." I asked if he would put that in writing, and he agreed. Then he called medical records and instructed them to release the files to me. We drove over to medical records, but they sent me back to the legal office. This was repeated about three times. I was going round and round in a circle, and I was never able to get the records. During my last trip to the legal office, we heard taps being played as the flag was lowered. Everyone is supposed to pull over and stop when taps are played. On that day, I just kept driving—something I had never done. I was so disgusted with the military and their runaround, I didn't care.

When we left the base, James checked into the psychiatric hospital where Daniel had been since March 10. By the next day, James had become very upset. He said he was afraid of the other adolescent patients, druggies and suicide attempts. There were three counselors involved now, and I heard something different from each of them. So on March 15, I brought Daniel and James home.

The evening of March 16, Sam called to talk to the boys. James and Daniel said little, just "Uh-huh," "no," and so on. At 4 a.m. Sam called back, threatening me. He was bragging about Jane's testimony again. I was so exasperated at that moment that I forgot he was probably taping the conversation. I said, "I'll get her for this; she'll do you no good in court." He said, "Is that a threat?" I answered, "Yes, I'll expose her for what she is, a welfare/food-stamp fraud." Again, Sam said he was coming right over to kill me, along with his usual threats. I hung up and called the police. They said there was nothing they could do, that they had no record of a restraining order. I insisted there must be a TRO on Sam, but they were quite definite with their no.

Connie had never filed it. They told me, "Call back when he's in the apartment with his hands on you." What a cruel joke. How is a woman going to make a phone call when she's being beaten or raped? All I could do was sit up and try to stay awake as I listened to every sound and watched every shadow.

I tried to call Connie the next day about the TRO, but I never was able to talk to her. That night, March 17, Sam called again about 4 a.m., saying he was coming over "to screw your brains out." I threatened to call the police; "there's no way you can explain being here at 4 a.m.," I told him. He said, "I'll say I came over to see the kids and to talk to you." He wasn't making sense and sounded drunk. I tried to make a deal with Sam: "I'm so tired of fighting, Sam. If you'll just agree in writing to pay child support, I'll agree to stay here so you can see the kids and I'll forget about the house and my share of the retirement. Let's just stop the fighting." Sam laughed, then continued with his threats. Finally, I told him I had my gun, that it was loaded, and not to try it. Again I sat up all night, knowing I had to be in court at 10 a.m.

On March 18, I wanted to shower, but I was too frightened. So I washed my hair in the kitchen sink and took a sponge bath to get ready. God, I was tired of living like that. In court, I was so sleepy that my head felt foggy. Sam's attorney asked for everything. He said Sam owed too many bills to pay child support and that after I got both boys, I stuck them in a psychiatric hospital to get rid of them. He said that since I lived in a one-bedroom apartment, both boys had to share a room, which wasn't acceptable. Sam's lawyer accused me of neglecting and abusing Daniel because he didn't have his own room and was sleeping on the floor. Connie slipped me a note, saying "Get a two-bedroom apartment *now*; that will show how hard you're trying." Then she consulted with Sam's attorney, and the neglect/abuse accusation was retracted. Connie explained to me that Sam faced a stiff fine if his accusation was not verified by a court investigation. That's why Sam retracted his accusation.

Nevertheless, the court ordered an investigation, additional counseling, and more psychological evaluations of the boys. Sam and I had to split the cost of all this, which came to about $200 each. This plus getting a larger apartment—more rent and added deposits—literally took food out of our mouths and more of my time away from the kids. It meant I had to work more hours and take on more assignments, anything to earn more money. "What are they trying to do to me?" I thought. "How can the judge be so unfair?" Sam was making $2,500 per month, while I was lucky if I made $800. He should have been paying $500 or $600 per month in child support. But no, because he had run up all his credit cards, the court ruled he only had to pay $350, with the first payment of $175 due on April 1 and the other half on April 15. Connie told me to run up my charge cards as Sam had done, but this went against my better judgment. Why run up bills I couldn't pay and jeopardize my credit? Paying for the bare essentials was enough of a struggle for me. I remembered when we first moved to Vegas and Sam had stuck us all in a two-bedroom trailer. Then all three boys shared a room which was much smaller than the bedroom two were sharing now. But that was different; Sam could do whatever he wanted.

As we left court that day, I told Connie, "The next time we go to court, ask for the house. The kids want to live in their house." Connie agreed that I should try to get the house for the kids' sake. I really didn't want to live there and knew the only way I could possibly afford it was for Sam to pay the maximum child support. Somewhere deep inside, I hoped that if Sam saw I meant to stand up for my rights, for my fair half of our properties, he would be reasonable.

From the courthouse, I went immediately to my apartment complex leasing office to sign up for a two-bedroom apartment. The rent was $398 a month instead of $325. The difference of $73 may seem small to some people, but to me, it was a week's worth of food. There was only one two-bedroom immediately available. I took it, even though it was on the ground floor and I would have felt safer on the second floor. I smiled and agreed to pay, but I felt as if my back was breaking. "Where does this end?" I asked myself.

If I thought Sam's harassment was bad before, all I can say is that after court, it got worse. I borrowed a tape recorder, thinking that if he could record calls, so could I. I hooked the machine up to my phone but got almost nothing on the tape. Either the batteries were dead or one of the kids had turned off the recorder. Most of the time, I was so distracted, I didn't think of the recorder until it was too late. God, I was so weary, but I was afraid to let myself sleep. I could deal with all the other pressures—money, job, kids, court—but Sam's constant threats to kill me were driving me crazy.

The evening of March 24, Sam had Daniel for a visit and dropped him off in the parking lot about 9:30 p.m. He told Daniel he was going straight home. It was a school night, and Daniel hadn't done any of his homework. I helped Daniel get settled into his homework, then I tried to call Sam. Daniel's grades had fallen, and one of the reasons was that when he was with Sam, Sam ignored Daniel's homework and didn't get him off to school on time. I wanted to ask Sam to make it a rule for Daniel to do his homework before play.

I kept trying to call until 2 a.m., but Sam never answered. I don't know what possessed me, but I decided to drive over to the house. Sam's car was not in the drive. I parked a short distance down the street and waited until he pulled into the drive. Immediately, a small white car pulled up and parked in the street—not in the cul-de-sac. As I watched, Sam got out of his car, walked over to the white car, and a woman got out. Arm in arm together, they went into our house. I waited about an hour, went to a 7-Eleven for coffee, then drove back by the house. Both cars were still there and the house was dark. Obviously, she was spending the night. I didn't feel jealous, but I was curious and totally confused. If Sam had another woman, why wouldn't he leave me alone, just let me go peacefully? As I drove home, I felt a tiny glimmer of relief and hope that now he might let me go.

On Saturday, March 26, after I got off work, we started moving into the two-bedroom apartment with the help of some friends. It took every penny I had to pay the extra deposits and rent, so there was no way I could miss work. We kept dragging stuff over until about 1 a.m., and then we collapsed. I remember saying, "I'm just like an ant; I'll work until I fall over dead." Early the next morning right after breakfast, we went back to work on moving and getting the new place organized. We were finished except for a few small things by 2:30 p.m. when I had to leave for work. I was facing a ten-hour shift. After I got to work, the boys called me, very upset. They had left the mother guinea pig with her four babies sitting in a glass aquarium in front of the sliding glass door and two of them had died. This was another blow to the kids. I tried to comfort them and told them I'd find a place to bury the guinea pigs later. Monday was my day off, so I'd have time for a few extras.

That Monday, March 28, I arranged with Sam to pick up Daniel's bed and chest, along with the rest of the boys' toys and clothes the next night, Tuesday. This had been court ordered, so it wasn't as if Sam was doing me a favor. On the phone, Sam talked sticky sweet, saying, "Beth, just you and the boys come on over tonight; I won't do anything. You don't need any witnesses." But I had already asked Larry and Debra to go with me on Tuesday after work, and Larry was going to use his truck to haul the bed and chest. Besides, I had a strong gut-level feeling not to trust Sam. For months he had threatened to kill me and now he was too sweet for words. For once, I followed my own better judgment; I didn't go.

Tuesday evening, the kids and I parked our car at Debra's. Larry pulled the truck up into Sam's drive, and we all went up to the door together. Sam met us at the door, arms crossed, saying, "You can't take anything; I've changed my mind." I told him we were taking our own things, that the court had ordered it, and that I had witnesses to his behavior. Sam let us into the house but followed me as I went to the bedroom closet to get my clothes. I found the closet empty, all my clothes gone. When I asked him where my clothes were, he grabbed my hands, twisting them behind me as he gritted his teeth and started swearing. Debra was coming down the hall, and he turned me loose. Daniel begged his dad for his bed and toys, but Sam screamed, "No fucking way! You can't come in the house and get anything unless you have it in writing. You got nothing in writing—you get nothing." Daniel and I were crying as we all left the house and returned to Debra's. Larry moved the truck back to his driveway. Then we called the police. It took them about two hours to get there.

At first, we all just talked as we waited for the police. Larry and Debra said they had both spoken with Sam to ask if it was OK for them to help me move. He had told them, "Sure, no problem." They were amazed at how he turned on all of us. As the wait for the police stretched into hours, I became hysterical. Why couldn't anything ever work out peacefully with Sam? How could the boys and I ever have a life? How much harder could I try? And how much longer could I struggle?

When the police arrived, we all went back over to the house. Sam still had a smug, smart-ass attitude, his arms crossed over his chest. But after the police talked to him a while, he agreed to let us take Daniel's bed and chest. No toys, no clothes, nothing but the bed and chest. By the time we moved Daniel's furniture into the apartment, I had cried so much I was sick, throwing up all night.

10

A No-Win Result

The next weekend would be Easter, and I expected a hassle from Sam about taking the boys. But, no, he surprised me by announcing he was going to Mina to visit his family over the weekend, and he never mentioned taking the boys along. Something about his trip plans did not ring true to me. "What is he up to now?" I wondered. When I called my attorney to report how Sam had acted Tuesday night, I also told her that some friends had invited me to bring the boys out to their country home for the Easter weekend. She encouraged me to go and to tell Sam I would be out of town. I decided to go, knowing I needed a rest from Sam's constant threats.

Sam's barrage of threatening calls increased during that week. Daniel visited him one day after school, as specified by the court; James refused to go. I tried to call the house on Daniel's visitation day, when I thought he should be home from school, but I could not get an answer. Finally, worried half out of my mind, I called Sam at work. He told me Daniel was supposed to go to Jane's to get the house key. Boy, was I furious. I thought of the way Jane treated her own kids—like dogs. She called them bastards, sons of bitches, even "little fuckers." "How can you subject Daniel to that witch?" I asked him. Sam just laughed and hung up. Later that evening, Daniel told me that when he went to Jane and asked her for the key, she stood in her door and swore at him, told him to get over in his yard and wait for Sam.

It tore me apart to see Daniel subjected to Jane's abuse. I couldn't understand why Sam didn't give him a key to the house. I had given both boys keys to the apartment so they could get in after school whether I was there or not.

On Friday, April 1, Sam's first child-support payment was due. I felt edgy, nervous, like something bad was about to happen. Sam had been calling me and making his death threats daily, not only at home but also at work. The only way Sam could have gotten my work number was by searching through Daniel's pockets. The family I worked for saw how terrified I was. I knew that part of Sam's purpose was to upset me and my patients so much that I'd be fired. Thank God for the caring and support of these Christian people. They did not fire me. Just the opposite, they did everything they could to bolster up my spirits. While I was at work on April 1, I got a call from James reporting that Sam came to the apartment, paid $175 in cash, and made James sign a receipt for the child support. Supposedly, Sam was on his way to Mina for the weekend. I didn't know whether to feel relieved or terrified. Sam had said over and over, "I'll kill your ass before I'll pay you child support." Now he had made the first payment. It just wasn't like Sam to accept or follow the court's ruling.

Maybe I'll never know the truth about what Sam did that Easter weekend. But I'm pretty sure he didn't go to Mina. His car was parked in the drive all weekend, and I called the bus depot and learned that no bus tickets were sold to Mina. It may be difficult for someone who hasn't lived it to understand, but I felt driven to check on Sam's whereabouts because of his constant threats. Somehow I felt safer if I knew exactly where he was. My guess is that he spent the weekend with his lady friend somewhere. Anyway, the kids and I had a peaceful weekend with our friends and a special Easter dinner.

Monday, April 4, was my day off, and I had my usual dozen errands to do. When I tried to use my car, the whole motor began knocking. I didn't get one block from my apartment before I had to stop and push it to the curb. I asked one of my neighbors to drive it up and down the alley to listen to it, but all he could say was, "It sounds so bad I wouldn't drive it if I were you." I had it towed to the Toyota dealer where it had been repaired for the oil leaks. After checking it over, the mechanic told me, "Someone who doesn't know what they're doing has been messing with this car." Several wires had been pulled loose and one spark plug was missing. I knew I hadn't taken the car in for repairs, and the only way to open the hood was to pull a release from inside my locked car. None of the locks had been forced, so obviously, Sam had kept a duplicate key and used it to tear up my car. The bill for this repair was $225. Then I understood. He paid the $175 in child support, but made sure I had to spend it, plus some, for car repair.

The next day, James and I discovered that someone had been in the apartment. Neither of us had moved my large file of records, but it was missing. James said that all his papers and clothes had been moved around, and later I noticed that one vial of my prescription hormones had disappeared. I recall standing there as all the blood drained out of my head, feeling faint. I couldn't stop the terrible things which kept happening. Like a light bulb turning on, it hit me, "We're not safe anywhere; we'll never be safe." I called my attorney, but couldn't get past the secretary. I hoped that Connie could report Sam's stepped-up harassment to his attorney, and maybe he could stop Sam. There was nothing more I could do. I couldn't even get my phone number changed because the court ordered that Sam have the number so he could talk to the kids.

At 6 a.m. on April 6, my birthday, I answered the phone to hear Sam say, "Happy Birthday, bitch. How do you like your presents?" Then he hung up before I could say a word. I got his message alright. Sam could destroy my car, he could get into my apartment when and if he wanted, and there was nothing I could do to stop him. I felt utterly helpless, vulnerable, hopeless.

The next day, April 7, I tried again to contact Connie and again I couldn't get past her secretary. I was so exasperated I said, "Tell Connie something for me—she's fired." By this point, I had already paid Connie $500, and I certainly couldn't afford to start with another attorney. So after I fired Connie, I called Sam's lawyer myself—no need to go through a lawyer anymore since I didn't have one. I told him about my car being torn up and my apartment being rummaged. He gave me no assurances, but I sensed that he believed me when he asked if my car had been locked. He agreed that "maybe Sam was a little bit out of hand." I stressed to this lawyer to keep Sam away from me, that I had a TRO against Sam. After talking to him, I felt a tiny ray of hope. Maybe now that Sam's attorney knew what Sam had done to me, he would take steps to stop the harassment.

My hope didn't last long. Sam was demanding that I give him my W-2 forms so that he could file a joint income tax return. I wanted to file under the option of married but separated.

Time after time, Sam called me at work during the next two days, badgering me about my W-2 forms. After hanging up from a call with him, I'd go out on the patio, trying to get control of my crying and shaking. As much as possible, I tried to protect my patients from seeing the hell I was suffering.

The next court date, April 11, was getting close, and now I had no lawyer. So I tried to gather information that I hoped would help me. I got computer printouts showing all the payments of bills for the house—the mortgage, the electric, the water softener, and so on. In the two years since we had bought the house, Sam had handled the bills. The computer printouts showed that every payment on every bill had been late. I inquired of John Hancock Insurance Company whether or not Sam had kept the policies on me and the boys in force since we had moved out of the house. Their representative informed me that our policies were still in force. In fact, Sam had increased the death benefits of my policy from $10,000 to $100,000. This was one more indication to me that Sam's threats to kill me were serious.

It was Sam's weekend to have Daniel, so Daniel went directly from school to Sam's on Friday, April 8. But Sam called me several times during that day and night. His threats were so menacing that I called the Domestic Crisis Hotline. There wasn't much they could do for me except listen, because my boys were too old to be admitted to the shelter, and I wasn't willing to leave without the boys.

Again on Saturday, April 9, Sam called me at work, threatening me so forcefully that I finally gave in and told him, "OK, you can take the W-2s if you'll promise to leave me alone." I don't know how I got through work that day as upset as I was.

I arrived home about 5:30 p.m. As I had every day for at least three months, I carried my gun with me, reassembling and loading it when I got into the apartment. I sat down on my bed, which was in the living room, and stuck the gun under it. I tried to call my sister in Arkansas as I did every other weekend, but her line was busy. I went into the kitchen to start cooking supper, taking the gun with me. The gun had become a part of me, like my arms and legs. James came home from seeing one of his friends, and we talked briefly, just catching up on the day. Then Daniel called to ask if he could be a few minutes late. "Sure," I told him, "today's Saturday, no school tomorrow." Sam got on the phone, talking sticky sweet, asking would I get the W-2s ready and would James be there. I asked James while Sam was still on the phone and James said no. Sam's voice took on a sharp edge as he pressured me to make James stay. I told Sam that was James's decision.

Sam must have called from a phone booth near by, because within ten or fifteen minutes they were there. James started out the door as Sam and Daniel were coming in. Sam grabbed him by the shoulder and asked him to stay, but James pulled away from him. Daniel was showing James a squirt gun Sam had given him. That was a slap in the face to me; Sam knew I didn't allow the boys to have toy guns. After a brief exchange with Daniel, James went on his way.

I was watching Sam intently. I had asked him not to come in, to stand outside the door while I got the W-2s for him. Sam continued into the apartment as Daniel hugged me around the waist, telling me about playing racquetball. Sam's voice turned gruff as he said, "Go to your room, Daniel." I knew then that he meant to hurt me. "I got you now, bitch," he said. "You don't have a lawyer and you can't afford to hire another one." I started crying as I asked him, "Why are you doing this to me, to your kids? How can you love them and do this? My God, your own son just walked by you, didn't even want to see you. If I just leave, not take the kids or anything, then will you leave me alone?" He was standing there real stiff, gritting his teeth, fists flailing, his eyes glaring with hate. "Never," he said, "never." He was between me and the door, and all I could think about was getting him out of my apartment. "Just take the W-2s and get out," I told him, hoping that would break up the argument. I backed away from him to the end of my bed and bent over to get the forms from my briefcase. I only took my eyes off him for a moment as I opened the briefcase.

Suddenly, he grabbed me by my hair and one shoulder and slammed my head down full force on the end table. Again, my head hit the table, another explosion in my head. I was foggy, almost blacked out, for a moment. My stomach came up in my throat as if I were on a roller coaster. I became aware of wetness; I had wet my pants. "Dear God, he really is going to kill me and he wanted both boys here. Why? So they would see it, or did he mean to kill them too?" So many thoughts flooding my mind at once.

Sam had me from the back, so I couldn't fight or protect myself. I felt a surge of adrenalin. I was never so strong in my life as I pulled away from him enough to grab a flowerpot and hit him with it. I'm not sure where it hit him, but I know I tried for his head. He let go then. I staggered back by the bed, reached down, and got my gun. Sam was facing me, arms out like a football tackle, coming at me. I pointed the gun at him and told him to just get out. He smirked as he kept coming. Scenes from the past flashed through my mind, times when Sam had simply reached out and taken the gun away from me. As I backed up, I said, "Please don't make me do this; please don't make me." I backed up more until I felt the bed touching my legs. I looked over at the phone, a long way away. I felt my body begin to pitch backward. I had one arm out to keep from falling because I knew he'd be right on me.

Sam kept coming, saying, "Get you, bitch! Get you, bitch!"

All I remember is screaming, screaming, screaming, and the sound of gunshots as if from far away. I can still see him coming toward me. Another shot, and he sort of reeled like maybe he was hit, but he was still coming toward me. More gunshots, I must have fired them, then I didn't see him anymore. I remember thinking just pull the gun up to your head and fire one time, just one time. I tried, but the gun clicked empty.

Then I heard Daniel screaming. I didn't know at that moment where I was. I remember blinking my eyes, trying to focus. I saw Daniel, standing near where Sam had been. I didn't even know he was in the room. He was screaming, "Mom, Mom!" The room was like a tunnel filled with gray, fuzzy fog. All I could see was Daniel going out the door, and I ran after him. Daniel was running down the alley screaming, and I was running behind him, yelling, "Stop, Daniel, stop." When I realized I still had the gun in my hand, I flung it away from me and continued running after Daniel. I knew I had to catch him and calm him before he reached Washington Street with its heavy traffic. Just as we got to Washington, I caught him. We were both screaming for help. I was short of breath, and my head felt like it was filled with cotton. We started back holding each other. As we approached the apartments, Daniel broke away and ran back into our apartment, while a young couple helped me upstairs to their apartment. I kept asking them to help me get back to my apartment because I was worried about Daniel being in there alone with Sam. I tried to walk but my legs buckled under me and I fainted.

When I came to, I was on the floor. Two policemen came in then and took me out on the patio to question me. I was shaking all over, my fingers and toes tingling from lack of circulation, my mouth so dry I had to pull my lips away from my teeth to talk. Someone gave me a glass of water. I told them I had fired the gun and wasn't sure whether or not I had hit Sam. My head was throbbing and I felt sick all over. One officer said to the other, "Maybe we'd better get her to a hospital," but the other said, "That can wait." I heard a lot of sirens and a helicopter hovering overhead. There were lights everywhere. I asked how Sam was, but the officers didn't answer me. When they told me they were taking me to the police station, I asked if I could change my clothes and grab my purse. They refused, so I had to go in my wet pants without my purse. They wouldn't even let me see or be with Daniel. My baby, my poor baby, what was happening to him? This all seemed so foggy, so unreal. Was I dreaming or was I crazy?

At the police station, they put me in an outer office and gave me some coffee. I told them I was hurt. My eyes wouldn't stay focused. After a while—I have no idea how long—they allowed me to go to the bathroom. I was bent over with the dry heaves, and when I straightened up, I saw myself in the mirror. I could barely tell it was me. My hair was pulled loose and stringy; my left temple bore a large raw bloody sore; red and blue splotches covered my entire face, with a larger one on my forehead; large swollen knots oozing blood covered my head.

The same two officers who had brought me in began questioning me. Repeatedly they told me to speak up, but my throat was so sore from screaming I could barely speak above a whisper. I asked them over and over about Sam. Once they told me he was in surgery, but mostly, they said, "No word." I prayed with all my strength, "Please, God, let Sam be alive; don't let me have killed someone. God, send me to prison for life; just don't let Sam die."

After what seemed an eternity, one of the officers told me Sam was dead. I remember looking at my right hand and thinking, "Cut it off, look what it did. I've killed someone, not just anyone, but Sam. I still have all this love for him, and now he's made me kill him." Feelings of horror and grief overwhelmed me.

One detective told me it looked like self-defense, but that I had to make a statement or they would be forced to lock me up until I could get a lawyer. I asked permission to call a lawyer but was told I couldn't until I was formally booked into jail. While this was soaking in, they went on to say they didn't know what would happen to Daniel. He was upset enough without knowing his father was dead. And if I didn't cooperate, Daniel would be sent to Child Haven. They told me they had James's personal phone book and had been calling around trying to find him with no success. "He's liable to hear this on the news," they told me, "Is that what you want? We'll have to call Juvenile Center and put both boys in there if you don't cooperate. The sooner you accept that and give us a statement, the sooner you'll be out of here to take care of your sons." I could hear Daniel crying off and on from another room. But the officers wouldn't let me see him if I didn't talk. It felt like blackmail.

My brain was on overload—hundreds of thoughts about Sam, Daniel, James tumbling around in my mind. The uniformed officer was in the questioning room with me, his head down, arms crossed, shaking his head, while the two detectives stood against the wall. I had the distinct impression that he didn't approve of the detectives' coercive methods. But I answered all their questions truthfully and signed a release for medical records. Even when I finished all that, they wouldn't let me see Daniel for another hour.

Finally, they let me in the room where they were holding Daniel. He cried as he hugged me and said, "Mom, it's not your fault; he was beating on you—he wouldn't stop." Daniel didn't know that Sam was dead, and I didn't want to tell him at the police station while he was so upset. I sat there holding Daniel, trying to comfort him, until one of the detectives took us home.

It was around 2 a.m. when we got back to the apartment; Sam had arrived there about 8 p.m.

I couldn't grasp what had happened. Sam was dead and I had killed him. In the span of one evening, our lives were turned upside down. And the future loomed ahead as an endless black hole, just as terrifying as Sam's sixteen-year reign of terror.

11

Go Directly to Jail

We went back to the apartment in the early morning hours of Sunday, April 10. Paula, a neighbor from another apartment, stayed with me a couple of hours. As we entered, I noticed some empty plastic containers from an IV starter kit scattered on the floor. I hurriedly picked them up so that Daniel wouldn't see them. I didn't see any blood, but the bullet holes in the walls were obvious. Later I found electrical tape covering a bullet's damage to the cord on my microwave oven.

I put Daniel to bed without telling him Sam was dead. I wanted him to sleep if he could, and I hoped that James would come home so that I could tell the boys at the same time. After Daniel went to bed, Paula helped me pick up the flowerpots and straighten up some of the mess. I happened to move the drape by the sliding glass doors and discovered Sam's shoes, socks, and glasses. I put them in a bag and threw them into the linen closet so the boys wouldn't have to see them. Then I noticed my purse sitting on the bed wide open. I checked my wallet and found that $200 was missing. It was my week's pay, and my stomach rolled over in panic as I wondered how I would manage without that money. I did not report it because I couldn't prove anything and I had no faith in the police. Paula called Sam's family to break the news; I just couldn't handle talking to them. She told me she talked with Sam's nephew, who didn't seem to believe the news of Sam's death.

When Paula left, I was sitting on the floor, leaning against my water bed, holding the phone and James's phone book. "Please, God," I prayed, "send James home so I can tell him before he hears it on the news."

I awakened a couple of hours later, slumped over on the floor. At first, I didn't remember where I was or what had happened. Then, with blinding flashes, the horror of the night started coming back to me. Wave after wave of nausea hit me. I shook so hard I could barely crawl to the bathroom. I knew I had to get control of myself. I made my way into the kitchen, put on the coffee, and called my sister in Arkansas. Talking with my sister and her husband helped me calm down a little. They promised they'd leave for Las Vegas as soon as they could get to the bank on Monday. I called my private patients and told them I wouldn't be there for a few days; then I called the nursing agency to explain what had happened. "Maybe the Armstrongs won't want me to work for them anymore," I said. Sarah, the agency coordinator, told me she had already seen Sam's obituary in the newspaper. "When I saw the last name," she said, "I held my breath, hoping it was Sam instead of you." That's when I began to discover that most of my friends and acquaintances expected Sam to kill me. I called the Armstrongs too. When I related the incident to them, they said, "take all the time you need, but we want you back as soon as you're ready. We'll pray for you at church today."

Relieved at hearing the Armstrongs' trust in me, I called Larry and Debra to ask if they would come and pick up Sam's car, still parked near my apartment. I didn't want his car there for the boys to see. While I waited, I called the Red Cross to get Matt home. I asked them to have a chaplain with Matt, but to call me collect so I could tell him. I also called Matt's girlfriend in Las Vegas so she wouldn't have to find out from the television or newspaper stories. It turned out to be a mistake to get her involved because she kept calling until she reached Matt. So Matt heard the news from her instead of me. That hurt me and created another breach between Matt and me.

Beth, about the time she met Sam, 1971.

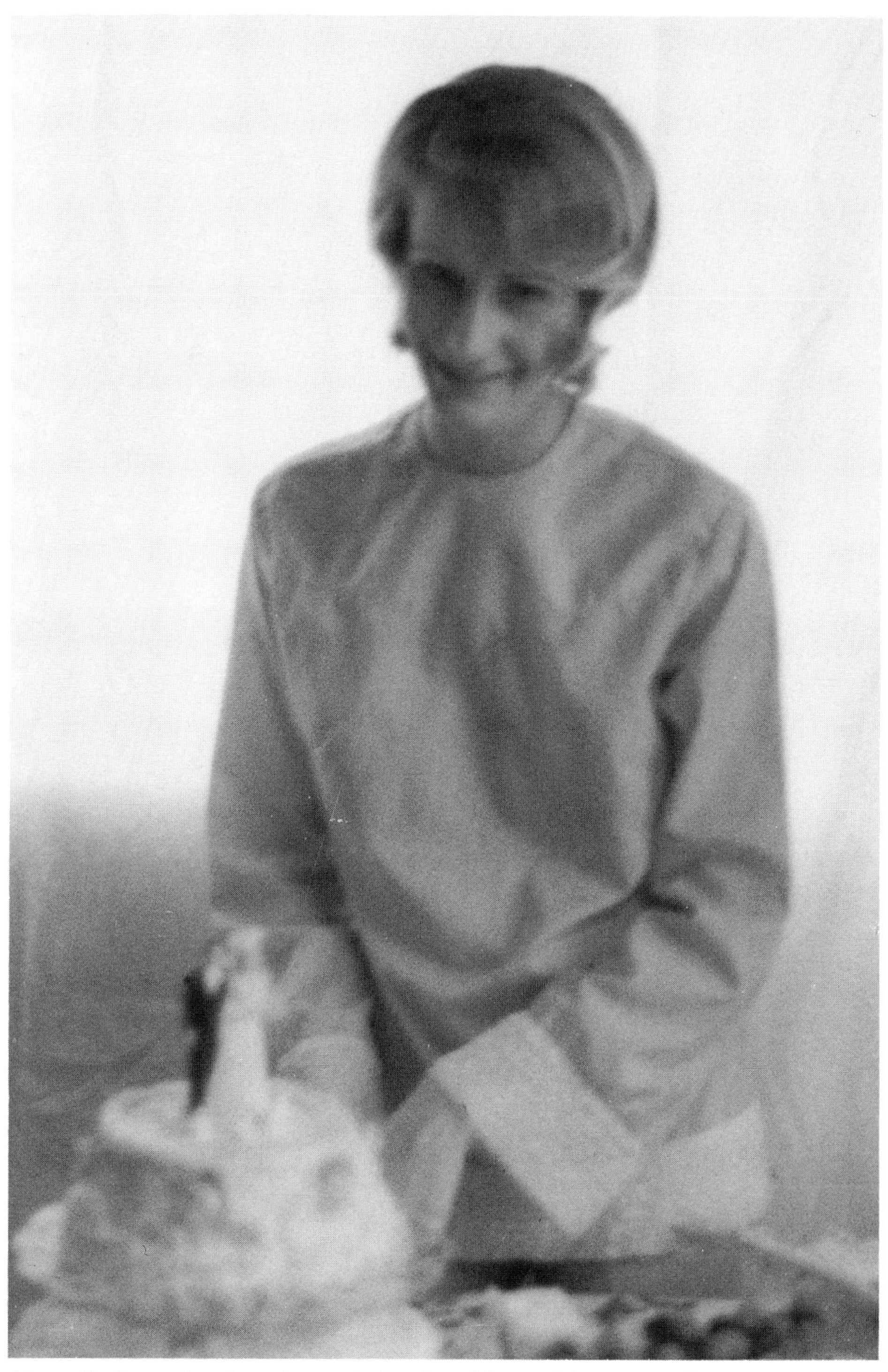

Above: Beth, cutting the cake at a belated wedding celebration with Sam's parents, 1971. *Opposite Page Top:* Beth and Sam kiss at wedding celebration, 1971. *Bottom:* Beth and Sam at the Reno airport, as Sam left for Vietnam, 1971.

Above: Beth with roses from Sam, shortly before the birth of their first child, 1972. *Top Right:* Beth with James, 1972. *Center Right:* Sam with James, 1972. *Bottom:* Beth gazing at Sam as he took her picture. She says, "I'm just struck by the way I'm looking at him." (1973) *Opposite Page:* Beth in photo taken by a neighbor in Utah after a severe beating, 1974.

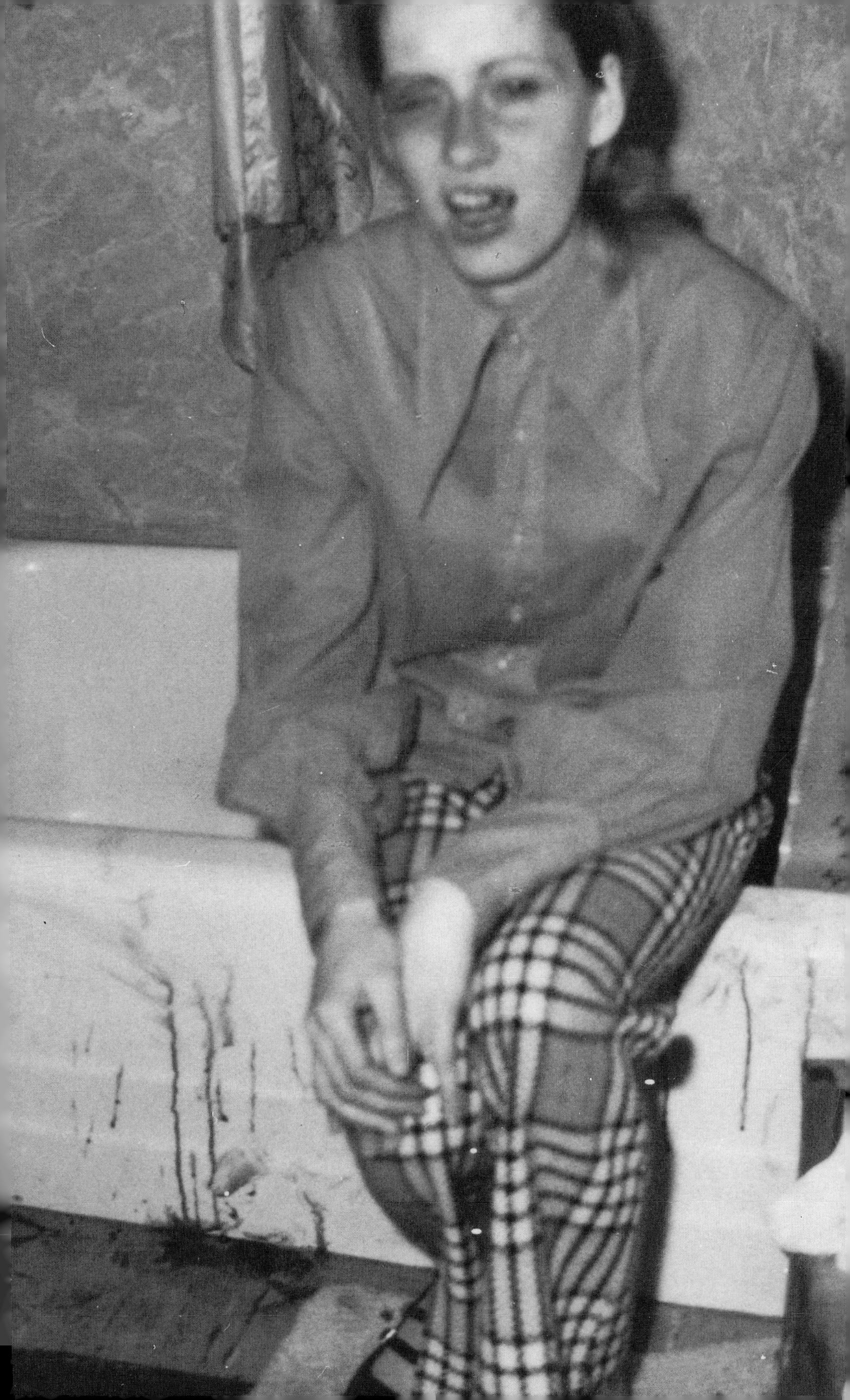

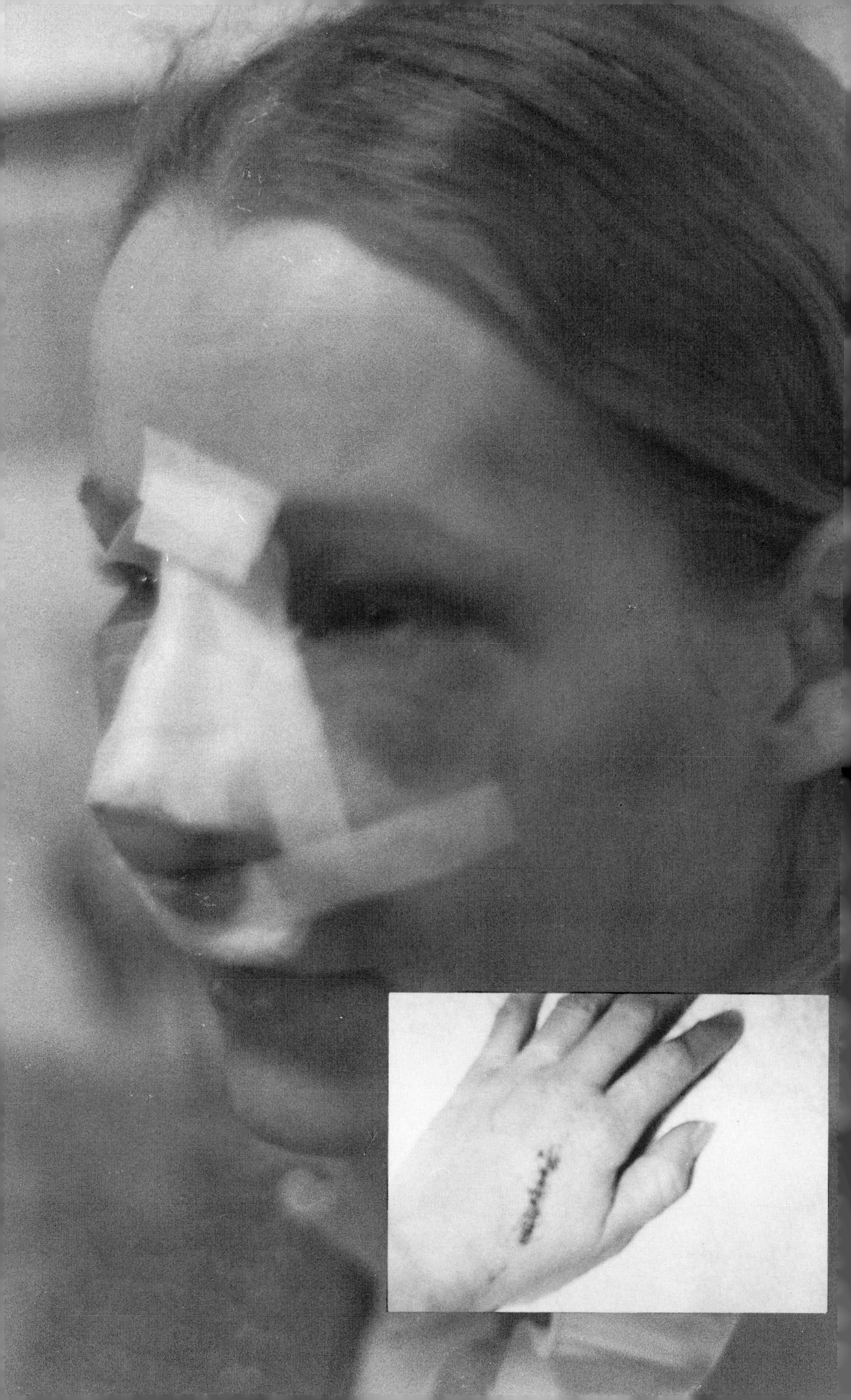

Top: Beth dressed for her role in **Crime Story**, 1986. *Center:* Beth and Sam, 1977. *Bottom Left:* Beth in Virginia, dressed for one of her cleaning jobs, 1977. *Bottom Right:* Beth and Sam, Christmas with his family, 1986. *Opposite Page:* Beth after surgery to repair her broken nose, 1979. Sam punched her in the nose again before she healed from the surgery. *Inset:* Beth's hand after it was cut with broken glass, 1987.

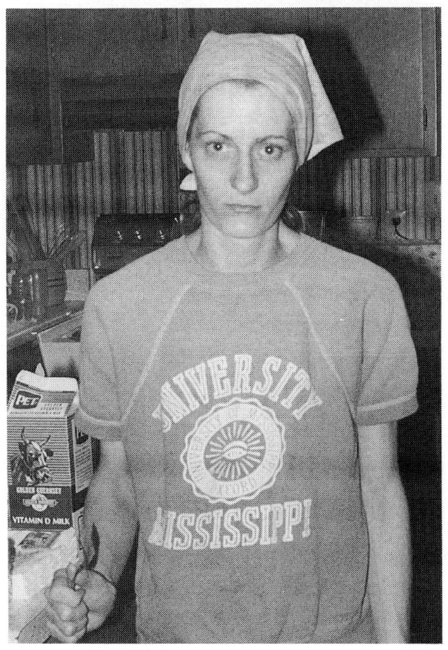

Beth in her new home, showing off newly born goat, 1992.

I was still sitting on the floor with the phone, trying to locate James when Larry and Debra arrived about 8:30 a.m. I felt comforted and reassured that they came right over. They were so thoughtful, bringing breakfast for everyone. Debra stayed with me while Larry drove Sam's car back to the house, and she helped me pull things together. I felt out of it, sort of disconnected from myself. When Debra mentioned my moving back into the house, I told her I couldn't afford it. "My rent here is only $398 per month and the house payments are $607. There's no way I could pay them." I guess I thought the house would just disappear. Anyway, I hated the house and did not want to move back to it. Debra helped me face reality. "Beth," she said, "you're responsible for the house now that Sam's dead. If you stay here, you'll be responsible for both the house and this apartment." Hearing that was overwhelming because it meant I had to move back to the scene of so many nightmares. But gradually I accepted moving back as my duty; whether I liked it or not, I would try to make the best of it.

A call came from Clara, the base mortuary affairs representative. She wanted to meet with me to make arrangements for Sam's funeral and burial. I told her, as Sam had told me, that the insurance was in his mother's name, so she would have to make these decisions. Clara informed me that as long as we were still married, the insurance couldn't be changed; that was just another lie Sam had told me. I agreed to meet with Clara about 1 p.m. Monday.

Then Paula, the neighbor who had helped me the night before, came to call me to her phone. She had left her number with Sam's nephew, and now Sam's sister was calling for me. When I answered the phone, Sam's sister started out by saying, "Beth, hon, what happened?" I was crying as I told her that Sam came into my place and was beating on me, that I grabbed my gun and fired. She kept asking, "Where? Where?" All I could say was "I don't know." I didn't know where Sam was hit. After I fired, I didn't see him, and no one told me where he was hit. Finally, I said, "I have to go now," and that ended the conversation.

When I got back to the apartment, Debra again urged me to go to the hospital to check on my head wounds. Even though I knew I needed to go, I felt I couldn't leave until James was found and both boys had been told that Sam was dead. I lay down on the water bed and my dizziness began to subside. Soon Larry returned, bringing a small tape recorder and Sam's briefcase, which he had found in Sam's car. I opened the recorder, but it was empty and there was no microphone hookup on it. The briefcase was locked, so I sat it on the floor and forgot about it. Daniel got up and came into the living room. He knew something was strange when he saw Larry and Debra there. I told him his Daddy was dead. He cried and hugged me real tight. "He was coming for you, Mom. You had to do it, Mom," he said over and over. I comforted him as best I could. We hugged each other for awhile; then Daniel went to get dressed.

In the meantime, Larry went back home again while Debra stayed with me. Within a few minutes, Larry called to report that John Jones was in my house. Larry had asked him what he was doing, and John told him that I had phoned and asked him to go into the house to feed the animals. I said, "Of course, he's lying." Larry went on to say that he could see John going in and out of my house, carrying boxes out and across the street to the Joneses. Earlier, Larry had checked all the windows and doors, so we knew they were all locked. Now, John was in the house and the back bedroom window was open. A chill went through me. Somehow I knew it was urgent to get him out of my house, that he was after something, even though I had nothing of value in the house and I couldn't imagine what he wanted.

I was so shaken when I hung up from talking to Larry that Debra called the police for me. They gave her some static about having no authority to call for me, but finally they agreed to send a patrol car to meet us at the house. Debra, Daniel, and I drove over to the house immediately. When the police arrived a few minutes later, John was standing in the middle of the road. I heard him tell the police that I had asked him to go into my house, and I yelled out, "No, I didn't." Then he said, "Oh, no. Sam's sister told me to." When the police asked about a key, John said, "They have it," pointing to Larry and Debra. I told the police, "No, they've never had a key." Then Daniel piped up, "I know where the key is." Daniel went to the porch and reached under a flowerpot, but he found no key. Until that time, I didn't know that Sam had hidden a key for Daniel. Daniel looked up at me and asked, "Mom, do you mind? Are you mad that I didn't tell you?" I said, "No, honey, if you promised Daddy you wouldn't tell anyone, then you did right not to tell me." God knows, I would never have used the key even if I'd known about it. Even when my lawyer told me to break in and get my personal belongings, I told her, "No way. You won't be the one the police arrest—I will."

In the midst of all this confusion, a county officer arrived with an order to seal the house. I pleaded with them to allow Daniel to go inside and take his hamster so it wouldn't starve; they finally agreed. Then they began putting red stickers on all the windows and doors. After they had applied the last sticker, they discovered a police officer still inside the house. They had to break the door seal to let him out, then reseal it. They were going to take my cats to the pound, but they finally agreed to let Debra feed them on the patio.

I wanted to file a break-in report, but the female officer snapped at me, "There's been no break-in." When I tried to press my point, she said, "It's not up to you to say it's your house." I told her, "Well, my name's certainly on the mortgage, which means I have to make the payments." But nothing I said made any difference to them. They did not protect my property.

Meanwhile, the police had ordered the Joneses back across the street. About eight of them dragged out lawn chairs to the edge of the sidewalk and sat there staring at us. I felt this was a gross indignity to me and Daniel. Why were the Joneses doing this? What did they want from us? What were they getting out of tormenting me? It was beyond my understanding.

Soon after Debra, Daniel, and I got back to the apartment, James came in. He was ghostly pale. He said that as he approached the apartment, the maintenance man told him that his dad was dead and that I was in jail. Debra helped me explain everything to James—all of us were tense and emotional. James calmed down somewhat and went to bed.

Only then could I think about my physical condition. When I bathed, I found dirt everywhere—in my hair, down my back, in my underclothes. After I got dressed, Debra drove me to the base hospital.

I brought in my medical records, which I had checked out to make copies for the divorce/custody action. When the doctor asked how I had injured my head, I told him it was abuse, "but you don't have to call the police; he's dead." They grabbed my medical records, saying that the OSI (Office of Special Investigation) had been there looking for my file. The doctor ordered X rays and administered precautionary treatment for my head injuries.

I barely recall leaving the clinic or the drive back to my apartment. When the doctor mentioned the OSI, he might as well have said the Gestapo. I felt overwhelmed; surely this was a nightmare and I would wake up any minute.

Early on Monday, April 11, I was awakened by the phone. Mr. Thomas, Daniel's school principal, called to express his sympathy. He had read about the incident in the newspaper. Mr. Thomas had shown a genuine interest in helping Daniel, who had academic and behavior problems at school. When Daniel moved in with me, I began working with Mr. Thomas. Right away, we seemed to see eye to eye. We both came from poverty-stricken areas of the South. Once, briefly, I had mentioned Sam's abuse of me and the boys to him. Mr. Thomas was a black man, and he told me several times that coming from the South and being black made him realize what a rough road life can be. His call at this time meant a lot to me—it was validation of my right to defend myself.

Soon after that call, the probate office called, telling me the house was mine, to come and pick up the keys. I called the mortgage company to see if the mortgage was insured—it wasn't. Little by little, I learned that none of Sam's loans and charge accounts were insured. All his creditors were coming after me; now I was responsible for all his debts. I left the probate office with the letter releasing the house to me and headed for my attorney's office.

When I reached Connie's office, she was on the phone with James. She had called to offer her services as soon as she heard the news about Sam. I was in bad shape, crying uncontrollably. Connie said she would still represent me, but that she was positive I would not be indicted. She told me that Sam's lawyer had already called her that morning. He informed her that Sam had "gone crazy on him" the previous Thursday, screaming, "Get her, get her!"

Connie tried to comfort me. "I know you were scared to death of him," she said, "He got up that day and decided what he was going to do. Whatever he was doing when it happened was his choice. His life was up. No matter what happened, his life was meant to end when it did." All I could do was cry and mumble, "Yes, but did it have to be by my hand?"

On my way back to my apartment, I stopped by the house. None of the keys would work in the locks. When I looked at the locks, I could see that bits of metal had been shoved into all of them. "Great," I thought, "this means more money to get a locksmith." Before I could leave, the police arrived, saying they had a report I was messing around my house. I was stunned, but I showed them the letter from the probate office, and they sort of grunted under their breath as they left. I knew the Joneses had called them. But it was beyond my comprehension why the Joneses were so intent upon harassing me.

I returned to my apartment in time to meet with the Air Force contingent to go over funeral arrangements. I remember that one of the guys kept staring at me and at the bullet holes. I didn't think he was very tactful. The female officer was going over Sam's benefits with me and seemed quite intent on how my first marriage had ended—did my first husband die or were we divorced? I dug out my divorce papers to show her. While they were there, James broke into Sam's briefcase, looking for some of the information they were requesting. It was hard for me to focus on everything they asked. The questions about my first husband seemed so irrelevant, considering I had been married to Sam for sixteen years.

After the Air Force people left, James and I went back over to our house. We still couldn't get the keys to work in the locks, so I went to Debra's to call a locksmith. While I was making the call, James punched a hole in the side door and got into the house. He said he felt so angry, he just had to hit something. Of course, the Joneses once again were standing at the edge of their yard watching. James and I both believed they had stopped up the locks.

When we got inside, papers were scattered everywhere as if a gale-force wind had blown through. I'll probably never know for sure just what the Joneses took out of my house. But Sam's guitar was gone, and the VCR was unhooked with the box it came in sitting open on the coffee table. Daniel had been watching the VCR just before he and Sam left the house on Saturday, so it was hooked up then. Several boxes of miscellaneous papers were sitting in the middle of the living room floor—bank statements, pay statements, bills, and so on.

That night, Larry, Debra, and a group of their friends moved everything out of the apartment back over to my house. They even cleaned the apartment for me. With the house in such chaos, I didn't know where to put anything. We just dropped everything from the apartment in the living room and one bedroom. By the time we got through with moving that night, we couldn't even walk in the house. I suppose I was still in shock, numb, just going through the motions of whatever had to be done.

On Tuesday, April 12, the police called, telling me I had to make another statement. Matt arrived home, obviously angry at me. He had said almost nothing to me when we talked on the phone after his girlfriend informed him of Sam's death. When he walked into the house, he still didn't speak to me, just said he wanted to talk to James and Daniel alone. Later, his words, "You had to go and kill him," cut me so deeply I had no response.

My sister, Nancy, and her husband, Jack, also arrived on Tuesday. They were a major source of comfort and strength during their stay.

On Wednesday, the 13th, Nancy accompanied James, Daniel, and me to the police station to make our statements. They made us sit in the waiting room for more than an hour. This made me frantic, wondering what more they could ask and worrying about all the things I needed to do at home. When Detective Barlow finally did take me into his office, he asked me about Sam's tapes and tape recorder. I told him there had been a tape recorder in Sam's car, marked "military property." When Larry found it, there was no tape in it, but there had been a package of empty tapes with it. Since the tape recorder belonged to the military, I had given it, along with the blank tapes, to one of Sam's coworkers. Detective Barlow told me that "all kinds of people have been calling me, saying you planned to kill Sam." I was too stunned to reply. He released me after a couple of hours, saying "it looks like self-defense—just a formality."

While the rest of us went to the police station, Jack had stayed at the house, organizing the checkbooks, bills, and papers and notifying the banks and credit cards. Later that day, two officers from the base came to get one of Sam's uniforms.

We noticed that every time we entered or left the house or looked out the windows and doors, we could see at least one of the Joneses standing on their porch, staring at us. This was odd, annoying, an invasion of our privacy.

It was also on the afternoon of the 13th that the funeral home notified me that Sam's body was ready. I had authorized open viewing, but the services here were to be private—no one but the family. The funeral home opened up the viewing room without letting me check to see that everything was acceptable. When we, the family, arrived, we saw that the Joneses had already been there and signed the guest book.

When we approached the casket, I saw large stitches on the back of his head. The last thing I remember was pushing my body backward because I knew I was fainting, and I didn't want to fall into the casket.

I woke up on the floor with Nancy pressing wet paper towels to my head. Several times, I tried to touch Sam, but Nancy said, "Just don't." She was trying to protect me, I knew. But I remembered touching my father, even kissing his forehead, when he was laid out in his casket. Somehow I wanted to kiss Sam good-bye, although I knew Nancy was right. I just couldn't take any more at that point.

April 14, the day of the funeral, was a blur. We had a private service in Las Vegas for the family only. I felt I owed it to Sam to follow his wishes, and he had always said he wanted to be buried in his uniform, no cremation, following a full military service. I had given the funeral home the phone number for Sam's mother so they could contact her and make arrangements for the service in Mina, where Sam would be buried. I wanted to be fair and do what was right. I felt that we deserved to have a private service here, but that Sam's mother deserved to do whatever she wanted also—just keep the two services separate. "I have sons;" I thought, "I'd want mine back." The service was brief and simple, conducted by a Catholic priest from the base. Afterward, a military representative escorted the body to Mina.

April 14 was also James's birthday. I felt so sorry for James, having his dad's funeral on his birthday. But we couldn't have it the day before because the coroner hadn't released the body in time. And we couldn't push it forward to the following day because the body was deteriorating, and there was still to be a service in Mina.

Nancy and Jack started their drive back to Arkansas about 5 a.m. the next morning. John was standing out in his front yard watching as they left. As soon as their car pulled away, I walked back into my house, and I noticed that John went back inside his house. Immediately, my phone started ringing. When I answered, there was no response, but I could hear someone breathing. This happened three or four times before I took the phone off the hook. I was at the edge of falling apart. With my sister gone, I felt so alone. If it hadn't been for Debra, I guess I would have cracked. Utterly exhausted, I lay down on my bed to rest for a few minutes. When I opened my eyes, I had slept twelve hours.

I looked around at my house and thought, "I have to get things in order." But I didn't know what "getting things in order" was any more. I felt as if I were in the eye of a tornado, with everything just swirling around me. Matt and James were planning to drive up to Mina to the graveside service on Saturday, the 16th; Daniel complained of being "so tired" and said he didn't want to go with them. I sat up all that night cleaning and getting the boys' clothes ready, including Matt's uniform. I could hear a commotion outside about 1:30 a.m., and when I looked out the window, I could see John and Jane loading at least half a dozen large boxes into their car. It seemed strange, but then the Joneses had done a lot of strange things.

Matt and James took off for Mina about 4 a.m. Saturday morning. After they left, I tried to keep busy cleaning and organizing the house, but my anxiety steadily increased throughout the day. It was a terrible day. I kept wondering what was going on in Mina. I felt that I had sent my husband off, away for someone else to bury. I felt hurt, ashamed, angry, because no matter what had happened I should have been there to bury him. But I didn't want to trouble his family, and I didn't want trouble with them.

About 2:30 p.m., the boys called to say they were starting home. At the 1:30 p.m. graveside service, the military had presented James and Sam's mother with flags. I was worried about their drive back because it was raining and the roads were slick. But they arrived home about 6 p.m., safe but shaken. James had recorded the graveside service, and I felt somewhat comforted, being able at least to listen to that.

The boys told me that the Joneses had been at the service, acting real cozy with Sam's family. So then I knew that they had taken at least some of the items they stole from our house to Sam's family. When the Joneses returned home late Sunday afternoon, all they took out of the car were a couple of small bags, no boxes.

The next morning, Monday, I called the nursing service, notifying them I wanted to return to work. I needed money more than ever now—all Sam's bills were due. The water was shut off the day we moved back into the house, although Sam had told Daniel he paid it. His phone bill was $80. Sam was behind for the electric and gas, for the water softener, for everything. I had to pay $240 for my part of the funeral. After that, I was flat broke. Yet everyone was calling and demanding money. Since the divorce had not gone through, I was still Sam's wife and therefore responsible for all his bills, bills I didn't run up or know about. Insurance premiums were due on both cars, but I dropped the insurance on Sam's car and went to the Department of Motor Vehicles and turned in the tags.

The boys and I went out to the base to take care of some of the necessary paperwork. I had notified Sam's boss to hold out Sam's last paycheck before it was automatically deposited in his bank account. But when I tried to pick it up at the base, I learned that the check had already been deposited to Sam's account and almost immediately taken back by the Air Force. I was told that the Air Force had a hold on all the money Sam had coming, including his last paycheck, three months worth of leave pay, and all survivor's benefits. I felt like a rat in a maze. Every path I tried was a dead end. It was clear I wouldn't get any immediate help from the Air Force. While we were at the base, we picked up Sam's personal belongings, which had been brought to the Mortuary Affairs office. At the time, I really couldn't look at the stuff. We just threw the box in the back of my car.

That day, I noticed a female civilian employee because she seemed to look at me with sympathy. Every time I looked up, we made eye contact and I could see the kindness in her face. As we finished our business there, she handed me a piece of paper with the Temporary Assistance for Domestic Crisis (TADC) phone number and suggested that I call. When she told me she had gotten help there, I knew my intuition had been right. I took the paper, thanked her, and said, "I guess there's no reason for me to go now; the abuse is over." She encouraged me to call anyway.

As soon as I got home, I did call. I remember telling the receptionist, "I don't know what kind of help I need; I'm just trying to survive." She was very kind and told me she had someone who could help me. She set my first appointment for April 26. This was scary to me as I remembered the last counselor we had seen for family therapy. Week after week, it had been "gripe at Beth" sessions. The counselor sat there and did nothing. In fact, she actually helped Sam. When we would leave the sessions, I felt abused and more hopeless. Thus I halfway dreaded facing a new counselor.

I was so upset during this time that everything became fuzzy. I know I worked a few days that week, on call with different patients. On the 22nd when I came home from work, Matt and James reported they had been in our backyard, shooting fire crackers, when the police surrounded them with drawn guns. The officers told them that some woman reported there had been one shooting at our house, now there were more gunshots. So when the police arrived, they were ready to shoot. All I could do was thank God they didn't kill one of my kids.

The next day, Matt returned to his Army post. In a way, I was relieved that he wouldn't have to be so involved in the aftermath of Sam's death. In another way, I was sad because there was such a strain in our relationship.

About this time, we began getting weird phone calls, as many as twenty a day. When we answered the phone, no one said anything, just someone groaning in a low voice as if from the dead. It reminded me of a horror movie. The sound itself didn't scare me, but the idea that someone would be vicious enough to make the calls was terrifying.

In the meantime, I heard nothing from the police. Larry and Debra, other friendly neighbors, coworkers, employers, and neighbors at the apartment complex were all waiting to be questioned by the police. But the police never contacted them, never questioned anyone who really knew me. The police didn't seem interested in hearing from people who had witnessed the abuse or who had seen my injuries. I tried repeatedly to contact Connie to ask what the police were planning to do, but she neither took nor returned my calls. I was too upset to eat most of the time. When I did eat, I threw up most of it anyway.

The next week, the week of April 24, three good things happened. I returned to my regular duty with the Armstrong family. They seemed overjoyed to have me back, and I was glad to see them, too. At least when I was working, I knew what I was supposed to do. At home with everything in such chaos, I didn't know what to pick up or try.

The second good thing was that the Air Force Assistance League issued me a check to cover the April house payment plus the late charge. It was called a grant, so I didn't have to pay it back. I still don't know exactly how they arranged that.

The third good thing was starting counseling at the TADC outreach office. My frame of mind was such that I would look at myself in the mirror and think, "You're dead; what are you doing walking around?" With my counselor, Evelyn Hall, I began to get the therapy I had needed so long. There I found support and encouragement.

Evelyn spent about half an hour explaining domestic violence to me. I sat there amazed to hear her describe everything that Sam had done to me. When she finished, I asked, "Do these men go to abuse school?" I could not mention Sam's sexual abuse that first day, because I still thought that it meant something was wrong with me that my husband would treat me like that. At the end of that hour, I knew I would return. In my notes for this period, I wrote, "This is about the only thing holding me together."

During the evenings, I began trying to organize the mountains of papers Sam had accumulated. The checkbook was a mess; from what I could see, it hadn't been balanced during the last six months. I was bewildered to see that Sam had been paying the Joneses' bills. Yet the stubs of our bills were missing for the last six months. Every day, I got more calls from bill collectors, demanding payment or a lawsuit or garnishment of my paycheck. Even the doctor who had done surgery on my nose two years ago had never been paid and was still sending bills. Sam had a balance of $900 on his Sears charge and a balance of $1,500 on one Mastercard. "How did he keep all these people off his back?" I wondered. As I looked through his checkbook, I could see he hadn't made monthly payments on any of these accounts. At first I tried to be nice, reasonable with the bill collectors, explaining that we had been separated and that I didn't know anything about these bills. But after awhile, I was totally stressed out and told them, "Bill the Air Force; they have Sam's money, not me."

The deeper I dug, the more I ran into odd records and receipts among Sam's papers. He had another account in Denver, and the bank there was taking out payments every month for his Checkstra Card. There were dozens of receipts for X-rated movies, and he had checked out two particular movies over and over again—*Death Wish* and *Death Wish Two*. Every time I found another of those receipts, I felt a chill run through me. There was a computer printout of how much of his retirement pay I had earned for every day we were married. There were stacks of business cards with girl's names on them—Bunny, Candi, Delilah, Rita. I called the Health Department to get information and learned that all of the phone numbers were for current brothels in Nevada. Totally embarrassed, my face was on fire as I talked with them. After that call, I knew I had to get myself tested for AIDS.

Day after day, I was literally standing in my house staring at endless piles of paper and clutter, asking, "What do I do? Where do I start?" I found credit card charges that made no sense to me—a charge of $40 for flowers dated 2-13-88, a charge of $100 to a gourmet restaurant, a charge of $200 for jewelry. Debra was a major source of comfort and help to me during this time. She made the connection of the charge for flowers with Valentine's Day. All these bills pointed to Sam's involvement with another woman or other women. It crushed me to think I would have to pay these bills, especially when Sam had never shown me that kind of consideration. These particular bills were salt in my wounds, proving that in his eyes I was worthless.

Perhaps the most chilling discovery was finding my large expand-a-file, which had disappeared from my apartment weeks earlier. There was no longer the tiniest doubt that Sam had broken into my apartment and taken my file. Most of my papers were still in it, but not all. He had removed James's juvenile court records and the bills for James's care from a civilian doctor.

He had also taken Daniel's report cards, made five copies, then whited out the grades on the copies. He had done the same thing with one of my bills at a medical supply store. He hadn't written anything in the whited-out spaces, so I couldn't figure what he was trying to accomplish with this.

During this time, I was bouncing off the walls, crying at least a dozen times a day. Anything could trigger it. I'd hear one of *our* songs and cry, then get mad at Sam. I'd run across pictures of us together and sob. Why the hell did he have to do this? Why couldn't he just let me leave? No, he had to push, push, push me, never letting up.

In my sessions with Evelyn, she explained to me the traits of an abusive man. I had never ever heard this information. When Sam did such terrible things to me, I was afraid to tell anyone. I thought I was the only one it was happening to and that if I told people, they'd think I was crazy. I was convinced that *no one, no one* had ever had a husband that did these things—not the beatings, the mental anguish, the sexual torture, the attempts to drive me crazy. Sam would give me something, then take it away. He'd promise me something, then deny it. He'd tell me something, then insist he'd never said it. Lies. Lies. Lies. He'd say, "I won't hurt you again," then say, "You're crazy, I never said that. Look at you, you're cracking up." Telling me, "Bitch, I can't stand you. The only way I can fuck you is to hurt you." Sometimes forcing sex, then denying we'd had sex. Killing my dog, denying me something I loved. Keeping me awake at night or waking me up from a deep sleep. Denying me family or friends, keeping me isolated until I got so depressed I didn't want to make friends anymore. After all, if I got close to anyone, I'd have to explain the bruises. His "I'm better than you, bitch," attitude pushed me down so far that I referred to myself as "bitch." Sam was so powerful; he had always had power over me, always in control. I couldn't even control the money I earned. I had to give most of it to him so he could write checks to pay bills—bills that he later claimed to have paid or never paid at all. I couldn't get out of it. Every time I tried, he went off the deep end.

On May 3 after my session with Evelyn, I asked about attorneys and she gave me three names. The first one I called was only interested in discussing plea bargaining. I was not willing to consider that because I had done nothing except defend myself. The second one I called was Bill Smith. When I called Bill, I learned that he required a $500 retainer up front. I didn't have $500, didn't know how I could get that much money, and wasn't sure I needed a lawyer. So I didn't call to make an appointment with him, and I abandoned the idea of getting my own attorney, at least at that time.

Just trying to sort through the mess in our house continually flooded me with visions of all Sam's abuse. My mind was like a movie theater where they show the same movie over and over and over. Waking or sleeping, I couldn't escape the bitter violent memories.

I stayed in contact with the child custody worker who had been investigating Sam and me in our divorce action. I didn't quite understand why she was still on the case, since there was no longer a custody question. She let me know that she was in almost daily contact with the detective investigating Sam's death, and although her words were reassuring, I became increasingly uncomfortable. Day after day, she told me, "I'm sure the investigation will close tomorrow and then we'll close our file." I asked my sister, Nancy, if they would take James and Daniel should I be arrested, and she agreed. I then asked the child custody worker to please let me know if the police planned to arrest me so that I could arrange flights for the boys to my sister's beforehand. She informed me that the police were going to complete their investigation May 5. She also told me that the police might indict me, but probably would not arrest me. Still I worried. If I had to be locked up, I wanted to know that my boys were with my family.

I had called Detective Barlow on May 3 or 4 to ask if the investigation was finished. He said, "We've talked to your husband's coworkers and friends, and they have a whole different story to tell." I said, "I'm sure his friends would; have you talked to any of my friends?" He replied, "We don't have to. It's coming down, and it's coming down bad." I hung up, shaking uncontrollably.

On Wednesday night, May 4, James became quite upset and ran away. I was worried sick, but I didn't dare call the police. In spite of my confusion, it seemed clear to me that I had to get my boys to my family. I could just see them in foster homes with no one to get them out, no family to care for them.

On Thursday, May 5, I got Daniel off to school; then I had to go to work. James was on my mind all day; where was he, was he OK? I cashed my paycheck on the way home from work to buy plane tickets. As I turned into the cul-de-sac at home, I noticed a white car, no occupants, parked in front of my house, but I thought nothing of it. As soon as I pulled into my driveway, another unmarked car pulled in behind me to block the drive. When I got out of my car, Detective Barlow said, "We're here to arrest you." I said, "OK, just let me arrange for my kids." He said, "Your kids are taken care of." Just then, my front door opened and out walked the child custody worker with another woman and Daniel. I was crying as I turned to her and asked, "Why did you do this to me, to my kids?" She sort of mumbled, "I didn't have time to let you know." Daniel was clinging to me, hugging me, as the police grabbed me and propelled me into their car. Later I would learn that Daniel was taken to Child Haven. I asked the police what would happen to James, and they said, "We've got a warrant out for him. Now you'd better understand that anything you say can be used against you." After that, I shut up. I just sat in the backseat, crying quietly.

The police didn't allow me to take any of my things or arrange for my animals to be cared for. I was wearing a pair of white cotton pants with a uniform top and lab jacket. They took me just like that. Thank God for that lab jacket; without it, I would have frozen in that drafty jail.

When we got to the jail, Detective Barlow pulled me out of the car and handcuffed my hands behind me. He said he didn't want to put them on in front of my boy. In all my dealings with him, that was his only kind gesture.

Inside the jail, I was taken up to the booking desk. I was shaking so hard that my whole body jerked and my teeth chattered. They took mug shots of me in the middle of the hall, where male prisoners whistled, jeered, and yelled out, "Hey, Mama, come to me." I was utterly humiliated. The police had taken my purse when we left the house. Now they dumped the contents on the desk and inventoried it. I was relieved to see my money from cashing my paychecks was still there, but I worried that it might "disappear" before I could be released.

From there I was taken to the lockup cell, which I shared with approximately twenty other women. It was a dingy, barren concrete room with two wooden benches. The larger, stronger women occupied the benches; the rest of us sat on the cold concrete floor, stood against a wall, or milled around aimlessly. The floor was filthy, mostly with cigarette ashes and butts. Once each morning, we had to stand on the benches while the floor was swept. One girl threw up on the floor and the vomit was left there until the next morning. No one received medical care. Our bathroom facility consisted of a stainless steel commode and water fountain in one corner, slightly screened by a chest-high partition. There was no toilet paper. The room reeked with foul odors, yet we were expected to eat there.

The second day, the guards took me with two others to be fingerprinted. I never dreamed fingerprinting could be so involved or take so long. When they asked us for distinguishing marks, one girl dropped her pants to reveal a tattoo on her butt. I could feel my eyes bug out in shock.

I felt so out of place, so alone.

My third night there, Saturday, guards took me out of lockup just before bedtime. They strip-searched me, which included making me bend over and spread the cheeks of my butt. Then I was taken upstairs to the recreation room. About forty of us slept in there on wall-to-wall pallets. Each of us had one wool blanket and one sandbag pillow. I was told the pillows were made of sand so they couldn't be used to smother anyone. Even though the pallets and sand pillows were crude, they were much better than sitting up all night on the cold floor. Upstairs, we were allowed to shower. After two and a half days in lockup, the shower felt wonderful. I liked the rec room better than lockup for several reasons. It was cleaner because we cleaned it ourselves. We all had rotating chores, so we had something constructive to do. Our street clothes had been taken from us and stored in plastic bags on a dry-cleaner conveyer rig. Once upstairs, each woman was issued one pair of pants, one shirt, one dress, one pair of socks, one pair of tennis shoes, one bra, one slip, and two pairs of underwear. These clothes gave me some sense of everyday hygiene, which had been missing since my arrest.

I was instructed to keep the dress nice for court by rolling it up and putting it under my pillow. At that time, I weighed about eighty-five pounds, so none of these clothes fit me. The only way I could keep the pants up was to roll the waistband three or four times. Still, it was better than feeling grimy.

Throughout my five and a half days in jail, I tried to keep a low profile—stay quiet and mind my own business. But there was one woman who made fun of me, called me "Little Miss PTA." She told me, "There's a lot more to your story than you're letting on; you're going to prison, Baby Cakes." After we were transferred upstairs to the rec room, she started acting too friendly, trying to pat me on the back or grab my arm, anything to touch me. When meals were served, she'd say, "You don't want this, do you?" then take my food. One day, I got so aggravated that I told her, "No one is going to force me into anything again. I'll die first." She smirked at me and answered, "Me and my friends will have our way with you when you get to Carson. I've got lots of friends there." All I could do was shudder inside and pray, "Please, God, don't let them send me to prison." I knew I would die if that happened.

I was told I would be arraigned on Monday and that meant going before the judge to determine whether or not I would be held. A man from Intake Services interviewed me to get information about how long I had lived in Las Vegas, where I worked, who my employer was, and so on.

Sunday was Mother's Day, and I was allowed to make a phone call to Daniel. We both cried and cried. I had never been separated from my kids on Mother's Day. There had been no news of James, and that was a constant worry. I told myself over and over, "You've got to hang on for your kids." Being there for my kids had kept me going for sixteen years; I prayed I could survive even though my world was crumbling around me.

Before going into court on Monday, I was strip-searched again. I was strip-searched every time I was taken out or brought back upstairs; that was the rule. I was so upset I didn't understand what happened in court on Monday except that a time was set for me to go back Tuesday afternoon. Just before leaving for court, I found out from the child custody worker that someone was trying to get custody of Daniel and that if I didn't make arrangements for his care by Tuesday morning, I could lose him, maybe forever. I was frantic that morning because we were on lockdown after breakfast at 4 a.m. until 10 a.m. That meant we weren't supposed to move off our pallets. But I had to call Debra, so I sneaked to the phone in the corner. While I was talking, the guard told me to get off the phone and started pulling out her nightstick. All the other women prisoners stood up on their cots and said, "Leave her alone. She's trying to take care of her kids." The guard backed off then. I had to sign a statement that as long as I was unable to care for Daniel and James, I authorized my neighbor, Debra, to care for them. Debra had to wait six hours downstairs in the jail for them to bring up the paper for my signature. In spite of the return strip search, I was relieved to learn that Debra had picked up Daniel from Child Haven and he was safe with her.

On Tuesday, I was chained with another woman and several men, then taken into court again. I tried to look my best, but I had no makeup and no way to curl my hair. One of the other women was going to french braid my hair, but the guard interfered. When we were taken into court, I made eye contact with a man sitting in the spectator's section. He seemed to be staring at me as I sat there waiting for my case to come up. My case was the last one, so I was very edgy by the time my name was called.

In total amazement, I heard the prosecutor say that I was charged with first-degree murder and that I was a flight risk because I lived in Denver, Colorado, and drove back and forth to work here. I spoke up and said, "Your Honor, this is all wrong. I've lived and worked in Las Vegas for the last four years." Then the judge said he had read all the material, that I had been abused for sixteen years, and that he didn't know how I had lived with Sam all those years. "I'm going to do something I've never done in all my years on the bench," he said. "I'm releasing you on your own recognizance." As soon as the judge ruled, the man who had been watching me and one other man ran out of the courtroom. I assume they were reporters, because the next day each local paper carried a brief article about my case. I broke down, sobbing with relief. I had no tissue to wipe my eyes and nose, and forgetting I was handcuffed, I almost broke the wrist of the woman I was chained to, trying to get my hands to my face.

After court, I was taken to lockup while I waited for my paperwork to be processed so that Debra could pick me up. After what seemed like hours, I heard a male cop outside the door say, "Where's that murderer?" When he opened the door and saw that I was the only prisoner there, he said, "You?" in disbelief. Suddenly, it registered with me that in the minds of many people, I had already been tried and convicted. I left the jail with mixed feelings—relief to be free even temporarily, but with a greater sense of impending doom. I was stuck in an endless nightmare.

12

Presumed Guilty

On May 10, I was free after the most degrading, humiliating experience of my life. When Debra picked me up from jail that night, she had Daniel with her in the car. We hugged and cried, overcome with relief, sorrow, joy. On the way home, I learned that James had returned the previous night. When he started to enter the house through the back door, he heard the police radio, got scared, and jumped into the storage shed, locking himself in.

Within minutes, he heard the policemen outside, discussing whether or not to break down the door of the shed. It was terrifying for him, thinking they might come in shooting. After they left, he spent the rest of the night in the shed. Then he called my sister, who advised him to go to Debra's house. I breathed a silent prayer of thanks for Debra's friendship. She had cared for my boys when there was nothing I could do.

When we arrived home with pizzas, James was cleaning the house. I was so happy and relieved to see him and to know he was alright. We all gathered round the table and ate the pizza. For just a moment, we could be happy to have each other and be together as a family. After Debra left, I felt so dirty that I bathed with lava soap. Then I slept soundly for the first time in five days.

Early the next morning, I went to Intake Services to meet the requirement of checking in within twenty-four hours. I learned that I had to check in with them three times each week, once in person and twice by phone. I was told a public defender would be appointed for me, but not until five days before the date of my preliminary hearing, scheduled for July 25. The intake workers were very pleasant to me; in fact, they seemed sympathetic to my case. At that time, every tiny crumb of kindness or encouragement meant the world to me.

At home, I was constantly bombarded by reminders of the turmoil in my life. Every place I looked, another mess, another problem to handle. Yet, I couldn't seem to get a grip on any of it; I couldn't finish anything. I began to call myself crazy; I felt crazy. In my dreams, I saw myself dying or dead. A picture of driving myself off Boulder Dam flashed through my mind frequently.

Work helped to distract me because I knew exactly what to do there. Bathe my patients, feed my patients, record their vital signs, see to their medication. Almost daily, more problems arose to distract me from my grief over Sam's death and my horror of being charged with first-degree murder.

On May 12 at 4 a.m., I received a call from a woman I had met in jail. She told me her husband had beaten her and kidnapped her children, that she had no place to go. I felt so sorry for her that I let her spend the night in my spare room. She arrived driving a truck; I was thankful that at least she had her own transportation. I put her in touch with the women's shelter and Legal Aid, but once she was in my house, she wouldn't leave.

Within twenty-four hours, I wanted her out of my house, because the next night she came in stoned on drugs. At the same time, I didn't want any trouble with the police, but I didn't know how to make her leave. This woman promised me she would leave early Saturday to go after her children. She would only be staying two days, so I thought I could handle that. Just as I had always had a soft spot in my heart for stray animals, I now had a special place in my heart for battered women.

I came home from work the first day after she moved in to find her bouncing around my house in a see-through teddy. I was shocked and told her to put clothes on before one of my sons could see her. The next day, she came home with several large bundles of new clothes from the most expensive department stores. When I asked her how she got the money for them, she gave me some vague answer. I had so much on my mind, like defending myself against a murder charge, I didn't push it. I told myself, "Just hang on one more day and she'll be gone."

On Saturday, to my relief, she did leave. But she came back in the middle of the night, banging on the door and scaring us out of our skins. At last, she left Sunday night and did not return. I thought that was the last I would hear of her. It was some comfort to me to think I had helped her, and I prayed she would be able to get her life together.

During her stay, Matt called, saying he was AWOL. I couldn't believe what I was hearing. He asked me to write a letter, stating that he was upset about his father's death and that I needed him at home. I wrote the letter and mailed it Federal Express.

On Monday, May 16, Matt arrived home. Part of me was relieved to have him home; part of me was worried about another mouth to feed. The night of his homecoming, after the other two boys went to bed, I had a serious talk with Matt. "I can't support you," I told him. "I need you to get a job and get it quick." Matt agreed, but somehow a job never materialized.

I had gotten several calls from a private insurance company that had written a policy on Sam. Although I had told them repeatedly, "I can't discuss this case with you," they persisted in sending an agent to my house on May 16. I was able to arrange for the TADC advocate, Sarah Jacobson, to be with me for this meeting, and she arrived before the agent.

We had talked on the phone several times, but this was our first meeting. Just as I had pictured her, Sarah was warm, caring, and comfortable to be with. She commented on how nice and clean the house looked, then asked to use the bathroom. She left her purse on the couch while I went into the kitchen to pour us some coffee. We both came back into the living room about the same time, then froze as we saw Sarah's purse darting to and fro on the couch with a furry blonde tail hanging out. Sarah calmly picked up her purse, pulled out my ferret, and said, "Well, my goodness," as she set the ferret down. She was matter-of-fact, as if this were an everyday occurrence. We both laughed, and I knew I had found another friend.

When the insurance agent arrived, he told me his company "had to have the facts." All I could say was, "I cannot discuss this case with you before it goes to court." He pressured me until Sarah said, "Beth, why don't you call your attorney?" With that, the agent left.

By the time I got to my session with Evelyn on Tuesday, May 17, I was falling apart, but I felt safe letting go with her. She noticed the large red splotches which had developed on my upper arms and told me she was concerned that I was becoming anorexic. She stressed how important it was for me to eat several times a day, even if only a few bites.

On Wednesday, May 18, Sarah accompanied me to meet with Attorney Bill Smith. My first impression when I walked into his office was, "Dear God, how can I possibly afford this lawyer?" Bill seemed to be very capable and forthright, but somewhat leery of me. I felt comforted and reassured that Sarah was with me. I explained to Bill what had happened on April 9. He said that in his opinion there was no basis for the prosecutor to pursue the case. He asked me how far I was willing to go with the case, and I said, "All the way." I gave him a check for $500 that I had borrowed from my sister. The check bounced because the bank had made an error in my new account. I was embarrassed and relieved that Bill didn't drop me as a client.

When I returned to work after my meeting with Bill and Sarah, James phoned to inform me that the Albuquerque police had called my home, saying, "We've arrested Bethel Sipe." I called Albuquerque immediately. They informed me they had arrested a woman using my name, and that she had my credit cards, my sheriff's card (an ID necessary for many jobs in Nevada), and my military ID. I kept all those cards in a dresser drawer and rarely looked at them. The woman from jail I had befriended had stolen these cards and a book of checks on a bank account which had been closed for more than three years. I began checking all these accounts and soon discovered she had written checks totaling $1,500 and charged over $2,000.

Here was more stress when I was already overwhelmed. I had to go to the police station, pick up forgery forms, get my signature notarized on all copies, then take one to every business where she had charged on my credit cards or forged checks. Trying to straighten this out involved at least one hassle per week for the next six months, endlessly. Even as late as January, 1990, I was getting calls from people trying to collect this money from me. I was sad to think I could trust animals more than people, but that's what I learned from the woman I befriended.

My mind and my world were chaos. I don't know how I appeared to my kids or others; probably I scared them. At times, I felt afraid of my own children. But I had people I could call for help—Debra, TADC, my employer, and my family, even though they were far away.

In my more lucid moments, I knew I had to raise money to pay my attorney. Privately, I sold Sam's most expensive toys—guns, 35mm camera, telescope, car. On Sunday, May 22, my day off, I had a garage sale. I sold anything, everything that would sell—the stereo, antiques, crystal, dishes, my jewelry, clothes, the dining room table, even my wedding rings. I ended up with $2,000, including my paychecks, which I paid on account to my attorney. I didn't know how we would eat the next week, but I had to defend myself. Debra's mother gave me a jug of nickels, her gambling money. She also filled my freezer with food. We would never have survived without the help of these good people.

I had missed a week's work while in jail, so I was short of money to live. I remember my brother telling me, "The hell with the house payment. You have to pay your lawyer to save your life." I found out it would take about six months for the mortgage company to foreclose. So I didn't make the May house payment of $607. Still, it was just one more thing hanging over my head.

The next week, I saw Bill Smith alone. I remember him saying, "I have to ask you in private; did you murder your husband?" I answered, "Absolutely not." In Bill's office, I related all I could remember of the events of April 9. Bill also wanted to see the apartment where I had lived or an identical one. A few days later in an identical apartment, Sarah, Bill, Daniel, and I reenacted the night of April 9. In spite of Bill's gentle questioning, this was very painful for Daniel and me. For the first time since that night, I began to have flashes of what happened, but I couldn't remember it all.

Bill gave me a list of things to do which included writing my autobiography, focusing on my sixteen-year marriage to Sam, in as much detail as possible. That assignment scared me to death, but I had to try.

The days and weeks following fused into each other. On Tuesdays, I saw Evelyn, reported to Intake Services, took James and Daniel to counseling, and handled as many errands as I could. The other days were pretty much the same—work all day, cook dinner, then spend all night poring over old calendars, files, receipts, pictures, letters, piecing together my life history with Sam. Once Matt found me sobbing amid all the papers. He put his arms around me and comforted me until I cried myself dry. Words cannot express how much his kindness helped.

Still, night after night, I'd sit among piles of papers, sobbing, talking to Sam, reliving the pain of years past. Morning after morning, I'd awake stiff and aching, still surrounded by piles of paper. I began to have flashbacks of violent incidents with Sam that I had buried in the back of my mind. At times, the pain of having to remember was so sharp I thought it would kill me. "Just get this mess over with," I'd tell myself, "then you can die peacefully."

By the time I saw Evelyn for my regular appointment on June 28, I had completed twelve of the sixteen years with Sam in my autobiography. Evelyn told me straight out, "Beth, your condition is worsening. I'm arranging for you to see a psychiatrist. Perhaps some medication will help." I wasn't eager to see a psychiatrist, because I knew I was distracted and at times disoriented. I was afraid the psychiatrist would tell me I was crazy and lock me up. But I trusted Evelyn, so I agreed. I saw a lady psychiatrist later that day who proved to be kind and sympathetic. She gave me a prescription for Elavil, which did help me sleep.

Fortunately, I had always kept pocket calendars of my work hours and appointments. Reading through my calendars was bittersweet—some dates brought up sweet memories, and I could see Sam and the kids smiling; others triggered terrifying memories. But either way, they made me cry. Yet these calendars provided a framework of specific dates into which I could fit the day-to-day pattern of our lives. I had also kept many medical records and reports that documented Sam's violence. Of course, many had to be requested or written for.

The process was slow because I couldn't resist stopping to read every word. I had kept all Sam's letters and poems to me, and reading through them at that time cut like a knife. Amazingly, as I dug through all these papers, I found that Sam had kept all my letters. We'd always had our troubles, but for most of those years, I'd clung to the belief that Sam loved me. His letters gave me tangible proof for that belief. Excerpts from a few of his letters show how loving he could be.

> March, 1972. Dearest Beth and Matt: I'm sorry it's taking so long to get straightened out (my allotment) and that you're having to do without quite a bit of stuff you'd like to have and need. I think you're pretty wonderful to put up with it so well especially with the stresses of carrying the baby and us being apart. I guess that's one of the many reasons I love you so much. And I do love you with all my heart.

> August, 1972. Dearest Beth: I miss you so very much. I look at your pictures constantly, wishing I was looking at you instead. I love you!! Well, Lady, it's almost 11 and I've got to try to go to sleep. I probably won't be able to get to sleep until about 2 o'clock. I'll probably just lay there and think about you. About your body, about all the things I'd like to do to your body. The kissing, the hugging, feeling your body next to mine, running my hands over your body . . .

> May, 1973. Dearest Beth: Hi Love! God I miss you. I've been thinking about you all day. Beautiful joyous thoughts about how wonderful it would be to have you sitting in my lap playing kissy face and huggy bod and other neat stuff. I love you, so I guess it's alright to have such ungentlemanly, nasty, juicy, perverted, luscious, wonderfully exciting thoughts about you. It will be nice to get home!!!

> March, 1976. Dearest Beth: I had this outstanding dream last night. I don't remember all of it, but I do remember I was holding you in my arms and it felt so good. You were so warm and I could feel the baby just starting to grow. We were watching Matt and James playing or something. It seemed so real. I can remember how content I was holding you and

watching my kids grow and play. When I woke up, I felt so warm inside. It was a wonderful way to wake up.

August, 1976. Dearest Beth: Hi. I've been sitting here for about 3 hrs. trying to write you this letter. I've been trying to think of something to say but all I can think of is how much I love you and how much I wish I were with you now instead of trying to write you a letter. I miss you very much. I think I'm becoming more and more aware of how much I really do love you.

February, 1984. Hello Sweetheart: Miss ya!! Not much to say since we got off the phone just a little while ago, but I wanted to say I love you. The kids miss you, but not as much as me. I hope you are putting your heart into being on vacation. You don't get many like this one. I miss you and your body and am awaiting anxiously your return.

Such bittersweet memories were stirred as I reread all Sam's letters. Now he was gone, along with all my dreams for a "normal" happy marriage and family. During all his absences on military duty, I had lived for his letters, reading and rereading them until the paper on which they were written was literally in tatters. His letters provided little comfort for all my shattered dreams.

Through endless nights, I forced myself to dig back through the mountains of papers. At the same time, I had to face the suffering and anger of my boys, powerless to help them. The boys screamed and fought and knocked holes in the walls. The anguish I felt as I watched them act out their pain is beyond description. I knew they had learned that from Sam; what else could I expect from them?

Through Bill, I obtained copies of Jane's statement against me, apparently the district attorney's primary "evidence" for charging me with first-degree murder. Jane's statement consisted of half-truths and blatant lies—reports of threats I never made, affairs I never had, allegations that I raised black widow spiders to extract their poison and that I grew deadly cultures in my refrigerator. Everything whirled in my mind like food in a blender.

One night in my murky confusion, it hit me that I needed to see Sam's grave. Maybe if I said good-bye to him, I could let go. I began packing to go to Mina. Daniel watched me for a while before he said, "Mom, what are you doing? You can't go anywhere." In a trance, I stopped and sat down, frozen, immobile.

After the boys went to bed, I sat like a stone, thinking, "It's all too much. I just want to go to sleep and never wake up." In my medicine cabinet, I found several vials of prescriptions—painkillers, sedatives, sinus medication. I emptied them one by one, swallowing every pill. When I finished, the vials were neatly lined up and I lay down to sleep, my mind totally at peace.

Some time later, I awoke vomiting. Wearily, I cleaned up the mess and went back to bed crying. I still hoped I had digested enough of the pills that I wouldn't wake up again. When I did awaken about twelve hours later, all I wanted was ice water. It took me a few minutes to realize that I was still alive. "It's too damn bad," I thought, "There's no way out for me."

On Sunday night, July 17, James ran away after a big family argument. We were all yelling at each other. In his depression, James said, "Mom, we ought to just get in the car and gas ourselves." Although I had experienced the same feelings, I was shocked to hear those words from the mouth of my son.

Later, I learned that James had seen my personal calendar where I had written "My life ends" beside July 25, the date of my preliminary hearing. After James ran out of the house that night, I found poems and lyrics he had written about suicide and death. Chills ran down my spine as I realized how upset James was.

The next day while at work, I was notified that the police had picked up James. He was being held at the Juvenile Center until I could get there. I arranged for coverage at work and called Sarah, who agreed to meet me there. James didn't seem rational, so he was transferred to a psychiatric hospital. At least he was safe for the moment. When I took his clothes to the hospital later that evening, he was furious with me. All I could say was, "I hope you'll understand some day." It grieved me deeply to see him so angry, but I had no answers. "Lord," I prayed, "give me a sign, an answer. When, how will this all end?" I knew I was close to the end of my endurance.

About this time, the base chaplain I had consulted several times called, informing me that OSI had completed their investigation and ruled that Sam's death was justifiable. Off the record, one investigator had stated, "The son of a bitch deserved what he got." Much later, I would learn that Detective Barlow never so much as requested the result of the OSI investigation.

When I saw Evelyn on July 19, I took in two dresses on hangers to get her opinion of which to wear to my hearing. She was so concerned about my physical and mental condition that she recommended I go into a psychiatric hospital. Mostly, I was relieved that someone else had said it for me. I had tried to hold everything together, but I could no longer hold myself together. I was ready to turn everything over to someone else—the bills, the bill collectors, the house, work, the kids, the case, the Air Force. I wanted everything to stop, stand still.

Even so, before I could check into the hospital, I had to arrange for Daniel to stay with Debra, arrange for the pets and yard to be tended, arrange for coverage at my job, notify Intake Services, meet with a base chaplain, and buy groceries for Daniel's stay with Debra. I was so preoccupied that day that I drove three miles past Nellis before I realized it.

When I got home, I saw a police car with two officers parked at the entrance of the cul-de-sac. Apparently, someone had reported me to the police again, probably because I had taken the dresses with me to my counseling appointment. I guess they assumed I was skipping town. Upset and angry, I called Sarah, who suggested I offer the policemen some coffee. I walked down the rise in my yard to the patrol car, rapped on the window, and offered coffee. The policemen declined and soon drove away.

This may sound brazen to other people, but following Sarah's suggestion defused the situation for me, helped me see a humorous side. Later, Bill told me he had gotten a call from the district attorney's office that day, saying I couldn't be very sick because I was out running around all over town. It wasn't just my imagination that someone was out to get me!

On Wednesday afternoon, July 20, I loaded all my valuable papers and records into my car; I couldn't trust leaving them in my own home. Sarah came to my house, followed me to my employer's home where I left my car, then took me to the hospital to be admitted.

13

My Cup Overflows

Although I trusted Evelyn and I could feel myself falling apart, I went into the hospital with misgivings. Debra begged me not to admit myself because she had had a friend in a violent relationship who had admitted herself for alcohol treatment. Once she was admitted, the hospital had committed her and kept her in a locked ward. After forty-five days, when her insurance benefits ran out, the hospital released her.

Debra told me, "Beth, if they get you in there, they will not let you out." This scared me, but I was more scared of falling completely over the edge of sanity. There was just too much coming at me from every direction.

The admittance procedure is hazy in my mind. I remember answering a lot of questions as the nurse filled out the admission papers. My military ID was copied and returned to me. Then I was taken into the adult ward, or unit as it was called. I recall a sinking feeling as I realized that I was locked in, but I was told the lock was more to keep people out than to keep people in, that being locked in only applied to a few patients, and that I would be allowed to come and go to the cafeteria and hospital activities, that I could go out on passes. That information eased some of my anxiety.

When I was shown my room, my anxiety started to rise again; I was to sleep on a cot between two other female patients, one of whom I soon learned was violent. "I have to get out of here," I thought. When Evelyn visited me in the late afternoon, her calmness and encouragement soothed me. She suggested I discuss my objections about my room assignment with my hospital therapist, Lori. Lori was kind, attentive, and sympathetic to my feelings. Very quickly, she arranged for me to have my own bed. I began to feel calmer, more comfortable, and I decided to stay for treatment that I knew I needed.

That was Wednesday night. During the next couple of days I began to relax a little, getting accustomed to the hospital routine. I found myself crying more, but feeling safe to do that. Evelyn visited me and constantly encouraged me to let my grief out, as I participated in the hospital therapy groups. I felt encouraged by visits from several people from church, even couples. In my experience, usually only the women visit people in the hospital. Even my employers, the elderly couple I cared for, visited me.

At times, I felt overwhelmed by everything outside—my sons, my home, my job, so many bills, my case preparation. Because I had always attended to responsibilities and work inside and outside the home, being in the hospital felt like neglecting my duties. I had to remind myself constantly, "Focus on getting better. That's what you're here for—you can deal with everything else later."

I began attending group therapy on Thursday. There were groups for almost everything—stress, grief, women's issues, relaxation, even a Gestalt group. After attending the relaxation groups, I noticed an increase in flashbacks of violent encounters with Sam. The flashbacks were just like reliving all those fights, some of which I hadn't remembered in years. The adrenalin rush from these flashbacks was overwhelming—filling me with dread and jitters. As the flashbacks increased, so did the nightmares. Lori was very good at helping me process this flood of memories and feelings. I was not allowed to attend the assertiveness group for some reason I didn't understand then and still do not understand. At first, I didn't have much to say, but I learned a lot by listening and soon felt comfortable enough to participate.

On Saturday, July 23, I was taken into a psychologist's office for neuropsychological testing. By this time, I was medicated with Stelazine and Vistaril. Because of the medication, I was having symptoms of drowsiness, muddled thinking, thick tongue, dry mouth, blurred vision, bed-wetting, and reversal of numbers and letters. I just knew I didn't feel right, but under the circumstances, I guess I expected to feel strange.

When I entered the psychologist's office, he said, "By the way, I was on staff at Nellis Air Force Base when your husband bought the farm." A shudder ran through me. The office was very small, no windows, and I felt like a trapped animal alone there with this strange man. Being around men was intensely uncomfortable for me at this point, especially Air Force men. This man struck me as a typical military man; his general attitude was snippy, crude, and arrogant, as he bragged about his credentials. "I'm the only psychologist in Las Vegas who can do this kind of testing," he said. I may be ignorant, but my thought was, "Why does he have to toot his own horn so loud?"

He began with a few tests of word associations and memory of number progressions. Then he blindfolded me, and I had to touch differently shaped blocks and place them in the correspondingly shaped holes. I broke out in a sweat. All I could think of was trying to maintain my composure with this stranger. I was so shaky, drugged, sleepy, tired. I said to him, "I don't think I should be tested in my present condition." He said, "No. It's fine. This testing needs to be done immediately."

I still wondered why it had to be right then on a Saturday, why I couldn't sleep in longer. At the end of the hour, my hands were so sweaty, they were dripping. At that point, I wasn't thinking about the test results. All I could think about was getting out of that room and getting away from that man.

Later that Saturday, I was allowed to meet with James and his psychologist. Looking back now, I realize that neither James nor I was in any condition to face each other with our feelings. The meeting did not go well and ended with our saying things to each other we didn't mean. I went back to the adult unit with my spirits dragging, more anxious and worried than ever about the future.

From the very first meeting, I felt uncomfortable with the psychiatrist assigned to me. Before I met with him the first time, I overheard him ask the nurses, "Why did they give me this case?" That made me feel like a reject, a hopeless case. In sessions, he had the saddest facial expression, as if he were grief stricken. Frequently, he shook his head, shaded his eyes with one hand, and rubbed his forehead as if he had a headache.

In our first session, he referred to the night "you murdered your husband," and told me, "Don't incriminate yourself in your own guilt." I felt I had already been judged and convicted by this man. What was he talking about? Murder? Guilt? Later, when I discussed this with Evelyn, she suggested that maybe I felt remorse and sorrow rather than guilt. Hearing that was like a brilliant light switching on in my mind, and I felt relieved, less confused. I had no reason to feel guilty; I was only protecting myself from a man in a mad alcoholic rage. But I certainly did feel tremendous remorse and sorrow.

My contacts with my psychiatrist steadily went downhill from that first meeting. Usually, he would see me the last thing on his shift, often at midnight. Several times, the nurses made me wait up to see him, and he never showed—just left it to the nurses to tell me he'd left the hospital. Even when I did get to see him, I was in a zombie-like state produced by the late hour and the medication. In that condition, it was difficult to organize my thoughts. Sometimes after waiting up so long, I couldn't go to sleep for the rest of the night.

One night, I explained to him how the Stelazine was affecting me. He dismissed this with, "It will level off." He told me I could not attend the assertiveness group but pressured me to attend the addictions group. That made no sense to me; I was not an addict, so I refused to attend. Of course, he was not pleased with that.

And always, there were his nervous mannerisms—holding his head, shading his eyes. One day, I remarked, "I seem to be stressing you out. I don't think you can handle all this." He didn't have a response for that, just seemed more nervous, uneasy.

It took a couple of weeks for me to realize the major reason for my distrust of my psychiatrist. He reminded me of Sam. His face, his height and size, but primarily his way of talking down to me as if I were a moron/slave and he were God—all echoed Sam. Once I identified the similarities, I approached each session with fear and trembling. It is not surprising then that I did not benefit from my psychiatrist's "treatment."

Fortunately, I had the groups, Lori, Evelyn, Sarah, and church friends. I began releasing feelings, and some of my confusion cleared. I resumed making calls, trying to get the necessary documentation for my case. During the second week of hospitalization, I began to go on passes for a few hours away from the hospital—to church, out to dinner, or to check on things at home. The passes provided relief from the hospital regimen and opportunities to spend time with Daniel. I could feel some inner strength returning, some hope that I had a future with my sons.

Evelyn visited me one night as I was preparing to go on pass and complimented me on how pretty I looked. It meant a lot to me that my efforts to improve my grooming were noticed. I still broke down in tears a lot, but Evelyn encouraged me, saying "You need to grieve; just let it out." Grieving was no longer fearful; it was a process I had to complete in order to survive. I was making progress, getting better.

Watching the other patients was interesting, enlightening, sometimes scary, sometimes funny. One young woman, also battered, also an Air Force wife, was assigned to my room. Her husband had her committed for overdosing on pills, but they never pumped her stomach. How much of an overdose could it have been? She seemed so hurt and vulnerable. She reminded me of myself in that Virginia hospital. I tried to comfort her and give her encouragement.

Another young woman sat and cried all the time for the first two or three days in the hospital. She talked about wanting to die and told me she had no therapist, so I went to Lori and told her I would give up my time if she would just see this woman. That same afternoon, she was assigned a therapist and given some antidepressants, and her mood lifted almost immediately.

A rather sophisticated man who said he was a therapist was admitted one night. We all teased him, saying, "Don't you get enough of us every day?" After he took his first dose of Stelazine, he went over to a corner of the dayroom and pulled down his pants as if to urinate. Two attendants grabbed him and took him to his room. We didn't see him again for a day or two.

There was another young man who stood out because he was so "out of it." One minute, he'd seem fine. Then his talking would get faster and faster, louder and louder, and he said things like, "Santa is trying to land here right now, but his landing field is frozen over."

I mention these other patients to illustrate how different we all were and thus how difficult it was to relate to each other. At times, we were frightened of each other; at other times, we all tried to comfort and encourage each other. Patients were discharged and new patients admitted almost daily. I began to see a pattern in how quickly patients "got well" when they had no insurance benefits left.

During my first two weeks in the hospital, a couple of things happened which made me uneasy. Before my life with Sam, I had listened to my intuition or sixth sense; usually it protected me. I'm sure I either learned or inherited this ability from my mother. Sam ridiculed and punished me if I dared to mention my premonitions, and after the first few years of our marriage, I ignored my inner alarm system. Now my intuition was coming back.

My first inkling of intuition was uneasiness about the neuropsychologist and his panicky insistence that I complete his tests. I couldn't face another session with him; some inner voice kept saying, "Don't do it! Don't do it!" I brought the subject up with my attorney, and he advised me to wait if I felt that strongly about it. Later, I mentioned it to Evelyn and she began checking with four other psychologists, particularly asking about the testing conditions.

According to those psychologists, medication and depression definitely interfere with neuropsychological testing enough to invalidate the test results and conclusions. Evelyn relayed this information to my attorney, who then instructed me not to cooperate further with this testing.

The other matter which set off my intuitive alarm concerned Daniel. On the third or fourth day after admission to the hospital, Helen, a new church friend, came for a visit and told me that Debra had informed her she was no longer willing to keep Daniel. Helen volunteered to take Daniel into her home. She had a son about Daniel's age and assured me she would be happy to care for Daniel for the duration of my hospitalization. With so much on my mind, I was relieved and grateful to Helen.

I tried dozens of times to call Debra, but all I got was the answering machine. I left numerous messages, but Debra never returned my calls. That wasn't like the Debra who had been my friend for two years. I felt hurt and rejected. I wondered if Daniel had done something so terrible that Debra couldn't tell me, but when I questioned Daniel, he swore there had been no incident.

Only after a month had passed would I learn the truth from Debra. Helen had gone to Debra and told her that I had instructed her to take Daniel, that I didn't want him staying with Debra. Of course, Debra was hurt and puzzled too. Even today, I do not understand why Helen found it necessary to lie to me and to lie to Debra. How could she have thought she was being helpful or acting in a Christian way?

When I went out on pass with Helen, her son, and Daniel the evening of August 2, I didn't know anything about Helen's lies to me and to Debra. I was eagerly looking forward to seeing Daniel and getting some work done at home. That afternoon I had called the homeless man who was staying in my house—supposedly taking care of watering the lawn and feeding my cats—to tell him I would be coming home that evening with my friend and our boys. Since I was trying to avoid any further friction with the Joneses, I asked this man to leave the back sliding glass door unlocked so I could enter the house that way. Later, Helen would drive up to the front of the house with the boys.

The outing started off well with all of us in a happy mood. When I entered my house through the sliding glass door, I found the man with another guy nude in my bed. Pillows covered the living room floor and an open bottle of generic vegetable oil was near the pillows. Through clenched teeth, I ordered these men out of my house. They threw on their clothes and ran out the back door.

Before I opened the front door for Helen and the boys, I grabbed the salad oil and took it to the kitchen. I was so upset I could hardly control my shaking. We sent the two boys out back to water the lawn, and I began to wash the sinkful of dirty dishes. A short while later, I went out back to see how the boys were doing and found they had dug a hole about three feet deep to bury the "cat poop." I told them it wasn't necessary to bury cat poop, to fill up the hole and get busy watering the dead spots in the lawn.

When I went back into the house, Helen was packing up all the canned goods she could find, saying she needed them to take care of Daniel. This confused me because I had already spent about $80 for the food I had taken to Debra's. During this time, I had no income because I hadn't worked for two weeks. Before I could say anything about this to Helen, Daniel came back in whining and pulling at me, insisting we go to McDonald's "right now." I told him we came home to clean things up first, that we would go to McDonald's later. When he began kicking me in the shins, I got hold of his shoulders, turned him around, and told him to go back outside and finish watering. He tried to punch me and I slapped him. The boys went back outside and forgot about it. Daniel wasn't even crying. I realized I was overwhelmingly confused, out of control, so I went into the living room and lit a cigarette.

The incident just got worse because Helen followed me into the living room, screaming and hollering hysterically. "I'm taking both the boys and leaving," she said. I told her not to take Daniel, or I would call the police and report her for kidnapping. She proceeded to take him anyway. I didn't try to stop her because I didn't want any more violence. I was worried she would have a wreck because she seemed too hysterical to drive. I was too scared to call the police, so I kept calling her house, asking her to bring Daniel back. She wouldn't talk to me, just kept hanging up.

There I was in the house by myself, past time to check back in at the hospital. As time went on and it became clear that no one was coming back, I called the hospital and tried to explain what happened. I was told I couldn't come back, that I was already too late. Added to everything else I was facing, all I could think was, "I'm in big trouble now."

A couple of hours later, I tried to call the hospital again. During the conversation, the phone went dead. I thought the nurse had hung up on me. Later, I would learn that my telephone line had been cut, but at that moment, I felt it was useless to try anymore. I sat down on the couch and mentally gave up. I stayed there all night, too agitated to sleep—so hopeless, so alone.

I spent all the next day hiding in my house, feeling like a trapped animal. About noon, I saw a police car at the side of the house, and when I looked out my kitchen window, I came face-to-face with a policeman, standing there looking in. I went to the front door and talked to them through the closed door. The officers said they were there to check on me. I asked if they had a warrant. When they said no, I asked them to leave me alone.

After that, I just curled up in fetal position on the couch, waiting for something, but I didn't know what. I couldn't go back to work; I didn't know where Daniel and James were; I didn't know where to begin to untangle the mess. I had always been able to get busy and do whatever I needed to do. That day, I didn't know what I needed to do or what I was facing. So I just sat there. From time to time, I tried to call Sarah or Evelyn, but the phone was dead. I drank a lot of coffee and chain-smoked my cigarettes until they were all gone. I found some of Sam's old pipe tobacco and rolled it in some old charge card slips. They were really fat cigarettes, and they tasted awful.

About 9 p.m., I couldn't sit there any longer. I went out the back door. I climbed three fences, got a big splinter in one hand, and almost got bitten by a dog, just to avoid being seen by the Joneses. I walked down to a pay phone in Lorenzi Park and called Sarah. I explained everything that had happened, and she said I could still go back to the hospital if that's what I wanted to do. I told her I wanted to go back, that I still needed the help I was getting there. She agreed to call Evelyn and then pick me up at my house. At the end of our talk, I felt somewhat relieved and not quite so alone and hopeless.

When Sarah and I reached the hospital, Evelyn was waiting for us, and I readmitted myself. All I remember about that procedure was having to pose for another identification picture and thinking how awful I must look. The hospital staff said my previous ID picture had already been destroyed. It had been more than twenty-four hours since I had paid attention to my grooming, and I didn't want my picture made in that condition, but I cooperated.

As soon as I checked myself back into the hospital, I had a sinking feeling, a sense of impending doom. It was from other patients that I heard, "Boy, are you in trouble now," and "How does it feel to be on lockdown?" It was horrible to hear that I was on "lockdown" because it reminded me of being in the county jail. It meant I couldn't leave the locked unit for any reason. I believed the other patients because I knew that the staff discussed all of us at the desk, and they didn't seem to care who heard them.

The other patients also told me they heard I had beaten Daniel so badly that he was hospitalized with a broken nose and that I had barricaded myself in my house with a gun, threatening to shoot myself or anyone who came near the house. I couldn't believe anybody thought these reports were true. I recall thinking to myself, "We're all in here for the same basic reason—because we can't cope. I'm no worse than anyone else in here, but everyone including the staff think I'm worse." Once again, I was filled with panic and hopelessness.

The next morning, August 5, my psychiatrist informed me that he had filed papers to commit me for at least six months. He told me that he was convinced on the basis of the psychologist's neuropsychological testing that I had temporal lobe brain damage and therefore was unable to control my behavior. I tried to explain the night of August 3 to him, but he didn't believe anything I said. I tried to reason with him, even pleaded with him not to commit me, but he was deaf to everything I could say. The whole world turned black—I saw no future for me.

At this point, I can truly say I felt crazy, mad, out of control. I threatened to starve myself to death and refused to eat. The food brought to the unit for lockdown patients was cold and stale anyway; "yesterday's food," I thought to myself. The staff said they would have to feed me intravenously. I threatened to tear out the IVs. The staff threatened to put me in restraints. Grudgingly, I began to eat again, but nothing tasted right. Most of the time, I vomited what I had eaten; my stomach churned so violently the food wouldn't stay down.

The only thing that kept me going was my contacts with Evelyn and Sarah. One or the other visited me every day, and I talked with both of them every day. Both encouraged me to cooperate with hospital procedure and to try to calm myself. I knew I could trust them and always felt better after our conversations.

Even so, I found it very difficult to maintain my composure in the hospital during this period. In so many ways, the staff treated me more harshly after I returned. I refused to take the stelazine upon my return, so then I couldn't even have a Tylenol for a headache. One day Evelyn visited me at lunch time and brought a sandwich. She ate half and I ate half. It was the first decent-tasting food I'd had in three days. Since the staff were recording my food intake, Evelyn went to the desk and asked them to record that I had eaten the sandwich. The nurse on duty blew up at her, saying, "You are not to bring food in here, and she gets no credit for eating it. That's against the hospital rules."

Evelyn also told me that the reports I had heard from the other patients and staff about Daniel were greatly exaggerated, that he had no marks or bruises, and that he was safe in Child Haven. I didn't get this news from my psychiatrist or the hospital staff; I heard it from Evelyn. It reminded me of the police letting me go on for hours believing Sam was still alive when they knew he was dead all the time. Here was the therapy crew letting me go on for days believing that Daniel was seriously injured when they knew he was fine.

There were inconsistencies in how I was treated. It sure made a difference who was on duty. One nurse appeared to sympathize with me, giving me a Tylenol for my headache and allowing me to eat in the cafeteria and to go swimming. It was about this time that another female patient told me that her therapist told her not to associate with me because I had murdered my husband. That cut me deeply because that therapist led one of the groups I attended, and I liked her.

One day, I caught sight of my open chart at the desk and saw the notation, "Patient did not participate in OT (occupational therapy) or RT (recreational therapy)." In fact, I was not allowed to participate in OT or RT because they were outside the locked unit. But these notations made me appear uncooperative and unwilling to participate. I was more than willing, I was eager, to participate in OT and RT. All I can say is that if a person wasn't crazy when admitted, the kind of treatment I got during this period could certainly drive anyone insane.

On the evening of August 8, I learned that James had escaped from the hospital and couldn't be found. Of course, this distressed me deeply. Pictures of him alone, hungry, and possibly being victimized tortured my mind. And there I was, unable to do anything but cry. My life just got messier and messier; everything was haywire.

The afternoon of August 9, I was called into a meeting with Lori, Evelyn, and my psychiatrist. The psychiatrist talked non-stop for about ten minutes about containment and increased containment. I felt confused; what was he getting at? Then Evelyn paraphrased in one sentence: "He's saying that if you can have four or five good days in a row, the commitment does not need to occur." Evelyn asked me to repeat this so everyone present would know that I understood, and I did. All present seemed in agreement. This gave me some hope for the first time since my return.

Clinging to that hope, I used all my energy to stay focused and calm and to cooperate in my therapy sessions with Lori and the groups. Lori helped me to understand the dreams I was having, and she always seemed kind and caring. On August 12, Lori made a special trip back to the unit to tell me that my psychiatrist had approved hospital privileges for me. I knew I had to wait until this order was charted, but my spirits soared.

The very next day, my psychiatrist informed me my commitment hearing would take place on August 17 and that I would be taken there in a wheelchair with my arms and legs restrained. He also told me I would have no hospital privileges, that he had not made that promise to anyone, and that his approval was contingent on approval from the nursing staff. Once again, my spirits nose-dived.

Later that same day, I was "evaluated" by a second psychiatrist. He began the interview by calling me "Ethel" and stating, "It's my policy never to go against another doctor's opinion, so I'm recommending you be committed for six months." I asked, "Without even talking to me?" He replied, "Obviously you're still very depressed." I said, "I'd have to be very mentally ill or a retard not to be depressed with what I'm facing." He said, "Well, you're better off committed. I've been a forensic psychiatrist for years, and you'll never get off with a self-defense plea." That was the end of his "evaluation" interview; it lasted about ten minutes.

Devastated, I went to the desk and asked to see my doctor. He was seated in the alcove with his back toward me. When he heard my request, he whirled around in his chair with an angry expression on his face and, in an abrupt, curt voice, said, "I have no time to talk to you now." I said I just wanted some clarification, but he interrupted with, "You have no grounds privileges." That was it—no explanation, no kindness, no empathy.

By the time Evelyn arrived for a visit a few hours later, I was in tears, shaky, in a state of panic. We had hardly sat down in the consultation room before a male tech jerked the door open and curtly insisted the door must remain open because Evelyn was not a hospital therapist. Evelyn remained calm and soothing, which helped me calm myself.

I poured out my feelings of disappointment and betrayal—all my fears. She listened, accepted my feelings as natural reactions to a bad situation, and reminded me that I had survived countless other disappointments and betrayals. I told her how awful it felt to think of being restrained in a wheelchair for the commitment hearing, and she acknowledged how awful that picture really was.

Evelyn consistently reassured and encouraged me, always expressing her faith in my ability to maintain appropriate behavior and get through this. She told me she was consulting with other mental health professionals and my attorney, and that everything that could be done to protect my rights would be done. As always, she kept my hope alive.

First thing on August 16, I was served with commitment papers. My psychiatrist had written as fact:

> She is emotionally labile and unstable. She makes statements about dying, wanting to die, killing herself and statements about killing someone else with enuendo (sic) including examiner. Diagnosis of mental illness: Major Depression with Borderline Personality Disorder and frontal lobe neurological impairment.

My mind was whirring; "He said this didn't need to happen if I had four or five good days in a row. He lied! He lied! He's committing me in spite of my improvement."

Before I could get my bearings, the hospital administrator came to me, demanding I give her my military ID. My ID had expired, and I had given it to Sarah to hold for me. This administrator seemed so excited when I couldn't give it to her that I suddenly had a brainstorm. I called the 800 number to Champus, my military insurance, and reported that I was being held illegally, that my ID had expired, and that the hospital was still charging for care of James although he had eloped from the hospital on August 8. I had no idea what Champus would do, but I felt better for taking some action of my own.

I then asked to see the head of the hospital. Instead I was allowed to see the head nurse. I appealed to her to release me, that I was rational and that the hospital was interfering with my preparing myself for my court case. I even threatened to sue them. "You can't hold me forever," I said, mustering up all my courage. "Sooner or later, I will get out, and then I will sue you for malpractice." Again, I felt a bit better for taking some action, although I could see this nurse wasn't moved.

After phoning Evelyn and Sarah to tell them what was happening, I watched the desk for sight of my psychiatrist. When I did see him, I asked why he was proceeding with the commitment, but he refused to give me a reason or discuss anything with me. Still I determined to maintain. I didn't see any other option. I knew Evelyn would come to visit me later that day, and I knew she and my attorney would attend the commitment hearing. I tried to bolster my spirits and comfort myself with that knowledge. And I prayed.

Evelyn came to visit about 1:30 p.m. While we were talking, my psychiatrist interrupted with a request to see Evelyn. After another fifteen to twenty minutes, I was called into the room. My doctor informed me that since I had been stable for the past six or seven days, he had gotten agreement from a third staff psychiatrist to evaluate me that afternoon. He added that "if that doctor finds you appropriate, perhaps we can cancel the commitment hearing, and you could sign yourself out AMA [against medical advice]." He stated, "I'm not making a promise, just a possibility." This time I registered on the "perhaps" and "possibility," but my hopes began to rise.

About 4 p.m., I saw the third psychiatrist. This man had always treated me with kindness and respect in my occasional contacts with him. He told me he felt I was appropriate and that he would recommend the commitment hearing be canceled, but that my doctor still had the final say.

By 7:15 p.m., my anxiety was rising, so I called Evelyn. To me, it seemed like another of my psychiatrist's tricks. For the third time, he had raised my hopes with carefully qualified promises. Twice before—when he said the commitment did not need to happen and when he told Lori I had hospital privileges—he had reneged on his words. Was this just another setup? By reneging on his implied promise that he would cancel the commitment proceeding, was he hoping I would blow my cool, go crazy? Evelyn encouraged me to maintain my composure no matter how difficult it was and to begin preparing for the commitment hearing tomorrow as scheduled. I agreed and felt calmer after our talk. I went to my room and began to prepare.

About 8:30 p.m., I was called to the desk and informed I was now off commitment status and therefore in the hospital illegally. The nurse asked me to sign a Voluntary Admission Form to make it legal for me to be there. A hundred alarm bells sounded in my head; if I was there illegally, why should I sign myself back in? I certainly didn't want to be there. Did they really expect me to subject myself to more of their crazy-making treatment? I said I'd have to talk to Evelyn before I would sign anything.

When I called Evelyn, she said she didn't know how to advise me, but that she would talk to my psychiatrist and to my attorney, then call me back. As I waited, I felt quite calm with a growing confidence that I would be OK.

Evelyn called back at 9 p.m. She reported that my doctor wanted me to sign myself back in and stay a couple of days longer, that it would "look better," and that "if there were no inappropriate incidents, he *might* release me." Evelyn asked me if I felt comfortable with staying there two more days. I said, "Yes, if they will definitely release me on Thursday, but I don't trust this doctor."

She told me that my doctor did not say he definitely would release me, just maybe. The whole situation felt wrong to me, so I told Evelyn I was not going to sign their Voluntary Admittance Form, that I wanted to leave the hospital. She agreed to pick me up within the hour. As I went to my room to pack my belongings, I felt a heavy, heavy weight lifted off my shoulders. I could leave the hospital, and there would be no commitment hearing.

Evelyn arrived about 9:40 p.m. She waited while I finished packing and signed myself out of the hospital. It felt so good to be free again. We stopped at Marie Callender's for pie and decaffeinated coffee as I unwound from the tension of that day. Every minute had been a cliff-hanger, but I had made it through; I had survived. Evelyn said, "Beth, I'm concerned about you returning to your house alone tonight. It's so late and you have no phone. Would you like to sleep on my sofa tonight? Then I'll take you home in the morning, you can get the phone repaired, and get settled in daylight." I replied with an emphatic, "Yes." Although I didn't sleep much that night, I felt safe. Now my attention turned back to the real issues, getting my sons back home and facing my preliminary hearing in October.

14

The First Rainbow

The next morning Evelyn took me to breakfast, then to my house, where Sarah met us. Larry, Debra's husband, walked over to explain that he had parked his truck in my driveway to make the house look lived in. I felt relieved and grateful that maybe we were still friends, although I still didn't know that Helen had lied to Debra about keeping Daniel. We unloaded my belongings, then Evelyn left for work, promising to call me later once my phone was fixed.

Sarah took me to pick up my car at the Armstrongs, but it had two flat tires from just sitting for almost a month. I arranged to get the tires fixed; then Sarah and I went to the hospital to pick up my medications and items which had been stored in the safe. They wouldn't return my medication (Elavil and hormones), and that upset me a little, but I kept my cool, still relieved and thankful to have escaped that place.

Later that afternoon when I saw that Debra was home, I went over to visit with her. It was then I learned how Helen had lied to her and how hurt Debra had been, thinking I didn't trust her with Daniel. We had a pleasant visit, relieved that the barrier between us was gone. The telephone company could not come out that day to fix the phone, so Larry was trying to fix it, but was not having any luck. I called Evelyn from Debra's, told her that I still had no phone, so not to worry. I had an appointment to see her at 2:30 the next day, and I knew I could call the shelter at any time if I needed help.

My plan was to get some food at the store, eat a good dinner, take a nice hot bath, and go to sleep early. But as my elation with release from the hospital wore off, all the grim realities of my situation hit me. I tried to sleep, but dreamed all night about Sam. He was chasing me and still had power over me. I felt so scared in that house alone with no way to call anyone for help.

The next day before my session with Evelyn, I received a copy of a petition to Juvenile Court, charging me with child abuse and asking that James and Daniel be made wards of the court. The petition even alleged that I had "threatened to kill the subject minors and a neighbor." Me? Threaten to kill my children or anyone else? Nothing could have been further from the truth. I felt like the target of one of those circus games—someone throws a ball and the target falls in a big tub of water. As soon as I could pull myself out and sit up again, boom, there I was back in the water, struggling to get out. Here was another crisis!

During my session with Evelyn, she set up a three-way call with Bill Smith. Bill related that he would handle the hearing about Daniel and James, scheduled for the next day, and that I would not have to attend. He also asked Evelyn to arrange as soon as possible for my testing to be completed and for an independent psychiatric evaluation. I felt very reassured after talking to Bill and hearing his plans.

Later in the session, I broke down as I told Evelyn about my first night back home. I felt afraid to go back there and stay alone. Evelyn called the shelter and verified that I could stay there. Sarah agreed to wait until we arrived to help me get settled. Evelyn followed me home, then led me to the shelter. The staff made me feel welcome, and for the first time in almost a month, I felt safe, protected.

In the Juvenile Court hearing on Friday, Bill was able to get the charges of child abuse dropped. He stipulated to the court that I was not able to take care of my children right then because of mental health problems for which I was getting the appropriate treatment. Although relieved that the child abuse charges had been dropped, I grieved for the apparent rift between my sons and me. I wondered if anything in my life would ever make sense again.

Later that day, I was informed that the district attorney had petitioned for my bail to be revoked. That hearing was set for August 25. Once again, I was threatened with being locked up. What had I done to deserve this? Bill told me it was because of the child abuse charges, along with an allegation by the Joneses that I had threatened them. The child abuse charge was an exaggeration that had been dismissed, but the allegation of my threatening the Joneses was a bald-faced lie. I felt harassed and panicky at the thought of being locked up until my preliminary hearing, now set for October. Talking with Bill, Sarah, and Evelyn reassured and encouraged me enough to keep going.

On Sunday, August 21, I returned to work. At first, I felt a bit strange, but overall, I was happy to be working. God knows I needed the money and some distraction from all my problems.

On August 23, my testing was completed by an independent group of psychologists. Most of the testing was conducted by a female psychologist, so I felt very comfortable during the testing. An appointment for an independent psychiatric evaluation was set for September 6.

Before my hearing on August 25, I was a shaking, nervous wreck, but I had a lot of supporters there—Sarah, Evelyn, the minister and his wife, the elderly couple I worked for, and other shelter staff and residents. The judge cautioned me sternly to avoid any trouble, but he did not revoke my bail. He seemed favorable to my case and stated, "This is the only instance in which I have ever granted OR (own recognizance) bail on a murder charge."

He also said the charge was questionable in the first place and mentioned self-defense. That was somewhat encouraging. Throughout this period I had frequent flashbacks, while digging through old papers and pictures, while driving down the road, when entering the house—just any time, these flashbacks would hit me. And dreams, every night the dream of Sam chasing me, grabbing me. Then I'd wet myself and wake up, unable to finish the dream. I still had trouble with eating, concentrating, relaxing; I was functioning, but barely.

Separation from my children was a constant source of pain. I had no idea where James was or if he was safe. Daniel was in Child Haven, and I wasn't allowed to see him. Matt and I were out of touch with each other. My sons had been my life, my main reason for staying with Sam, especially during the last six years. In spite of all our problems with each other, I felt lost without them. It was as if my purpose for staying in that reign of terror with Sam had been erased by the boys' absence.

I continued to live at the shelter, returning to my house only with a witness and only to water the grass or pick up something I needed. One thing I picked up was my sewing machine, so that I could do alterations of donated clothes for other women at the shelter. We all pitched in to do the cooking, cleaning, and necessary chores at the shelter. In spite of the turmoil I felt inside, I could still be helpful. I thought if I could spare even one woman from going through what I had gone through, my efforts would be well spent.

Toward the end of August, I got one piece of good news. Since June, I had been trying to straighten out the title problem on the land in Colorado which Sam and I had purchased in 1981. I retained an attorney who specialized in land deals, and he had sent a notice to Sam's mother that she would be sued if she did not quitclaim the land back to me, that Sam's quitdeed of the land to her was illegal. I had made all the payments on the land, so rightfully the land should be deeded to me. On August 29, this attorney informed me that he had received the necessary quitclaim from Sam's mother, restoring my name to the title. That was one less worry, one battle won.

On August 31, Evelyn and I met with Bill Smith to review all the records and materials received for my case. We made a list of sources who had not responded and who had yet to be contacted. Some of the records never came, particularly Sam's "sensitive" military file, which contained all his base arrests and disciplinary actions. Bill had already gathered an expand-a-file full of materials, at least a foot thick.

Bill's plan was to put together a packet of letters, documents, and records, appealing to the district attorney to acknowledge that I had acted in self-defense and to drop the charges. I left feeling somewhat reassured, but I could not believe the packet would satisfy the district attorney.

The next evening I was allowed to see Daniel for my first supervised visit at Child Haven. The visit went well, with Daniel hugging me and staying close throughout our hour together. When it was time for me to leave, Daniel begged me to take him home with me. I had to tell him I couldn't, that it was up to the courts. Daniel didn't seem to understand, just repeated, "Please, Mom, don't leave me here; take me home with you." I felt so sad to leave without him, but I had no choice. My boys were wards of the court now. It seemed my whole life was in the hands of the courts.

A few days later, Sarah accompanied me to Nellis for an appointment with the base attorney to get information about my benefits. He was sympathetic and truly wanted to help, but all he could say was, "Your benefits cannot be awarded until your case has been settled in the courts." His office was at the end of a long corridor, and as we left, every door along the corridor opened, and all the personnel came out into the hall to stare at us. I realized I was a spectacle to them, but I kept walking, my back getting straighter and stiffer with every step.

When we got out of the building, Sarah said, "I've got to hand it to you, Beth; you didn't let that bother you." It bothered me alright, but what could I do about it? I thought to myself, "I'd rather they think I'm a cold, hard, vicious bitch than to break down and cry in front of them."

From there, we went to renew my expired identification card. The sergeant we spoke with first said it hadn't been approved, but Sarah was firm and insistent. Finally, after several minutes of debate, the sergeant referred us to a civilian worker, who said the approval was there all along. One of the staff told me on the sly, "Once you get your benefits, you should sue the Air Force for hassling you." I replied, "If I get my benefits, I don't want to sue anyone. I just want what is coming to me." When we left, I had my temporary ID, but it had to be renewed every thirty days until my case was settled. I felt vindicated for a few minutes, although I knew I would probably have to repeat this humiliating process many times before everything was resolved.

On September 6, I met with another psychiatrist for an independent evaluation. He seemed sympathetic and humane, so I felt very comfortable with him. He understood post traumatic stress disorder and stated his opinion that my symptoms typified that disorder. His words and manner reassured me that I was not crazy, that my present condition was understandable and justified in view of the violence I had endured from Sam. I left his office with a tiny ray of hope for the future.

There was a Juvenile Court hearing about James and Daniel on September 15. The boys were officially made wards of the court as we expected. But Bill got it on the record that the social worker who had prepared the initial petition with all the false allegations of child abuse had to correct his report. That was some comfort to me. I was still worried sick about James, not knowing where he was or if he was still alive. At least, I could see Daniel occasionally.

And always there was worry, as well as work to be done on my case—calls, letters, meetings with Bill. After working all day, I spent my evening hours digging through the boxes of papers, searching for names and dates that substantiated Sam's abuse. At times, I cursed myself for lying to cover up for him, although I never felt I had any other choice.

September 20 was especially hard; that was our seventeenth anniversary. I was flooded with memories, both good and bad. Incidents I had blocked out of my memory came back. Again, I recalled the night Sam kept me at the kitchen table for hours with a loaded gun, both safeties off, threatening to shoot me, threatening to shoot the kids. I had to sit there and listen to him rant and rave, wondering when he would kill me, praying he wouldn't, praying he would. The next day I took the clips out of the gun, hid them one place and hid the gun another.

I remembered how Sam could put on his "super-nice guy" face to the rest of the world. I knew that people who saw that side of him would never believe his cruelty to me, and it seemed useless for me to try to get help from them. I felt so ashamed that he chose me to abuse when he could be so nice to others. It seemed better to keep quiet. That's what I did most of the time, especially during the first ten years. These thoughts and memories flashed through my mind all that anniversary day, bringing floods of tears.

Three days later, I moved home from the shelter. I was feeling better and getting tired of running back and forth to the shelter. But the main reason was the Jones clan. The night before, I had been home watering the lawn and feeding the animals. When I left to return to the shelter, I noticed a vehicle following me. I slowed down and let it get close enough to recognize two members of the Jones family.

I was afraid of leading them back to the shelter. That address was secret for the protection of all the women and children. I didn't know what the Joneses intended, but I did know I couldn't lead them to the shelter. I drove around in circles for almost an hour, but they stayed right behind me. I was already panicked, but with them following me, I became more and more frightened. Finally in desperation, I saw a police car parked in front of a donut shop and pulled in beside it. I waited there until I was sure the Joneses were gone before I returned to the shelter. That incident was a sign to me that I should leave the shelter and move back home.

Living in that house again wasn't easy. A couple of nights after moving back, I returned home from the grocery store about 7 p.m. Our cat, Sissy, ran toward me with all her hair standing on end. The phone was ringing and when I picked it up, the line went dead. Then I noticed the back door was wide open. I turned and ran out the front door just in time to see one of the Joneses walking down Debra's driveway. I was certain he had been in my house, but why? What did they want from me?

I thought of calling the police, but immediately dismissed that idea. From all past experience, I knew the police would not help me. When I went back inside, Sissy never left my side all night. Because of that incident and because it was so lonesome all alone in the house, I went to the pound the next day and brought home a puppy, which I named "Baby." I shut off all the bedrooms and lived in the front part of the house with my cats and new puppy.

About a week after I moved back to the house, I finished my dream about that last night with Sam. As always, the dream began with Sam chasing and grabbing me. This time it continued. In slow motion, I saw the look on Sam's face, smirking, mocking me, the same look I'd seen during every beating. In my dream, I saw him rise up after the first shot, crouched like a football player, arms outstretched, hands palms up with fingers crooked and beckoning me to come on, like "I dare you."

I awakened from the dream about 4:30 a.m., drenched in a cold sweat, shaking as if I had a chill. I threw on some clothes, got in my car, and started driving. I had no idea where I was going or even where I was; I just drove automatically. I don't know how long I drove, but it was daylight when I realized I was half way up Mount Charleston. I got out of the car and screamed until I couldn't scream any more.

From my work with Evelyn, I knew this was a milestone for me, something I had to work through. But it was so painful and terrifying. I wondered how much further I had to go—if my life would ever be settled and "normal." Suddenly it dawned on me that it was Saturday and I had to be at work by 9 a.m. Work was the one thing in my life that seemed normal. That day, I couldn't wait to get there.

About that time, Matt called and we reconciled with each other. He was working, making it on his own, and I felt proud of him. Daniel's twelfth birthday was coming up, and I had approval to give him a small party at Child Haven. I baked him a special birthday cake and bought a few small gifts. Then Matt, Debra, and I went to Child Haven to celebrate with Daniel. It was pleasant, but in the back of all our minds was the preliminary hearing less than a week away.

The days began flying by and with every passing day, my anxiety and panic mounted. On October 1, I picked up a copy of the packet Bill had sent to the district attorney. As I read it, I became hysterical. All I could see was that he had left out so many documents. I called Evelyn, crying, raging, saying, "I'm going to fire Bill. He's left out the most important evidence." Evelyn listened, letting me get those feelings out of my system. "There's nothing we can do about this until Monday. I wish you would talk this over with Bill before you make such a serious decision." After thirty minutes or so of venting, I calmed down and saw the logic in what she was saying.

When I talked to Bill on Monday, he explained that the purpose of the packet was not to present my complete case, but rather to show the DA the extent of documentation available in my case. What he said made sense to me. Plus his voice was calm, patient, reassuring.

On Tuesday during my session with Evelyn, I showed her the packet. She read through it and thought it was excellent.

"Beth, there's nothing in here that could hurt you or damage your case. Everything here supports you and the view that you acted in self-defense." I mention all this just to show how emotionally taxing it was for me to face trial on a first-degree murder charge. As I approached the preliminary, I couldn't see the forest for the trees. I became super wary, even paranoid, of everyone, even my strongest supporters.

Evelyn gave me a word to describe my reaction—"hypervigilance." Because I had been betrayed so many times by Sam, the person I had trusted most in the world, I now expected betrayal from everyone sooner or later. This made me overly watchful and overly reactive to anything that even hinted at betrayal.

October 6, the day of the hearing, finally came. Sarah picked me up at 7:45 a.m. She carried my heart medicine in her purse, ready to administer it if needed. My heart and stomach were fluttering wildly with anxious agitation. I knew I would have to face Sam's family and the Joneses. I had no doubt that they blamed me for Sam's death. More important, I was facing a verdict, some kind of ruling on my case. I both dreaded and desired a ruling, some certainty about the future.

First, Bill got a ruling that anyone who might be a witness in my trial be excluded from the courtroom; the Joneses and two of Sam's Air Force buddies were escorted from the courtroom by the bailiff. There were only two witnesses, both called by the state.

During the district attorney's examination of the coroner, the coroner stated that Sam had been hit by two bullets, that one had been lethal, and that he wasn't certain which bullet had hit Sam first. He also reported that Sam had a moderately severe coronary artery disease; "this guy is set up for a heart attack before he's fifty," he said. It may be difficult for some to understand, but this news shocked and saddened me. I still loved Sam and had not yet fully accepted his death.

During Bill's cross-examination of the coroner, he introduced a photograph of Sam from the autopsy. When Bill held the picture up to the coroner, the light shone through it and I could see Sam clearly. I felt my stomach churn and thought I would either throw up or faint. I gripped the chair as hard as I could, telling myself, "Hang on. Just hang on." The coroner stated that the scratches and abrasions on Sam's forehead were "extremely superficial," and thus, "they certainly wouldn't have knocked him out . . . wouldn't have rendered him defenseless or unable to pursue the attack."

Bill assumed the position of a football linebacker in a crouched position ready to spring forward, and the coroner conceded that could account for the entry angle of the lethal bullet. The coroner further stated that Sam could have continued his attack on me even after "an absolutely lethal wound like that." He went on to describe a case in which an officer shot through the heart with a .38 drew his gun, fired six shots, walked across the street, and opened the door of his patrol car before he collapsed. Bill also got it on the record that Sam's blood alcohol content at the time of his death was .15.

Daniel was called to testify immediately following the coroner. The judge asked the bailiff to bring a phone book for Daniel to sit on because he was too short to see or be seen over the witness box. There is no way to explain the agony I felt about his having to testify. "I'd rather be dead than see him put through this," went through my mind for the ten-thousandth time. But if I were dead, what would happen to my boys then?

My whole purpose in life had been to raise my kids. They still needed me, especially Daniel. He looked so small, so vulnerable, as he entered the witness box. What was this doing to him? I was so anguished about my son, I couldn't register what he was saying. Only by going back and reading the transcript can I report Daniel's testimony.

During the district attorney's questioning, Daniel described what he had seen. The district attorney seemed gentle in her questioning of Daniel. By that I mean she did not try to lead or confuse him, and I was thankful for that. After a five-minute recess, Bill cross-examined Daniel. Through Bill's gentle questioning, Daniel described Sam's behavior on April 9 as "weird . . . he wasn't acting like his usual self." Bill introduced a diagram of the apartment, including the furniture, to make it easier for Daniel to describe what happened.

Daniel testified that Sam had ordered him to his room soon after arriving at the apartment, and he had obeyed but left a crack of his door open so he could hear what was going on between Sam and me. This was one indication of Daniel's fear of Sam's violence. Daniel went on to describe how I "would block off the door with all the furniture" and "sleep in the same bed" holding him after Sam's threatening phone calls. Daniel stated that he came out of his room after he heard a crash and my "shrill scream." Daniel related his terror as he grabbed onto Sam, trying to stop the fight. He demonstrated his dad's stance, crouched like a football player ready to tackle, saying Sam then stepped forward toward me.

Daniel recalled that I continued to scream and that he had never heard me scream like that before. Referring to the diagram of the apartment, Daniel pointed out that there was no way for me to get out except to run past Sam, and that was impossible. In response to Bill's question about how I looked and acted at that time, Daniel said, "She was crying, shaking. . . . I had never seen her that way."

In Bill's concluding statement at this hearing, he said, "Two witnesses put this woman in fear of her life reacting in four seconds. The deceased was in a position where he had taken a step forward in an attack." The judge's response was, "I'll make my final ruling at the completion of the hearing," which was then set for November 8. The judge turned to me and said, "For a matter of record, the defendant will continue being on an OR release from custody, which I granted her several months ago, and all the conditions of the OR still remain the same. Do you understand that?" "Yes, sir," I replied.

Court was over for that day, but still nothing was settled or certain regarding my future or that of my children. I could breathe a sigh of relief for only a minute before I had to gear myself up again to fight for my sons, to fight for my own life.

15

The Second Rainbow

That same afternoon, October 6, the welfare worker called to inform me that James had been picked up in Denver and would be flown back to Vegas the next week. She went on to tell me that Daniel had been placed in a foster home and that all visitation would have to be arranged with the foster mother. *Foster mother*—the very words sent tremors through my body. "I'm losing my kids," I thought. "Everything in my life is out of control." In spite of assurances from Bill, Sarah, and Evelyn, I couldn't get rid of these terrifying thoughts.

That was pure torment for me. I was not allowed to have the phone number or location of the foster home. Thereafter, I had to depend on the welfare worker to arrange for my visits with Daniel. I couldn't even speak to Daniel on the phone unless the foster mother arranged and monitored the call. I called the caseworker every day for a week with no results. She kept telling me, "Visits have to be at the convenience of the foster mother. I have no control over her; I can't make her do anything." Feeling that that was a lie, I argued with her; "Yes, you can," I said. "You all have taken over my kids, so now do the job spelled out in the court order. I'm supposed to have weekly visitation, and Daniel is supposed to see his counselor weekly." My arguments got me nowhere.

By the second week, I could see a pattern developing. Daniel was not taken to his counseling sessions, and no visits were arranged for us. I became more and more frantic as the days passed. I called the caseworker's supervisor, who assured me he would check into the situation and try to arrange for a visit. Still nothing. I was trying to follow their rules to the letter, but welfare wasn't playing by the rules of the court order. I then called the supervisor's supervisor, who promised to straighten out the situation. But later that evening, this man left a message on Evelyn's answering machine, saying, "Mrs. Sipe has made unwarranted slanderous accusations against a number of people. This cannot be tolerated, and I plan to proceed legally against her." What was he talking about? It was now October 11; I had been trying daily for almost two weeks to arrange a visit with Daniel. Was it considered an accusation to report that no visit had been arranged? It was not an accusation, but fact that the caseworker had not followed the court-ordered treatment plan for Daniel.

Even my closest supporters, Bill, Evelyn, and Sarah, did not understand how crucial regular contacts with my sons were to me. They all told me about the same thing; "You can't take care of the boys right now. Let welfare handle it. Concentrate on your own case." I know they meant well, but no one could grasp what my kids meant to me, what seeing them made wards of the court meant to me. I didn't trust the welfare system and every contact with the welfare people fed my distrust. I began preparing a written account of all the inconsistencies I had experienced with the welfare people.

I felt a desperate need to explain my actions and to expose the negligent way Daniel and I were being treated. Later that evening, I learned that James had been flown in and was being held in the Juvenile Detention Center.

On Wednesday, October 12, at 9 a.m., another Juvenile Court hearing was set. Bill couldn't be there, but Evelyn agreed to meet me there. Bill instructed me to ask that the hearing be continued to October 17. Matt, now nineteen, accompanied me, and Evelyn was there waiting for me. After checking in with the central bailiff, we sat and waited for almost half an hour before the caseworker approached us. I tried to talk to the caseworker about my concerns and all the inconsistencies, thinking I had a better chance to get some answers with Evelyn there as a witness. The caseworker didn't have answers for any of the issues I brought up, but she did volunteer that she had talked with the prosecutor's office the day before, and "they say you can talk to your sons only with a monitor."

We waited for over an hour. Then the caseworker went to ask why the case had not been called. She returned about 10:15 a.m., saying that the case was called before I arrived and since I wasn't there, it was continued until October 20. I had taken off work again for nothing. I was upset and asked to see the judge, but he was not available. Then I asked to see James, and the caseworker said no. I persisted, and Evelyn took me to one side, trying to dissuade me. But I was determined and I told her, "You can all quit, but I am going to fight for my kids." Evelyn left for work and I knew she wasn't pleased. "Nobody understands, not even Evelyn, that my kids mean everything to me. They're my life," I thought. But I was still determined to fight.

I told the caseworker, "I'm not leaving until I see James, and if that means I have to sit here all day, then I will." I sat there, alone, waiting for what seemed hours. Finally, I was allowed to see James. He was so glad to see me and said, "Please, Mom, take me home." It tore me to pieces that I couldn't. He was so thin and sick looking, coughing throughout the visit. I felt his forehead and it was burning with fever. I was certain he had bronchitis, possibly pneumonia, but he was getting no medical care, and there was nothing I could do for him. Our fate as a family was in the hands of welfare and the courts. We cried together when I was told to leave.

I drove home crying all the way, my thoughts bouncing around in my mind like the balls in a bingo machine. The only goal that was clear to me was to save my kids. I gave up on saving me and gave up on trying to prepare my case. I called and left a message for Evelyn that I wouldn't be coming in anymore because "no one will help me fight for my children. For the last seventeen years with Sam, that's what I've been fighting for. I'll just plea-bargain with the prosecutor and take whatever they will give me." I left similar messages for Bill and Sarah.

After I made the calls, I felt scared and totally alone. I told myself, "If those people can't understand how I feel about my kids, I don't need them. I'll have to fight this battle alone, just like all the old battles with Sam. I can't depend on anyone." I sat there on my living room couch as if in a stupor for hours, wondering what to do next. I didn't have a clear plan of action, just determination to be in charge of my own life. Sam had been in charge of me for seventeen years; then it seemed that all my "helpers" were trying to control me. I wasn't going for it.

Sometime during the evening, I got the idea to call the prosecuting attorney. I found her telephone number listed in the directory and called her. I told her I was giving Bill permission to let her read my autobiography and was willing to plea-bargain just to get the case over with. I also told her I planned to contact the media and that by tomorrow morning, "it will all be over."

What I meant was the case would be finished, but the prosecutor took it as a suicide call. She called the TADC crisis line and the police to check on me. About half an hour later, I answered the phone, but hung up as soon as I recognized Evelyn's voice. I was scared, angry, desperate, betrayed, panicky—I couldn't handle any more confrontation with anyone.

The next couple of days passed in a blur. I made several calls to the caseworker, trying to set up visits with Daniel and James. All the caseworker did was put me off; there was always some excuse. I talked with my sister, Nancy, trying to get the boys transferred to her care before I went to prison. I had resigned myself to that fate. Nancy was planning to fly out for a visit on November 4, a few days before my hearing on November 8. I held onto that, counting on their support, feeling I had lost the support of everyone else.

Except for the calls I made, I talked to no one else during these two days. If the phone rang, I didn't answer it. I had made my choice—my kids—and I didn't want to defend myself for that. If that meant cutting myself off from the rest of the world, then so be it.

On October 15, much to my amazement, I received a letter from Evelyn, stating her concern and opening the door for me to resume counseling. That was the first time in my life someone with the authority I attributed to Evelyn validated my right to make my own choices, accepted my anger, and still held out an open hand to help me.

I picked up the phone and called Evelyn. I told her, "You and Bill have to understand that I was pushed too far about my kids; they're my life. Without them, nothing matters anyway. Without them, I have no life, no future." Evelyn acknowledged that and apologized "for losing sight of your right to make your own decisions." She remained encouraging and supportive as she thanked me, saying "I've learned an important lesson from this." Talking to Evelyn gave me a renewed spark of hope. Maybe I had a future after all. At least I knew I could call Evelyn or Sarah to talk out my feelings. I wasn't totally alone.

With every aspect of my life up in the air, it didn't take much to upset me. For example, I became very upset when I saw the letter sent out by Bill's secretary asking numerous agencies and individuals for records and information. The letter stated that I had shot and killed my husband. "Beth states that he was pulling her hair, so as you can see, this may be a case of self-defense." Why say all that? Why not simply request all available records or information? The statements in the letter were both too much and too little—too much because I didn't want the entire world to know I was charged with murder and too little because Sam was doing much more than pulling my hair in his final attack.

Even more upsetting was the continued runaround I was getting from welfare about the boys. They had me scheduled for hearings at Juvenile Court on October 18, 20, and 21. How could they reasonably expect me to take off work three days in the same week? Why couldn't everything on the same case be handled at one hearing? To make it even more confusing for me, the caseworker told me to forget about the hearing on the 21st, which was the only date for which I had a subpoena. Days were passing and still I had no visitation with Daniel, none since September 30.

More details about the shooting filtered back into my awareness. I recalled Daniel holding on to Sam, saying, "No, Dad, no!" Sam had shaken him off and Daniel had grabbed him again. I remembered that one of the bullets had whizzed past Daniel's head, just missing him, and that Sam was raising himself up on his arms when the gun emptied. It was then that Daniel ran out and I ran out after Daniel, thinking that Sam was coming after us. Horrible, all of it was horrible. I wondered if I'd ever have peace of mind about having killed Sam and nearly killing Daniel. I had no idea where I was firing. In my terror, it didn't register in my mind that Daniel was standing there struggling with Sam.

The day before the October 18 hearing, Daniel was allowed to call me. He was crying, choked up because we hadn't talked in so long and because we had to have a monitor on the line. Talking with him was like an answer to my prayers. He told me how much he wanted to come home, how much he missed me, how much he loved me. Apparently my calls to welfare had done some good because we now had a schedule for phone calls. Daniel was to call me every Monday at 3:30 p.m. This call from Daniel gave me another ray of hope for the future—mine and my boys'.

As I approached the Juvenile Court hearing the next day, I held on to Evelyn's words, that whatever was decided then would not be permanent and that the ultimate goal would be to reunite my family. My attendance at court took up the entire morning, most of it just waiting for the case to be called. Welfare finally presented a detailed case plan for Daniel, and the judge approved it, to be reviewed in 60 days. That was it for the October 18; I still had to go back on the 20th for James. That hearing went about the same as the one on the 18th, except that the caseworker informed me Sam's mother had called the day before, wanting access to Daniel. I thought it odd that she did not mention James.

Later that night, October 20, I received a threatening phone call. An obviously disguised male voice said, "If you walk out of that courtroom, you're going to die, but you'll see James, that bastard son of yours, die first. See it, enjoy it, believe this." "Who is this? Who is this?" I cried into the dead phone. The man had already hung up. I called the shelter, shaken and crying. Then I called the police, only to be told, "Call the detective on the case." I knew that was useless, so I sat there alone in the dark, listening to every sound, watching every shadow until I drifted off into a restless sleep.

The next night, I heard a cat screeching in the backyard. I switched on the outside light and walked out to the edge of the patio, thinking to break up a cat fight. Something whizzed past my right temple as I registered the sound of a gunshot. I dropped to the ground, flattening my body, as I inched my way back into the house. Again, I sat rigid at the end of the couch, listening to every sound and watching every shadow all night. The next day, I found a bullet hole in my concrete block wall. I felt like a helpless sitting duck. The worst part was that I felt there was no one I could tell. It would only worry Sarah and Evelyn, and I knew the police would do nothing to help me.

Days passed, filled with work and hundreds of follow-ups for my case and for the kids. One bright spot in my life at this time was spending time with Matt. He volunteered to help me fix up the house, and he supported my resolution to get James and Daniel back home. The wedge that Sam had driven between us was melting away.

By November 2, James had been transferred to a group home, and I met with James's counselor. As we discussed visitation, he made a reference to my "murdering my husband," which blew my mind. Had I already been convicted? If so, by whom? When I saw the records of James's and my hospitalizations, I saw that the hospital staff had applied the word *murderer* to me. Now another agency had picked up the label and continued to use it. How dare they do that? I felt furious about this violation.

By November 4, I was all set for my sister to arrive. I had cleaned the house top to bottom, filled the refrigerator with food, and prepared some dishes ahead so that we could enjoy our visit. I was so looking forward to this time with my sister, just being with family again. My mind had been filled with pictures of myself in prison for life, possibly never seeing any of my family again.

That afternoon I received a call from my sister saying the trip had been canceled. Her husband was at that moment in surgery with an inflamed appendix. Nancy said she would fly out by herself as soon as her husband was out of danger, but I couldn't let her do that. Although it was comforting to know that Nancy was willing to come alone, I was disappointed, let down, by her news. "Fate is against me in this," I thought. I wondered if this was an omen that my hearing would go against me.

Finally, November 8, the date for completion of my preliminary hearing, arrived. First, the prosecutor spoke briefly, followed by a short statement from Bill, asking that the charges be dismissed. Then, in answer to my prayers and those of my supporters, the judge dismissed all charges against me. I can't remember every word, but in part, he said, "There is no evidence of wrongful killing . . . and the evidence is clear for self-defense." I felt my body sway slightly with relief, and I broke down sobbing as we left the courtroom. My hopes shot up, hopes for the future with my children. Maybe God had heard my prayers and answered them.

16

The Sun Comes Out to Stay

Before I could digest the judge's ruling exonerating me, Bill Smith, my attorney, phoned to tell me the prosecutor was planning to appeal the self-defense ruling, possibly through District Court, the Grand Jury, or the State Supreme Court. Bill reported that the DA was willing to let me plead guilty to involuntary manslaughter, but he advised me not to accept that offer. I was no longer willing to plead guilty to anything, because I wasn't guilty, and one judge had already recognized that. I realized, though, that I was still in jeopardy. Bill advised me to go ahead and apply for my military benefits, using the judge's ruling as evidence of my eligibility.

It was now seven months since Sam's death, but I still couldn't relax, still couldn't freely grieve his death, still couldn't get on with my life. In a way, I was caught in the same old familiar pattern I had lived with Sam for seventeen years. As soon as one crisis was over, another one hit. Evelyn explained to me that this pattern kept me in a state of constant battle-ready arousal, which was both physically and mentally damaging. She taught me systematic relaxation, even made me a relaxation tape, which helped some. But it was impossible for me to relax completely or for very long.

New threats came up daily, including dozens of weird phone calls. Would he or they really carry out the death threats now that the charges had been dropped against me, I wondered. None were as specific as the one threatening my life and James's, but the calls let me know that some person or persons intended to "get" me. Evelyn loaned me an answering machine so that I could screen my calls and still not miss important messages. That helped some, but I could still hear the phone ring and the machine click on, so I continued to feel threatened when callers left no messages.

After the self-defense ruling, something broke loose inside me. I found myself telling Evelyn about Sam's sexual abuse. I had never uttered a word about this to anyone before. I surprised myself the first time. I don't know where the words or courage came from to name the sexual acts he had forced on me. I hadn't even mentioned them in the autobiography Bill had me write. Not only had Sam sodomized me and mangled my breasts, as he called me every known gutter name. He had also taunted me, saying, "Whatever I got, I will give you, including AIDS," and "If I ever get a terminal disease, I'll take you with me." One of the first things I did after his death was go to the Health District and get tests for every sexually transmitted disease, including AIDS. I never told anyone I had done that until then. The tests were all negative, but I still live with the fear that AIDS may show up years from now.

By the end of that week, November 12, most of my energy and attention had shifted to James and Daniel. Thanksgiving Day, November 24, was less than two weeks away. I began trying to arrange home visits for the boys so that we could have Thanksgiving dinner as a family. We had never been separated on a holiday. While my visits with James at the group home were going well, I hadn't had a visit with Daniel since September 30, and he wasn't allowed to call me every Monday as promised. The foster mother continued to enforce the monitor rule even after the charges were dropped against me, so Daniel couldn't call me without her on the other line, and apparently she was usually too busy. At 3:30 p.m. on Mondays, I'd hover over the phone, willing it to ring, getting more and more anxious as the minutes slowly ticked away, with no phone call. Then I'd wonder what was really happening with my kids. Was this an omen that I'd lost the boys forever? I truly feared that Sam's family was somehow involved in an effort to take the kids away from me, that the kids would just disappear one day.

Juvenile Court had approved the case plan specifying visitations. How could the caseworker fail to follow the order? Of course, the case plan specified action on my part also. For one thing, I was ordered to take parenting classes. When I checked with the one agency in Las Vegas that offered parenting classes, I was told I was not eligible to attend the classes because my sons were too old. I was also ordered to "submit to a battery of psychological and/or psychiatric testing" and "to participate in and successfully complete a program of individual counseling." These orders ignored the fact that I had already completed exhaustive psychological testing and that I had been continuously involved in individual counseling since Sam's death. The fact that the caseworker had all this information in preparing the case plan added to my fears about losing my children.

On November 15, I asked Evelyn to call the caseworker, hoping that would get some results. The dozens of messages I left for the caseworker didn't even get a return call. The caseworker told Evelyn that she was trying to arrange a visit for me and Daniel, and that she would call her back at the end of the week. In spite of my disappointment with the caseworker, I was very surprised that she didn't bother to call Evelyn back either.

By Monday, November 21, I was getting frantic. I called Evelyn, crying my eyes out, because I couldn't get any definite word from the caseworker about Thanksgiving visits with James and Daniel. Evelyn listened and agreed to meet with me after she finished work at 7:30 p.m. that night. By the time I met with her, I had cried myself out, but I knew I looked terrible, eyes red and swollen. We talked for more than an hour as I vented my feelings about welfare's stalling and changing stories from one day to the next. Evelyn suggested meeting at the welfare office the next morning at about 7:45 a.m., before the caseworker left on her rounds.

Evelyn's plan was for us to confront the situation together, so we would both hear the same information. She told me her approach would be to ask for the caseworker's help in clarifying procedures I was to follow. This sounded good to me.

The next morning, I met Evelyn in the parking lot in front of the welfare office at 7:45 a.m. We weren't taking any chances about missing the caseworker. When the doors were unlocked at 8:00 a.m., we entered a large waiting area with chairs lining the walls. We asked to see the caseworker, then sat down to wait. After about fifteen minutes, the caseworker appeared and sat down to talk with us. Evelyn told her that we wanted to work with welfare for the benefit of children, but that there seemed to be some confusion about procedures, specifically about getting visitation with Daniel. This caseworker had the gall to say, "It's up to the mother to schedule visitations. The reason Mrs. Sipe hasn't seen Daniel since September 30 is because she has not requested a specific date for a visit at least a week ahead of time." I bit my tongue to keep from screaming at her. I had been calling at least every other day, sometimes every day, for almost two months. But I knew my anger would get me nowhere, and I saw that Evelyn was taking notes of our conversation, so it wasn't just my word against the caseworker's any longer. The caseworker said it would be fine to pick up Daniel for Thanksgiving, but she didn't know yet about James, that it was up to her supervisor's supervisor, and that she would get definite word and relay the decision to Sarah at the shelter by the end of the day. That was Tuesday, November 22, two days before Thanksgiving.

Well, the caseworker never called anyone—not Sarah, not Evelyn, not me. By 4:30 p.m. on Wednesday, I was frantic, wondering what welfare's decision would be about James's visit. Finally, I called the caseworker, only to be told she still didn't know. This was torture for me. Obviously, James's visit wasn't approved, so why not tell me that instead of dangling a thread of hope right up to the last minute? I wept for hours that night—tears of despair and anger. I fell asleep, consoling myself with the thought that at least Daniel could come home for a visit.

On Thanksgiving Day, I picked up Matt and then Daniel about 12:30 p.m. The foster mother had called and given me directions to their house. We were all three so happy to see each other, hugging and crying and laughing. We stopped at a 7-Eleven store, bought some hot dogs (Daniel's choice), then went to see *Land Before Time.* Throughout the movie, Daniel held onto my hand, but when the baby dinosaur said, "I am all alone; I am," Daniel tightened his grasp and snuggled into me. I thought, "That's how we all feel, separated this way." After the movie, we went home for awhile, just enjoying our reunion.

Late in the afternoon, all three of us went to have dinner with James at the group home. All the boys were so happy to see each other, the first time since July. I was surprised when one of the counselors took me aside and said, "James's behavior is fine; he really doesn't belong here." As we ate dinner, I told the boys, "I'm getting an attorney and I'll do everything I can to get you out of welfare's jurisdiction and back home."

The next day I was too sick to go to work. I couldn't recall the last time I had been that sick. Bottom line, I went to work whether I felt like it or not. But, physically, I could not force myself to work that day. All the tensions of dealing with the welfare system in trying to arrange a family Thanksgiving had gotten to me. But the drive to raise my children which had propelled me for seventeen years was still operating beneath the surface. Later that day, I called TADC for recommended attorneys and was given three names. Before the day was over, I had an appointment for the following Tuesday with Nora Rains. I determined to push this as far as I legally could.

On Saturday, the 26th, Daniel called me from a friend's house. He said he had permission to visit his friend, a few doors from the foster home. Something in his voice didn't sound right, but I couldn't put my finger on what was wrong. On Sunday, I spent the day cleaning house, then cooked some of James's favorite foods and took them to the group home. About 10:55 p.m. that night, Daniel called again. I was surprised to hear his voice, because his bedtime was 9 p.m. He sounded miserable, but all he would say was, "Mom, I don't want to be here." I reassured him I would do everything possible to get him home, and reluctantly ended the conversation by telling him, "Now, go to bed and dream sweet dreams. You need your sleep because tomorrow's a school day."

On Tuesday, November 29, I met with Nora. I was totally impressed with her empathy and fighting spirit. Instinctively, I knew that I had found the right lawyer to help me regain custody of my children. She reviewed the information I gave her and said, "Welfare isn't doing its job. Your family belongs together." I had scraped together $500 to pay her, and as I left her office that day, I felt confident she would handle the December 6 hearing successfully.

On Wednesday, November 30, the caseworker called to inform me that Daniel had run away from the foster home Sunday evening, that he had been found with one of his friends in Moapa, a small town fifty miles northeast of Las Vegas, and that he was being returned to the foster home that day. He had been missing when he called me, and I hadn't even been notified. I asked her why no one had bothered to tell me that Daniel was missing. Her reply was, "They are (my boys) not your problem. They're under welfare's jurisdiction." Hysterical, I called Nora, who said, "This is just one more reason to get welfare out of this case and get your children back home." I wasn't even allowed to speak with Daniel. "He's in big trouble," I was told. "He's being punished, so he can't use the phone." Again, I tried appealing to a welfare supervisor, but was told that person was out of town until next week. So I was left hanging for another endless weekend.

On December 6, we all appeared at Juvenile Court, but the hearing was canceled. The judge was out sick, so Nora, my attorney, substituted as the juvenile judge that day and for obvious reasons could not both present and hear our case. The hearing was rescheduled for Tuesday, December 13. At least, I got to see Daniel for the first time since Thanksgiving. "When you ran away, why didn't you come home?" I asked him. "Because, Mom," he answered, "I knew they would look for me there, and I didn't want you to get into trouble." I understood his reason. What I could not understand was the fact that no one had looked for him at home. If they had, I would have known he was missing.

That Sunday, I cooked several of James's favorite dishes and took them to the group home. James had been missing our cat, Sissy, so I hid her in my bag and took her along. James was thrilled to see her. We had a very nice visit, and I told him again how sure I was we would all be together after next Tuesday.

Later that night, I heard a lot of noise coming from the Joneses' house. I looked out the kitchen window and saw a young guy standing in front of their house, pointing a rifle at my house, and yelling "Bang! Bang!" This confirmed in my mind that the Joneses were responsible for many, maybe all the other weird things that kept happening. Rocks were thrown at my car while it sat in my driveway. Cars pulled onto my front lawn, shining lights into my house. Rows of jagged scratches appeared on the driver's side of my car. Hang-up phone calls occurred constantly, and the doorbell often rang in the middle of the night. Frequently, one of the Joneses followed me to the store, to the bank, anywhere. One freezing night, someone turned on all the sprinklers in the backyard, and everything was covered with icicles the next morning. My sprinklers were manual and had to be turned on individually. It wasn't just my imagination; someone had gone to a lot of deliberate trouble to turn them on.

There was nothing I could do about it. Every time I tried to report these instances of harassment, I was told, "You have no proof." All I could do was sit there with my fear and pray. With all the problems I had to face, I didn't need all the harassment. It certainly intensified my constant state of agitation.

On Tuesday, December 13, Matt accompanied me to Juvenile Court. Evelyn and Sarah were there for support and to testify in my behalf if called. The caseworker was not there; instead welfare sent two supervisors. As we entered the courtroom, the young bailiff said, "I've got to hear this one," which set me to wondering why. Nora pointed out all the delays and inconsistencies I had encountered with welfare. She said, "Welfare is alienating the family rather than following the court-ordered plan for reunification. We ask that the children be returned home now." She referred to our family life with Sam as a *Burning Bed* situation. I had not seen the movie, but had heard that it was a story about a battered woman who killed her abuser. The judge interviewed everyone, including all three boys. Then he ruled that the boys would return home immediately, saying, "I'm taking welfare out of this case and placing it in the hands of Child Protective Services." Family and individual counseling was ordered for all of us, and Child Protective Services would make home visits twice a month. We left the courthouse together, jubilant, a family again with renewed hope in the future. We were all crying and hugging each other. I felt God had answered my prayers.

A couple of months earlier, I had come upon an original cashier's check for $1,000 among Sam's papers. The check was dated November 1979. When I inquired at my bank, they informed me the check would have to be thoroughly traced to make sure it was never cashed. That procedure would take sixty days. On December 14, 1988, the bank notified me that the check had never been cashed and that I could pick up the money any time. Talk about prayers being answered. With that check I was able to catch up on several bills and give the kids a real Christmas.

On December 18, my day off, the kids and I went shopping at the Meadows Mall. We must have hit every store on both levels, doing more looking than buying, but truly enjoying each other. We ate in the commons, a large dining area of the mall surrounded by five or six different fast-food places. The day had been pleasant, fun, just celebrating being together. Suddenly, I felt someone staring at me and looked up to see Mary Jones across the commons, giving me the finger. I did not acknowledge that I saw her, but it dampened my spirits a little because it reminded me I would probably be charged with murder again.

The boys were all excited about Christmas, and their enthusiasm was catching. They wanted to go out for dinner on Christmas to have lobster, so we did. We didn't go to a fancy, expensive place, but to one of the casinos which offered a special on lobster. It was the first Christmas Eve I'd ever been able to enjoy as an adult. Always before, I was rushing to finish last-minute shopping and wrapping, cooking for the next day, or packing everything to visit Sam's family.

The next morning, we got up and opened our presents leisurely and peacefully. Daniel had always wanted a flocked tree, so we bought one. We were free to try new ideas and to start new traditions for our family. Several times throughout that Christmas Day, I remembered last year and how Sam had made everyone miserable. It was so sad to think that had been our last meal together and that Sam's drunken rudeness had made it barely tolerable. Now we were building a new life and I vowed to myself to make it a good life for all of us.

A few days after Christmas, the ax fell again. I was notified that the district attorney had appealed the dismissal of charges against me and had again charged me with first-degree murder in District Court. The hearing was set for January 17, 1989. Once more, I was thrown into turmoil. "How many times can they do this to me?" I wondered. "Can they continue to hound me like this forever?" As always, I got total support from Sarah, Evelyn, and Bill, and that support helped me through the darkness I felt.

In the meantime, I still had to work and take care of my kids and the household. I also made countless calls and filled out stacks of paperwork, trying to get our military benefits. There was always something else to do, but I was learning to handle my financial affairs. By this time, I had caught up on all my bills and had paid off many of Sam's. Sometimes, I was amazed at myself. At the same time, it made me wonder what Sam had done with all his money. His salary had been $2,500 a month. He was always late paying the bills, and we never had anything. If I didn't work, we didn't have decent food on the table, and I never had even a few dollars for pocket money. Where had it all gone? Here I was making the house payments, supporting myself and the kids, taking care of everything on time, with less than half his income.

Early in January, I saw the prosecutor's Opening Brief of Appeal to the Justice Judge's decision to dismiss charges. The brief stated, "The victim was not armed. The victim did not threaten nor attack Bethal [sic] on April 9, 1988." Of course, that statement upset me because it was not true, and it ignored information brought out in the October and November hearings. Reading that statement made me feel as if I had already been convicted, sentenced, and executed. It took days for me to work my way through my feelings of doom and gloom. Bill, my attorney, explained to me that there were two sets of issues to be addressed. One was whether or not the prosecutor was entitled to appeal the dismissal. The second was whether or not the ruling to dismiss had merit. His manner as he explained this was calm and reassuring, but I still felt that my very life was threatened.

As always, I had to brace myself before going into a court hearing. This meant days of trying to reason with myself, constantly trying to calm myself.

When we went to court on January 17, 1989, we found that the case had never been entered on the court docket. It had been continued to February 6. What a letdown! I knew I'd have to go through all this agony again. On top of this, the Juvenile Court hearing scheduled for January 26 was canceled and continued to February 9 because welfare did not submit its report on time.

But I continued to work and, more or less, just mark time, waiting for the next court date. At least once every couple of weeks, I had migraines, making it even more difficult to function. Toward the end of January, I woke one morning with blood in my ears. My arthritis, which had started in childhood, flared up worse than ever in my chest and all my joints. The pain was so intense, it kept me awake many nights. Besides these health problems, another form of harassment began.

Several times at night, a small white car pulled into my driveway and sat there idling for five to ten minutes. I could never see the driver, but I believed it was the woman I had seen Sam with back in March. One night, a woman who would not identify herself called and said, "You killed the only man I ever loved." It confirmed my gut-level belief that Sam had another woman. But then why didn't he just let me go? Why did he persist in threatening and attacking me? These questions went round and round in my mind, and I never could make sense of it.

A few days before the February 6 hearing, it was canceled and continued to February 22. More delay, more torture for me to go through. I wondered how much more I could stand. At times, I was tempted to give up, just plead to whatever, and get it finished. But there was too much at stake, especially for my children. If I gave up, they would lose all their VA benefits. So I determined to hang in there, to keep fighting.

In the midst of all this confusion, a wonderful thing happened. The Air Force released Sam's back pay. This not only helped me catch up on some of my debts, it also relieved the immediate pressure of just scraping by to put food on the table. It gave me hope for the future, keeping alive my will to fight for my children and for my freedom.

On February 9, the Juvenile Court judge reviewed our case and commended Child Protective Services for their handling of the case. We all continued in individual and family counseling, and things ran fairly smoothly at home. Not that we had no problems, but we didn't have life-threatening crises. We were learning to solve our problems.

About this time, the Joneses complained to the prosecutor that I was harassing them. This time, however, at my attorney's insistence, the Joneses were closely questioned. The only form of harassment they specified was that I "stared" at them. I knew

I had done nothing to harass them, but I was upset to see how determined they were to make trouble for me.

I felt certain they were responsible for most of the harassment I have previously mentioned, including vandalism of my property. Yet the police refused to take those acts seriously. Bill reassured me that their report about me staring at them merely discredited them with the prosecutor.

We went back into District Court on February 22. At that time, the judge considered only our Motion to Dismiss the prosecutor's appeal. In his ruling, the judge stated, "Inasmuch as the action of the Justice of the Peace in dismissing the Justice Court case resulted in a final judgment, the State of Nevada may thereafter appeal from such an Order of Judgment. . . . Defendant's Motion to Dismiss . . . is hereby denied." Another hearing for the merits of the appeal was scheduled for March 6. More waiting, another cycle of getting myself pumped up for court. Would this nightmare never end?

I tried to relieve some of my frustration by doing heavy yard work—digging, weeding, planting. The ground is very dry and rocky in Vegas, so gardening requires a lot of muscle and sweat. Tending the yard was the most effective physical activity for me in terms of relieving stress and frustration. The added bonus was that I loved it so much, seeing the grass and plants come back to life after being neglected for so long. My roses bloomed again, and it gave me so much pleasure to share them in small bouquets with others. Gardening was still in my blood, one way I had of feeling connected to the roots of my childhood—happy, carefree, innocent days before I knew Sam.

Dreams of Sam still haunted my sleep. One night I dreamed he was living in an apartment and invited me over. When I got there, some woman's clothing was strewn around the living room, evidently for me to see. I woke up crying, hurt, confused. Another night, I dreamed I was all dressed up in a tap-dancing outfit—satin and sequins. Sam was barking orders: "Clean the kitchen, scrub the bathroom, change the baby, iron my uniform." I was dancing in faster and faster circles. Suddenly, my outfit was transformed to a simple white cotton gown, I stood very still, and said, "I'm dancing as fast as I can." I woke up crying each time because these dreams always triggered flashbacks of abusive episodes I had blocked from my memory. Although painful, these flashbacks helped me move through my grief. The March 6 hearing was continued to March 22 and then March 29—three more cycles of buildup, two more cycles of letdown. On March 29, 1989, the District Court judge ruled, "It is hereby ordered that the State's appeal from the decision of the . . . Justice of the Peace, rendered on the 8th of November, 1988, . . . is hereby denied."

The judgment to dismiss all charges against me had been upheld. That was another victory, another milestone in my journey through hell to freedom. It came just eleven days short of a year after Sam's death.

Through Bill I learned that the prosecutor planned no further action against me. And while that was a great relief, I live with the knowledge that the State could bring me before the Grand Jury at any time for the duration of my life. Supposedly, the State must have new evidence in order to do this, but the original charges and the appeal were brought against me with no evidence. So, because there was no trial, I will never be completely free of this threat. Heavier than this for me is living with the knowledge that I took a life, a life of the one person I loved the most. Of that, I can never be free.

I CHOOSE TO LIVE

You chose the bulb; you planted it.
In the spring it started to grow,
to push through the snow and ice.
"Look at me, I want to be beautiful for you."
You put your foot on the tender buds before
they ever bloomed.
You stomped, you smashed, you destroyed.
"Look at me, I'm ugly, I'm broken. I am no more."
I slept. I withdrew. I was nurtured within
a safe, warm womb. Spring came and you weren't there.
I pushed and fought my way through the ice and snow.
I saw the sun. It warmed my face, it warmed my soul.
"Look at me, I'm beautiful and I'm alive and I will
not allow anyone to stomp or smash me again."
This is the first spring of the rest of my life.

—Beth Sipe
March, 1990

Afterword

Another year passed before all the issues in Beth's case were resolved. Ultimately, Beth was validated and vindicated in all instances. Full custody of her children was restored and the involvement of Child Protective Services was terminated. She was awarded her full widow's pension by the Veteran's Administration. James and Daniel were awarded their Veteran's Administration benefits. Finally, Beth was awarded the death benefits from Sam's Federal Service Life Insurance policy. Those victories required numerous reports and court hearings, which prolonged Beth's trauma. But she persevered and she prevailed.

Today, she resides quietly in a remote rural area, tending her gardens and a menagerie of farm animals. Her greatest joy is her freedom, her independence, her sense that she is in control of her life. Her sons are all adults now, living on their own. They prefer not to be identified.

Commentaries

The Counselor's Perspective

Evelyn J. Hall

Counseling a battered woman who has killed her abuser requires attention to the same principles outlined by Schechter (1987) for counseling any battered woman. The focus is on empowering the woman through safety planning, validation of her experiences, exploration of her strengths, and respect for her right to self-determination. It means listening to her with compassion and acceptance, but without judging, blaming, or telling her what to do. As Beth's story illustrates, adherence to these principles is important, even if the woman begins treatment with the idea that it is too late for her to get help. The following sections will elaborate on these concepts.

An Immediate Focus on Safety

A battered woman who has killed her partner continues to need safety planning. The counselor cannot assume that danger of physical harm to the woman ended with the abuser's death.

He may have family or friends who threaten or attempt to harm her. Beth, for example, was harassed by callers who hung up after she answered and by threatening phone calls, prowlers, vandalism of her home and car, and gunfire in her backyard. Repeated unexpected appearances by the police at her home added to Beth's perception of imminent danger.

When the woman's safety continues to be threatened, safety options, such as an avenue of escape, shelter, safe storage and copying of important documents, and emergency phone numbers, should be discussed with her. Consideration of possible positive and negative consequences of each option should be part of this discussion. Rehearsal of her ultimate plan is helpful, and knowing what choices she can make in regard to safety also accesses her personal power.

Listening with compassion and acceptance to a battered woman's story is particularly important after she has killed her abuser. By the time death has occurred in a violent relationship, a woman has usually had many encounters with social services, mental health providers, and the justice system. Typically, these experiences have ranged from disappointing to disastrous, limiting her willingness to trust a new authority figure. This was certainly true in Beth's case. She had appealed unsuccessfully for help and protection many times throughout seventeen years of intense abuse.

At first, the woman may view the counselor as part of the establishment which has been nonresponsive. Consequently, the counselor's ability to maintain a nonjudgmental attitude is more critical than ever. Because the system has not responded to her cries for help, the woman may have concluded that no one cares about her safety. After she has killed her partner, she may give up hope of any future. In Beth's words during her first counseling session with me, "I don't know what I'm doing here. It's too late for me." For someone to listen to and accept her story gives her validation and may trigger some hope.

Another reason that acceptance is so important at this stage is the woman's emotional condition. As pointed out by Browne (1987) and Walker (1989), a battered woman usually kills only in self-defense after prolonged severe abuse; she usually has no intent to kill. Understandably, her symptoms of posttraumatic stress disorder (PTSD) are extremely severe after her abuser's death. Mixed with PTSD symptoms are her grief and remorse about his death and how he died. Like Beth, the woman is likely to be shut down, exhibiting flat affect, disorganized thought, disassociation, even indifference to helping herself. She may experience appetite disturbance, sleep disorder, and panic attacks that affect her physical health or become life threatening. She may view and label herself as "crazy." At some point, her anger about the years of abuse and about feeling forced to kill in self-defense will surface with a force that may frighten her. Like Beth, she may have sought counseling because someone else suggested or ordered that she do so.

The counselor—through nonjudgmental listening—offers her needed validation that she does matter and that her reaction is normal, not crazy. The counselor's role is to assist the woman in working through the maze of emotions in a safe, nurturing environment. Frequently, these emotions may surface in dreams, so the counselor should be prepared to do dream work or direct the client to a qualified professional who can.

Typically, a battered woman who remains in a violent relationship for a long period of time is viewed as weak-willed, masochistic, lacking intelligence, or all three. In fact, the opposite is true. She could not survive the years of abuse if she did not have great strength and resourcefulness. The counselor needs to assist her in identifying and exploring all her strengths. This task ultimately helps the woman reclaim her identity and self-esteem. Beth, for example, had demonstrated skill and persistence in her pursuit of education and medical training, as well as in her determination to earn money at any honest labor. Throughout the years of abuse, she was able to maintain relationships with her family and a few friends, so she usually had some support system. She was also a creative homemaker and devoted mother, budgeting limited monies and resources to ensure that her family always had the necessities of life.

Helping her to identify all her accomplishments was a critical step in her treatment. As she began to see herself as a person with strength and ability, she became increasingly motivated to handle daily tasks and problems, such as her job and her children. She also redoubled her efforts in her own defense.

Overall, Beth's level of functioning before the shooting was very high. In spite of extreme duress from Sam, she was able to maintain a full-time job as a medical aide, take on a part-time job as a movie extra, meet the demands of the court to get a larger apartment, and support herself and her children. Only in interactions with her husband did she exhibit signs of learned helplessness; she could excel in most other areas of her life. Thus, Beth clearly demonstrates that learned helplessness can be situational and limited to a battered woman's intimate relationship. For the counselor, recognition of this factor can help him or her maintain appropriate respect for the woman and her right to self-determination. The counselor should offer the woman maximum encouragement with minimal interference in her decisions.

Reconstructing the History of Abuse

Taking a complete history of the abuse experienced by a battered woman who has killed serves several therapeutic functions. It allows her to express her feelings about the abuse in safety, perhaps for the first time. Writing out this history is usually suggested as a means of confronting the reality of the abuse. Without a visible written history, the abuse remains shadowy, disjointed fragments in the woman's mind.

For a woman like Beth with so many years of abuse, addressing her history of abuse is a very emotional and lengthy process. It requires that the counselor balance therapeutic boundaries and structure with enough flexibility to respond to emergencies that inevitably arise while bringing such painful memories to the surface. There is a danger that the counselor can become so immersed in the woman's intense drama as to lose objectivity. Regular consultation with knowledgeable colleagues is not only helpful but also necessary for the counselor to maintain an objective perspective.

Through examination of her history of abuse, the woman may gradually complete expressions of feelings long buried and break free of her confusion about the relationship.

The counselor's role is to provide a safe, supportive environment and information about domestic violence as it is relevant. The cycle of violence, power and control tactics, characteristics of a batterer, and symptoms of PTSD are representative of subjects that almost always need explanations. The value of offering such information is evident in one of Beth's responses; that is, "Do these men go to abuse school?" Until she had access to this information, Beth thought she was a rare case. The information helped alleviate her feeling of shame about being abused and lessened the need for secrecy.

As instances of past abuse are processed, the woman begins to ask herself why she returned after separations and why she stayed in the relationship so long. These are questions Beth asked herself repeatedly. The counselor should allow the woman to identify her own reasons and validate those reasons through acceptance. The counselor can provide further validation by providing lists of reasons other battered women have given for staying or by suggesting written materials, such as Barnett and LaViolette's (1993) book on battered women leaving relationships.

Beth's primary reason for staying during the first ten years of her marriage coincides with the most frequent reason given by other battered women—love of the man. Although many people find this reason implausible, Walker (1989) points out that most people grew up in homes where physical punishment was linked to love. So physical violence in an adult relationship does not necessarily seem inconsistent with love to a battered woman or to the batterer. Exploration of different definitions of love may be helpful at this point, along with pinpointing what the woman expected going into the relationship. Conclusions she reaches about love and relationships may help her protect herself in the future. It may also help her come to peace with another recurrent question: How could he love me and treat me so badly?

Past Help Seeking

It is the counselor's role to raise questions, suggest options, and offer support for the woman, whatever she concludes.

Reviewing a battered woman's history of abuse usually reveals ineffective responses by various professionals to her attempts to get help. In Beth's case, there were numerous such ineffective responses. Examination of these responses provides strong reasons to stop victim blaming, as well as indicators for effective intervention.

In 1973, Beth sought professional help through counseling. At that time, little had been written about treatment for domestic violence. Both counselors the couple saw offered practical suggestions to reduce conflicts, but they did not address Sam's violent and alcoholic behaviors. This gave Beth some validation, but it allowed Sam to dismiss the counselors as "outsiders" and "just a bunch of bull." Today, the recommended procedure is to screen all couples for violence during the initial phone call. If violence is present, knowledgeable counselors do not see the couple together until the man has completed his own therapy to eliminate the violence. The practice of seeing a violent couple together encourages the abuser to blame the woman for his behavior and often increases the danger to the woman, as shown by the Sipe case.

Individual counseling, either with a mental health professional or with clergy, is another way a battered woman often tries to get help. Initially, her purpose is "to get him to stop hurting me." If she continues in counseling, she may rebuild her self-esteem and regain her identity.

This was true for Beth with the psychologist and the pastor she saw during her years in Colorado. However, it should be noted that the improvement of her mental health did nothing to retard or end Sam's violence. On the contrary, Sam's violence escalated as he tried to maintain control over Beth. Counselors who see a battered woman individually must constantly caution the woman that changes in her behavior, for example, assertiveness, may increase the danger of intensified attacks by the batterer.

The battered woman who kills her abuser has—in most cases—made frequent calls to police agencies for help. Beth, for example, called police for help more times than can be counted, starting with calls to Blytheville police in 1975. In that instance, the police appropriately returned the baby to Beth but did nothing about Sam's violence to Beth, his driving under the influence of alcohol, or endangering the safety of his child. Throughout the years of abuse, she continued to appeal to the police for help, but Sam was never given an appropriate consequence, such as mandatory counseling in a batterers' treatment program or jail time. This lack of consequences gives the man a clear message that his treatment of his partner is acceptable; it reinforces his battering behavior. Even when the Sipes lived in states (Colorado and Nevada) where mandatory arrest laws had been enacted, the police arrested him only twice. In those cases, the court did not apply an appropriate consequence, thereby increasing the danger for Beth.

Statistically, battering by an intimate partner is the single most frequent cause of injury to women in the United States. It is estimated that 22% to 35% of women seen in emergency rooms annually have been injured by battery (Chez, 1988; Isaac & Sanchez, 1994; Jones, 1993; Stark, Flitcraft, & Frazier, 1979). Yet the medical community has frequently failed to notice, comment on, or intervene in obvious cases of domestic violence. In the Sipe history, Beth was seen by numerous doctors for gross physical injuries, and not one appeared to question their source. Even when Sam slapped Daniel in the presence of medical personnel, nothing was said or done to intervene. Only the psychiatrist in a Virginia hospital seemed knowledgeable about domestic abuse and intervened appropriately by refusing to commit Beth.

The woman gets the message that no one cares about how she is abused and no one will help her. For the counselor hearing such stories, the task is to provide validation through empathy and a supportive atmosphere for the woman to release her pain and anger about such treatment.

Legal Defense Issues

Counseling a battered woman after she has killed her abuser will often focus on the subject of her legal defense. In most cases, the woman is charged with first-degree murder, even though she has no past criminal record. Several issues immediately confront her.

One issue is how police have treated her. The treatment Beth received by the police on the night of the shooting and afterward is typical of experiences reported by other battered women who have killed in self-defense. Specifically, she was not allowed to take her purse, which resulted in theft of her money.

She was not given medical attention even though she was clearly injured. She was given false information about the condition of her husband, and she was coerced to make a statement without counsel through false references to her son. When arrested and officially charged, she was subjected to strip searches and all the other indignities of incarceration. In short, Beth was treated as a career criminal. This treatment by the justice system when a woman acts in self-defense extends the wound created by the abuse.

The counselor is likely to observe the most severe symptoms of PTSD as the woman struggles to deal with her shame, degradation, terror, remorse, and anguish about all that has transpired. For example, Beth became anorexic and suicidal, both life-threatening conditions. The obvious solution of hospitalization had mixed results. The sense of safety along with individual and group therapy were helpful. However, "routine" medication, conclusions drawn from questionable testing, inconsistencies of treatment, use of the label of "murderer," and threats to commit her were damaging to her. At times, comments by the hospital personnel reflected more concern about Beth's legal status and their potential liability than about her mental health. Thus, when considering hospitalization in such a case, the counselor needs to screen hospitals carefully for staff who are knowledgeable about domestic violence before recommending an inpatient facility.

The point of these observations is not to criticize the hospital, but rather to emphasize the need for specialized treatment of a battered woman suffering from acute PTSD. Such a patient needs a secure, supportive environment. She needs psychiatrists, nurses, and therapists who thoroughly understand domestic violence and the importance of empowerment in her treatment. She needs to be screened so that triggers which cause flashbacks can be identified and either avoided or removed. Above all, she needs continued, regular contact with her counselor and advocates throughout her hospital stay. As long as her legal case remains unresolved, the woman continues to live in the trauma and therefore, to be at risk.

One alternative to hospitalizing a woman in Beth's situation is shelter placement. In a battered woman's shelter, she will have a secure, supportive environment with staff who are educated and experienced in dealing with domestic violence. However, the shelter will need to have the services of a psychiatrist to prescribe medication if necessary. After Beth's hospital experience, that component was arranged in cooperation with the local shelter.

Even in a protected atmosphere, the counselor must continue regular contact with the woman. The counselor can help to provide continuity, support, and advocacy, thereby helping the woman maintain a level of functioning high enough to survive the ordeal of defending herself in court.

Battered women also face paying for their legal defense counsel. This often taxes the financial resources of her entire family to the breaking point. The woman may work, sell off prized assets, or borrow money. In Beth's case, she used all three methods to raise money, including holding garage sales in which she sold some treasured items. Her financial crisis was intensified by bill collectors hounding her for payment of Sam's debts and by threats to foreclose on her house. These financial demands create more emotional stress for the woman, aggravating her already precarious emotional condition. Again, the counselor's focus is upon providing encouragement and support with reality testing as appropriate.

Protecting Her Children

Although concerns about her legal defense are constant, nothing may be as riveting for the battered woman who has killed as the welfare and future of her children. Often, the woman's perception that she is ensuring her children's welfare is a primary reason for her staying in the violent relationship.

Throughout her story, Beth demonstrates how strong this reason was for her. It is apparent how shattering the actions taken by social services were for her. The removal of her children from her care multiplied the impact of all her other traumas to the point that, for a brief period, she gave up hope and her will to struggle.

The counselor's role here is to interface with social service agencies when they are nonresponsive to the woman, without taking over for her. In Beth's case, this involved accompanying her to meet with a caseworker who did not return her phone calls.

Conclusion

Throughout counseling with a battered woman who has killed, the central focus should be on empowerment of the woman, and all techniques used should be consistent with this focus. The counselor must accept the woman's priorities and decisions as part of assisting her to become empowered.

The counselor's ability to maintain objectivity is of paramount importance and is likely to be challenging, particularly when involved in advocacy activities for the client.

The Lawyer's Perspective

William H. Smith

I saw Beth for the first time in May 1988, about six weeks after the shooting. She was referred to me by an advocate at the Las Vegas battered women's shelter who knew I had experience in this area of criminal defense. Beth's case gave me my first opportunity to handle a battered woman's murder case from the beginning, which I knew was the best place to start.

In 1986, I argued successfully before the Nevada State Board of Pardons Commissioners for early parole eligibility on behalf of a woman serving two consecutive life prison terms for murder. The woman had shot her partner while he was taking a shower and was convicted by a jury that rejected the testimony of Dr. Lenore Walker concerning battered woman syndrome. She was later released from custody.

When I met Beth, I was handling an appeal for another woman who was also serving two consecutive life prison terms for murder. This woman had shot her partner in the head with a rifle as he lay sleeping in their bed; she was convicted by a jury that also rejected expert testimony concerning the psychological effects of her abusive relationship. Her conviction was reversed in December 1988 by the Nevada Supreme Court (*Larson v. State,* 1988) because of her trial attorney's ineffective assistance (bad advice to reject a proposed plea bargain). She was released from custody about a year later as a result of a plea bargain for manslaughter that was finalized with the district attorney's office after the case was remanded for a new trial. In the last few years, I have represented two other battered women who shot their abusers. I hope my comments will be useful to others who prepare defense strategies in similar cases.

Beth killed Steven (or Sam, as he liked to be called) on Saturday night, April 9, 1988, in front of their eleven-year-old son, Daniel. The lead homicide detective prepared an affidavit dated April 28, 1988, to justify the warrant for Beth's arrest. In his affidavit, the detective referred to statements Beth and Daniel made to the police shortly after the shooting; to a crime report filed on February 8, 1988, that listed Beth as the victim of a battery by Steven and described Steven's arrest and release from custody for that offense; and to the physical evidence at the scene of the shooting—all of which suggested to the detective "that a justifiable homicide situation may exist."

The detective further stated in his affidavit that he told Beth at the police station that night the circumstances "may justify the homicide of her husband but that the decision to prosecute was ultimately in the hands of the district attorney's office and that it would be made at a later time." The detective further affirmed that after Beth asked for an attorney at the beginning of her initial interview, he told her that if she gave a statement to him, she would be allowed to leave police headquarters that night rather than facing probable arrest.

The detective's affidavit also stated, however, that the description of the shooting Daniel gave during his second interview with the police four days later suggested Steven was staggering and at least partially incapacitated at the exact moment of the shooting and may have been physically incapable of conducting a life-threatening physical attack at that moment. Thus, Beth may have had the opportunity to resort to an alternative to the use of deadly force, as she had allegedly done many times in her seventeen-year marriage. The detective opined that there was sufficient probable cause to believe that Beth's admitted actions did not constitute justifiable homicide. He requested an arrest warrant for homicide with use of a deadly weapon.

Even more troubling for Beth's defense was the detective's account in his affidavit of his interview with a woman who was one of Beth's neighbors. This woman and her husband socialized regularly with Steven. She said Beth had on more than one occasion made the statement, "I'll blow his fucking head off," and that one time Beth told her, "I'll blow his fucking head off, and I will get away with it because I will say he battered me." The woman also told the detective she heard Beth make threats to Steven to the effect that she would poison him and put black widow spiders in his bed.

Apparently these accusations of premeditation and subterfuge made by the woman, coupled with the speculative possibilities of escape and/or nonlethal recourse, persuaded the detective to recommend that Beth be charged criminally.

Beth was arrested on May 5, 1988. She made her first appearance in Justice Court on Monday, May 9, 1988, to be arraigned on the charge of open murder (which includes first- and second-degree murder) with use of a deadly weapon. The court referred her to the public defender's office for representation. Fortunately, the next day she was released from custody on her own recognizance. The presiding judge had read the detective's affidavit, recognized that Beth had suffered years of abuse, and was impressed that Beth was not a danger to the community or a flight risk. This judge's courageous decision was a portent of the events during the next ten and a half months, which culminated in Beth's complete vindication.

When Beth first came to my office, she was accompanied by her advocate from the battered women's shelter. Although Beth had received support from the shelter before and after her arrest, she was desperately in need of professional psychological assistance. I contacted the psychologist who testified in the *Larson* case mentioned above, but his caseload was too heavy for another major immediate commitment. He referred me to Dr. Evelyn Hall. Although I believe he would have been helpful in this case, I know that no one could have done better than Eve. This book and Beth's recovery are the products of Dr. Hall's sustained efforts throughout the past seven-plus years. Professionally and personally, I admire, respect, and like her very much.

It soon became obvious to me that Beth's seventeen-year history of abuse should be reconstructed and documented in detail to facilitate my efforts to obtain the eventual dismissal or optimal reduction and disposition of Beth's criminal charges and/or to prepare for a jury trial. At my request, Beth began to put her story on paper.

In late September 1988, my secretary and I met with the deputy district attorney assigned to prosecute this case. We presented to her a compendium of material that included letters from a forensic psychiatrist, from a therapist (Dr. Hall), from the executive director for the shelter, and from Beth's advocate. The material included numerous letters from people personally aware of Beth's history as a battered wife and reports that substantiated many of her allegations of physical abuse through the years. We also displayed Beth's good employment history, various medical and insurance records, and letters from her three sons.

Although I reasoned with the prosecutor for a voluntary dismissal of the charges, I realized that her team chief had prosecuted the woman I had represented at the Pardons Board and might not be receptive to my position. Battered woman's syndrome is not a legal defense to murder. No firm offer to settle the case had been made by the district attorney when the preliminary hearing began on October 6, 1988.

The same judge who released Beth on her own recognizance was still on the case. The prosecutor told him that she intended to present only two witnesses and then rest her case because she felt their testimony would be sufficient to establish the requisite probable cause to justify binding the case over for trial under existing Nevada case law. My associate's research revealed, however, that a recent case from the Federal District of Nevada (*Groesbeck v. Housewright,* 1988) held that "unlawfulness" is an element of the crime of murder in Nevada. Furthermore, in a September 1988 opinion (*Sheriff v. Gleave,* 1988), the Nevada Supreme Court stated that certain defenses may be presented and sustained at a preliminary hearing, which, if established, require as a matter of law that a criminal charge should be dismissed at that stage. Armed with those legal arguments, my goal at the preliminary hearing was to establish convincingly, through the prosecution's own witnesses, that Beth had acted in self-defense. I crossed my fingers that the presiding judge would have enough gumption to dismiss the case if I succeeded.

I had discussed the facts of this case many times with Beth, but my most important fact-oriented discussions were during my two meetings with young Daniel. Shortly after being retained, I went to the apartment complex where Steven was shot. Beth arranged for herself, Daniel, and me to enter an apartment identical to the one in which she and Daniel had lived. We reenacted the events of the night of the shooting from start to finish. Weeks later, I met with Daniel and his two older brothers in my office while Beth waited in the lobby. We again discussed in detail Daniel's recollections. Preparing Daniel to be a witness at the preliminary hearing was crucial to the ultimate disposition of this case because his testimony and that of the pathologist established an unrebutted case of self-defense for Beth.

The first witness was the chief medical examiner who performed the autopsy. He described two gunshot wounds: one bullet went into the upper right chest from right to left at a 45° angle, irreparably destroying the heart; the other penetrated the left upper arm from left to right and went into the chest at a 15° downward angle. The first wound surely was fatal; the second was life-threatening but survivable if prompt medical attention had been rendered. Minor scratches and abrasions on Steven's forehead were also described.

On cross-examination, the medical examiner said that the superficial scratches and abrasions on the forehead were consistent with Steven being hit over the head with a flowerpot from a frontal direction contemporaneous with the shooting. He also testified that the head injuries were relatively insignificant because they would not have impaired Steven by rendering him defenseless or unable to aggressively pursue Beth during an attack if that was his intention. He also commented on an excerpt in a book written by a famous forensic pathologist that cited a case history of a police officer who was shot through the heart with a .38 and then drew his own service revolver, fired six shots, walked across the street, and opened his patrol car door before he collapsed. The medical examiner's testimony was totally consistent with our theory of self-defense. On direct examination, the second witness, Daniel, gave a straightforward account of the shooting for the prosecutor. On cross-examination, he described an incident that occurred a couple of months earlier when Beth and Steven got into an argument and Steven pounded on her, swung her around, and threw her on the ground. Daniel recalled several earlier fights between his parents. He also mentioned recent telephone threats made by Steven to Beth and said she would block their apartment door with furniture while she and Daniel slept in the same bed.

Daniel also testified about coming home with his father during the evening of the shooting after he and his father played racquetball at Nellis Air Force Base; he said that his father had been acting "weird." He did not see his father drink alcohol earlier, but Steven's blood alcohol level was one and a half times the legal limit for driving when he died. Beth and Steven told Daniel to go into his room, which was about fifteen to twenty feet away from the shooting, and he described overhearing their conversation. It began normally and escalated into a loud argument and fight. Daniel described running into the living room and attempting to separate his parents. He saw the flowerpot crash, his father stagger backward, his mother get the gun, his father crouch, rise, and approach his mother, and the ensuing gunshots. This was a terrifying situation with his mother screaming and crying. He thought his mother was terrified because he had never heard her scream like that before. He thought his father would have hurt Beth if she had not shot him and probably would have beaten Beth badly. There was no way Beth could have escaped. Daniel ran out of the house and down the alley about 100 yards before Beth caught up with him, and he had never seen his mother that way before. She looked really scared. She was crying.

A few days later, I gave copies of the two recent cases that supported my oral motion for dismissal to the judge and prosecutor. Before the next court hearing, we met with the judge in chambers, and he told us that he was going to grant it. Another courageous decision. When the judge formally dismissed the case in open court, he stated on the record that the only witness to the crime was Daniel, whose testimony was not going to be contradicted. He sympathized with Daniel being in this terrifying situation and agreed with my analysis of the law. He said,

> I think that the testimony that was given to me in this preliminary hearing is overwhelming to show that the killing of the deceased in this manner was done in self-defense and was so overwhelming that I'm going to rule, as a matter of law, that this killing was done as a matter of self-defense and I'm hereby dismissing the murder charges against the defendant.

After the preliminary hearing, the district attorney's office appealed this decision to the trial court. The issues were fully briefed by both sides and the trial court denied the appeal.

Beth was lucky. Lucky to be released without bail to assist in her own defense. Lucky to appear before two judges who did not pass the buck to a jury and run the risk of facing adverse political consequences (judges in Nevada are elected).

I believe that the deputy district attorney who prosecuted this case was sympathetic to Beth's plight. She was moved when I showed her an old photograph of Beth sitting on the tub in a bathroom in one of her previous marital homes with blood streaming down her face from a busted nose and a thick big-buckled belt that Steven used for sadistic beatings. I did not learn about the rapes and other sexual degradations until after I read the manuscript for this book.

In most cases, when unarmed abusers are killed by their partners, strong sentiments for the deceased and his family coexist with those for the defendant. There are at least two sides to almost any story. A typical homicide case is examined and judged from the first levels of investigation, through the charging and plea bargaining processes, and through contested court hearings by an array of people in authority who are charged with the responsibility of making tough decisions. Sometimes, on review, these decisions appear to be arbitrary and capricious, especially in a death penalty context.

It is not an easy job to defend battered women accused of murder. Patience, understanding, diligence, and resources are necessary. Money is required for many services. The National Clearinghouse for the Defense of Battered Women in Philadelphia (215-351-0010) is a center that provides information and resource material to attorneys, battered women's advocates, and expert witnesses who are assisting battered women charged with crimes.

This was a relatively clear-cut case of self-defense. Most others are not so simple. Nevada has a rule of evidence (Nev. Rev. Stat. §48.061) that became effective on June 30, 1993, specifically permitting the introduction of evidence of domestic violence and expert testimony concerning the effect of domestic violence in criminal cases. The trend in this country is to admit such evidence in court. The extent to which it can mitigate a murder charge down to justifiable homicide or even manslaughter is uncertain. Defense attorneys and other advocates should be alert to develop the potentially powerful argument that sustained psychological abuse can be as much if not more threatening and devastating than immediate or imminent physical attack. The laws that govern the legal defense of self-defense in most states are still predicated on contemporaneous physical threats only. Changes in these laws by legislatures are needed to empower juries to render more humane verdicts.

Throughout this country, participants in our criminal justice system are becoming increasingly aware of the enormous toll that violence in the home exacts from our society. While education, intervention, and prevention are worthy endeavors, we who work in this system are presented too often with a fait accompli. We then must strive to achieve what is fair and just for both the living and the dead. I believe that what happened to Beth in court was about as fair and just as she should have expected. Without luck, however, her story might not have had such a bittersweet, happy ending.

The Fatal Flaw

Inadequacies in Social Support and Criminal Justice Responses

Susan L. Miller

It would be easy to focus on the horror of the abuse described in this book, and to ask, How could she still love him or why didn't she leave? That would be a mistake. It is far more instructive to look at the interactions between cultural, medical, military, and criminal justice institutions and battered women, and to explore how these shaped Beth's options and responses. Even more telling, but perhaps not as powerfully described in Beth's account, are the instances—and there are many—of Beth's inner strength, coping abilities, resistance, and resilience in the face of dehumanizing and violent behavior at the hands of her husband.

Beyond the horrific details of Beth's personal story, her experience is typical of many battered women who live in terror of their current or former male partners' violence and rage. Each year, it is estimated that the leading cause of injury to women in this country results from the violence committed against them by intimate partners or ex-partners (Bernstein, 1993). National victimization data indicate that the rate of violence committed by intimates is nearly six times greater for females than for males (Bachman & Saltzman, 1995). The focus on male-to-female violence here is *not* meant to suggest that lesbian or gay male relationships are violence-free (see Island & Letellier, 1990; Renzetti, 1992) but to limit the discussion to common dynamics consistent with Beth's experience.

Despite these statistics, battered women continue to experience frustration, dissatisfaction, or just plain ambivalence in their dealings with major social institutions in this country, such as the clergy, the medical system, social services, and the criminal justice system.

"Walking on Eggshells"

Beth's story vividly demonstrates the cycle of violence and the theory of learned helplessness typically experienced by many battered women, regardless of race, ethnicity, social class, religion, or sexual orientation. Understanding this cycle provides a partial answer to the question, Why did she stay? Walker (1979) developed these concepts in an attempt to explain how a woman could be "trapped" into staying in a relationship by the abuser's emotional manipulation, as well as his physical intimidation or violence.

Beth believed that Sam loved her, that he truly didn't mean to harm her, that he could or would change. At times, during their reconciliations, he actually became the guy she thought she had fallen in love with and married. As Beth describes Sam in the early days, "He could be the life of the party, making everybody laugh, including me. He could also be very kind, gentle, and loving. . . . No one had ever been so attentive and affectionate with me before, and I was filled with joy" (p. 11, this volume). She wanted desperately to believe that he would stay a loving father and husband.

The time immediately following the violence is often the hardest time for a battered woman to leave, because although the bruises may still be fresh, his promises sound even more sweet. It is also the most dangerous time for her to leave (see Mahoney, 1991, 1994): Over 50% of women who leave violent relationships are followed, harassed, or further attacked by their estranged partners (Browne, 1987). Another study indicates that more than half of the men who killed their wives did so following a separation (Barnard, Vera, Vera, & Newman, 1982).

Battered women want to believe their partners' promises not to hurt them anymore and try to alter their own behavior to forestall a recurrence of violence. As Beth said,

> It was hard to keep my hopes up, but I kept thinking I could do something to calm Sam down. It became a twenty-four-hour-a-day job just trying to satisfy him. It didn't matter any more whether I was right or wrong, just as long as I could pacify him. (p. 31)

Fueled by her religious convictions and her socialization as a female in this society, Beth embraced her role as caretaker and nurturer of the family. "Violence begins after a woman has made a deep investment of her love, energy, and self into the relationship" (Mahoney, 1994, p. 74). Although researchers call the abuser a "batterer," he remains the woman's "lover, husband, or partner—often, the father of her children" (Mahoney, 1994, p. 75). Cultural expectations in our society emphasize women's vital role in maintaining intimate relationships and taking responsibility for children, which pressures women to keep the family intact and foster closeness between father and children. For example, pending a possible separation, Sam told Beth,

> "How can you take my baby away from me?" . . . [so Beth explained] he really got to me. I began to feel guilty, confused, helplessly trapped. Finally, I told Sam I would come back if he would promise to see a marriage counselor with me. . . . He promised never to hit me again. (p. 35)

Despite how unrealistic the abusers' promises might seem, women latch onto them with anxious hope.

Beth also encountered many people—both professionals and lay people—who failed to offer her support or pretended not to see the abuse. Sometimes, Sam interrupted any progress she made in reaching out for help or friendship. Seeking help from her religion resulted in mixed messages. One priest told her to stop associating with a friend who had a drinking problem or else she "couldn't expect" her marriage to work—a message that troubled Beth because it was contrary to sermons he made preaching kindness to those less fortunate. Sam also used the priest's admonition against Beth to blame her for their marital problems. Another priest, who counseled her a couple of years later, told her that she had grounds for a divorce (with the beatings and infidelities), and that "no man has the right to beat his wife" (p. 78).

Sam repeatedly threatened to take her kids away, saying that she would not be able to get custody, a very believable possibility because he had exclusive access to financial records, resources, and a steady job. Beth's geographic isolation from her family, as well as the suspiciousness Sam had about her friendships, are also typical of the circumstances many battered women face (Walker, 1979). Sam's constant put-downs whittled away her self-esteem. Sam's calculated destruction of Beth's pets and property further emphasized his power and control.

Beth believed, "With me totally dependent on him, there was no place I could even get milk on my own" (p. 34) and "If I could have gotten away from Sam financially, I would have gone" (p. 37). Economic dependency on the abuser is real. Battered women and their children, once they leave the abuser, often face poverty, short-term shelter stays, inadequate long-term housing options for low-income women, and generally inferior housing and marginal financial help (Hoff, 1990), all of which is exacerbated if the woman has minimal job skills and/or dependent children.

The fear of stigmatization—if the Air Force found out—and the threat of Sam's losing his benefits or job were strong enough to deter Beth from pursuing help. When the tendon in Beth's arm was cut during Sam's attempt to shove her hand down the running garbage disposal and Beth begged him to take her to the hospital, Sam threatened, "You get me in trouble and I'll fix your face. You get me kicked out of the military and I'll kill you" (p. 41). Once at the hospital, the doctors accepted the fake story of "an accident." This denial of the abuse by professionals and their failure to ask Beth herself what happened were omnipresent.

At the base, everybody saw Sam as a good guy, a leader, and they wouldn't intervene. Beth describes the runaround she received when attempting to obtain medical documentation, following an encounter with Sam's immediate supervisor, who said, "From what Sam's told me about you, I don't blame him for beating the hell out of you" (p. 121). Beth became "a good military wife," covering up for him. Sam continued to advance in his profession; he clearly wasn't "out of control" with other people for he was able to select who and when he would abuse, as well as being able to target the more hidden parts of Beth's body at times. For instance, when she was pregnant, Sam beat her in her chest, head, and stomach for over an hour, thus causing her to miscarry. When Sam began hitting Beth in his sleep, he shrugged it off as a "battle-ready reaction from Vietnam" (p. 34).

Sam's family did and said nothing to stop Sam *or* comfort Beth, after witnessing physical and verbal abuse for years. Beth's own parents reacted to Sam's violence initially by saying "You married him and your kids need a father, so you have to live with him" (p. 35). This unsupportive attitude changed later and her family *did* help her leave Sam on several occasions, but if she couldn't find steady employment, she returned—or was coerced with his threats of losing her kids—to Sam.

Calling the Police Will Only Make It Worse

Police, prosecutors, and judges have routinely trivialized battering of women by men, thus reinforcing the social message that this violent behavior is acceptable, that somehow the woman "deserved" it, that she provoked his anger, that she could do something if she really wanted to stop it, or that she was trying to garner some attention for herself (Karmen, 1982; Stanko, 1985). Beth learned to not count on the police for help. Regardless of jurisdiction, they told her to call *after* he got into the house and had his hands on her. The police took Sam's side and accepted his explanations, even when Beth's bruises were visible.

One time, after Sam had broken Beth's finger and continued to punch her, one of their sons woke up, and Sam grabbed him by the shoulders and took him to another room. Fearing that Sam would hurt the boy, Beth grabbed Sam's gun and told him to let the boy go. Sam complied, laughing, and took the gun away and left the house. Two military police officers came back with Sam, guns cocked at Beth, and arrested her, refusing to believe her story or allow her to get medical attention. Over time, Beth learned that calling the police would only make things worse with Sam, and she also feared that if Sam got into trouble with the military, he would kill her.

I Wonder Where I Got the Strength to Function

The image of the helpless passive victim, who "chooses" to remain in an abusive relationship, contributes to stereotypes that belie another truth, namely, that remaining in an abusive relationship can also be viewed as a survival struggle in which a woman is desperately trying to shield her children from harm, maintain daily tasks, and figure out how and when to safely make the break (see Miller & Forest, 1994). Beth observed early in her marriage that, "Clearly it was up to me to find a place to live, find a job, and take care of my kids" (p. 25). Despite all of these attempts to break Beth's spirit or thwart her flight, Beth remained innovative in her dealings with the violence and aftermath of the violence. She writes of an inner strength that prevented her from giving up by committing suicide. Throughout the book, she describes acts of resistance, some minor, some major, all acts that speak to a kind of rebellion and resiliency, and a fierce concern for her kids: "I used all my strength just to meet their daily needs. I just tried to hold on, get through one day at a time, and believe that everything would turn out alright in the end" (p. 55). For instance, she enrolled in college-level classes. At various points, Beth opened her own savings account or hid money from Sam (sewing it into her bras) and supported the family—buying groceries, paying the rent or heat, when Sam refused to do so. Beth canned 500 quarts of vegetables from her garden one summer and prepared baby food from scratch to deal with her son's food allergies. Working at all kinds of jobs, at all kinds of hours, negotiating around child care responsibilities, Beth simultaneously kept the house clean and had dinner on the table for her children and Sam. Beth said, "I desperately wanted to work, because I had no access to our money. For most of my life, I had been used to working and the freedom of having my own money" (p. 33). In fact, Beth continued to take good care of her children even when suffering pain, broken bones, and severe lacerations. She was able to fly her youngest son to a hospital specializing in acutely ill children, eating nothing herself for the week she was there, and sleeping in a chair because she had no money. She learned there how to treat him at home and drain his lungs—consequently saving his life several times. Beth also passed her GED exam and state certification test for an oxygen technician position in the same week: "Sam didn't have one word of encouragement or praise for me, but he couldn't erase these achievements either" (p. 80). Later, Beth even challenged her "feminist" lawyer when her case dragged on, ultimately firing her, and Beth also challenged her confinement to a psychiatric hospital following Sam's death.

For years, Beth was raped almost nightly or otherwise humiliated by her drunken husband, yet

> in spite of everything, I finished my spring semester classes with all As again, passed my driver's test, and got my license. Sam was not too pleased with that, and he was even less pleased when I told him I had put in some job applications. He made such a fuss, I gave up on that for the time being. (p. 40)

> I was overwhelmed with a bittersweet feeling—torn between wanting to believe that he loved me and the kids, but at the same time, doing without the bare necessities and remembering the beatings. (p. 59)

What do the acts of resiliency and resistance mean? Hoff (1990) argues that once researchers *and* the public reject the stigmatizing image of *victim,* battered women can be seen as survivors who "struggle courageously" with little network support (see pp. 229-230). As such, women are no longer seen as passive victims in an unequal power struggle with their male abusers, but as long-term survivors and crisis-managers (Hoff, 1990). This alternative conceptualization of battered women's experience challenges the deflating concept of "learned helplessness" (Gondolf, 1988).

I Just Prayed I Could Hang on Long Enough to Get My Kids Raised

Women who use self-defense against violent men generally are treated more harshly by the criminal justice system (Browne, 1987). Part of this disparity involves a cultural double standard that warns women not to step out of their proscribed gender roles and be violent (like men). The other part concerns the law of self-defense itself. As Gillespie (1989) persuasively argues, the law of self-defense was designed by men, for situations involving typical male action. The law was developed to handle two basic circumstances: a sudden attack by a stranger or a brawl that escalates (Gillespie, 1989). The underlying assumptions are that both participants enter willingly, that they are of roughly equal size and strength, and that the event is an isolated incident occurring in a public place between strangers or near strangers where withdrawal or escape is impossible. Most women who kill their abusive partners in self-defense, however, don't fit into these situations:

> Her assailant is neither a stranger nor someone with whom she has voluntarily engaged in a fist fight. . . . The situations [battered women] face are light years from the kind of pugilistic combats between gentlemen that the law contemplates. Men and women are not of equal size, strength, and fighting ability. . . . She was entirely at his mercy physically; she knew it, and he knew it. Once he made up his mind to start beating

> her, nothing she did, or could possibly do, would stop him. . . . Nor was this a one-time only episode between strangers, with no past history and no future. She knew, with painful certainty, that his threats were not idle barroom bluffs; he was able and more than willing to inflict horrible injuries on her. She knew that if she submitted to him and "took her punishment," that would not be the end of it: he would not just walk out of her life like a stranger after a bar fight. Their life together would go on as it had before; he would be free to shackle her and beat her at will, and she would be powerless to prevent it. (Gillespie, 1989, pp. 4 and 7)

For sixteen years, Beth lived this experience herself. Sam repeatedly threatened to take her kids and kill her. He threatened to stalk her if she left, telling her "You'd better watch every shadow, because I'll see your ass dead" (p. 77). He told her how excited he was by snuff films. He loaded and unloaded his gun around her, pointing the barrel at her without the safety catch. When she moved out, he broke into her apartment, made harassing and threatening phone calls, saying things like "I'll see you dead before I give you a penny" (p. 120). And Beth certainly could not match his size or strength. The coroner's report stated that

> the scratches and abrasions on Sam's forehead were "extremely superficial" and thus, "they certainly wouldn't have knocked him out . . . wouldn't have rendered him defenseless or unable to pursue the attack. . . ." The coroner further stated that Sam could have continued his attack . . . even after "an absolutely lethal wound . . ." (p. 202)

Yet despite these conclusions by the coroner and the judge's dismissal of the case, the district attorney appealed the dismissal of charges and charged Beth a second time in District Court for first-degree murder. The prosecutor's brief said, "The victim was not armed. The victim did not threaten or attack Beth." Not only is this version untrue, but it ironically captures the gender bias in self-defense standards.

Policy Implications

The incidents in Beth's story are useful for generalizing to battered women's overall situation. When the focus is on helplessness and passivity and asking why she didn't leave, victim images cloud the character of the battered woman and raise credibility questions regarding her competency to care for her children and retain custody. Beth's powerlessness and stigma, first as a victim of abuse and next as a "murderer," contributed to the relative ease with which the state intervened and took her children. As suggested by Mahoney (1994), "exit" from the abusive relationship should *not* be the only evidence of agency. Focusing on failure to exit ignores all other coping strategies and should not be the sole social and legal measurement of victim competence (Mahoney, 1994).

The criminal justice system repeatedly failed to respond adequately to Beth's cries for help. Until the mid-1980s, police reticence to arrest was commonplace, as police training and (in)action reflected the belief that what happens in the privacy of one's home should remain private. The battered women's movement and victim advocates fought to have police arrest batterers and hold offenders accountable for their violence. Following the Minneapolis experiment in 1984, which suggested that arrest was a stronger deterrent to repeat violence than crisis intervention or mediation, many states enacted mandatory arrest policies; at the same time, research was funded to evaluate pro-arrest policies, but the findings are inconclusive (see Symposium on Domestic Violence, 1992). Arrest, however, is only one component of the criminal justice system continuum, and arrest policies cannot exist in a vacuum and can be circumvented by the unresponsiveness of other components, such as prosecution (Elliot, 1989). There is some evidence to suggest that once the prosecution takes on the onus of charging under mandatory arrest policies, battered women feel more free from retaliation, *and* the batterers are held accountable for their behavior (Lerman, 1986).

Early intervention programs are necessary to break the cycle of violence, particularly, in the case of children, to prevent disciplinary trouble or delinquency or school truancy in the future. The likelihood of a person's behaving aggressively toward a partner is influenced by exposure to models of aggression, such as witnessing aggression between one's parents, having been the victim of parental aggression, fighting with siblings or friends, and accepting aggression as a response to problems (see Miller & Iovanni, 1994).

Following a comprehensive primary prevention program for wife assault and dating violence undertaken in a London, Ontario, school system, research found that both attitudes and knowledge changed, as well as behavioral intentions (Jaffe, Sudermann, Reitzel, & Killip, 1992). Proactive strategies, such as dating violence awareness programs targeted for high school populations, indicate some success; typically the programs involve students, their parents and teachers, police, courts, peers, and counselors. Evaluations show that these efforts help to demystify intimate violence; decrease victim blaming; empower victims; teach self-protective skills; encourage and facilitate victims' communication with mothers; identify, educate, and coordinate resource people; and provide support to victims through the legal process (Prato & Braham, 1991).

We are a competitive society, stressing winning at any cost, particularly for males whose socialization experiences reinforce competitiveness, superiority, and aggression through team sports and other activities involving male camaraderie (Franklin, 1984; Miedzian, 1991). Male socialization has taught men that some aggressive behaviors are valid, rewarding, and above scrutiny (Farr, 1988). We need to adopt programs in primary and secondary educational settings that challenge traditional gender-role expectations, stressing alternative conceptions of manhood that do not support battering and unequal power relations, enhancing women's self-esteem, and teaching that women are to be taken seriously and understood as equals.

It is hard to acknowledge that after twenty years of efforts to address and eradicate battering in our society, there still exist archaic attitudes and policies from the very people or places geared to help battered women. For instance, as Beth discovered, shelters designed to help battered women by offering a respite and legal and counseling services, are often full to capacity and turn away women who are in need of help; some even have policies that do not welcome mothers with teenage male children.

Many women who seek shelter from their abusive partners are also dependent on the abuser for economic resources. These women need opportunities to develop their own skills so that more choices are available to them. Shelters are generally short-term, stopgap measures that provide limited opportunities for this because most shelters do not have the funds to provide long-range training and housing for all who need it. One model residential program in Madrid, Spain, combines immediate crisis intervention with long-term refuge and job training programs. This model shelter houses thirty women and their children (with a required six-month stay, renewable up to eighteen months) and provides child care and medical care while the women attain educational and job training experience (see Miller & Barberet, 1994). Assistance is also given for job placement and housing assistance upon departure from the shelter.

Doctors, nurses, emergency room technicians, and other health care professionals need to have better training to recognize injuries of battered women and provide information about services. They need to know how to maneuver the situation to facilitate talking to victims/clients out of earshot of the man who brought them in, no matter how loving and solicitous he might be acting toward his partner in front of them.

Research efforts have addressed some of the consequences of criminal justice policies, such as mandatory arrest (Miller, 1989) but have moved away from asking the victims themselves about *what* assistance would be most helpful. Ferraro (1995) has noted elsewhere that current research on battering typically suffers from the limitations of the strictly positivistic, empiricist approach. Often, quantitative studies fail to adequately address women's lived experiences (see Mahoney, 1994; Smith, 1987), despite the fact that these women themselves are the experts on their situations. This kind of qualitative approach in this book, which permits Beth to tell her story in her own voice, offers a way of going beyond the pain of violence to illustrate personal struggles and triumphs (see also Hoff, 1990, and NiCarthy, 1987, for similar qualitative research presentations).

Conclusion

Beth's story illustrates the inability of institutions and social safety nets to provide more effective assistance and interventions for battered women. Beth consistently demonstrated strength and resilience in the face of her husband's violence and the ambivalence of those from whom she sought help.

No one deserves to be treated the way Sam treated Beth, nor to be so without options that—even though she acted in self-defense—Beth now lives "with the knowledge that I took a life, a life of the one person I loved the most" (p. 223). As we move into the twenty-first century, let us take the findings of researchers, the knowledge of practitioners, and the experiences of battered women seriously, and continue to challenge, directly and boldly, the cultural messages and systemic practices that tolerate battering in our society.

Rule Making and Enforcement/Rule Compliance and Resistance

Barbara J. Hart

> If we are to end violence against women, we must profoundly transform the relationship between men and women in this culture. We must engage all justice and human services systems in ending this domestic terrorism.
>
> Jeremy Travis, Director, U.S. National Institute of Justice, July 1995

Rule making and enforcement are universally practiced by men who batter their wives and intimate partners. Although the scope and detail of the rules vary, the imposition of extensive, egregious rules by batterers on their partners is certain, as is the belief in the inalienable prerogative of batterers to impose and enforce rules. The tactics used to enforce the rules are influenced by the life experience of the abused and the batterer; they always involve coercion, intimidation, degradation, exploitation, and violence.

All rules are not equal. Batterers create a hierarchy of rules with a concomitant hierarchy of enforcement measures. The four rules invariably most important to batterers are the following:

1. You cannot leave this relationship unless I am through with you.
2. You may not tell anyone about my violence or coercive controls.
3. I am entitled to your obedience, service, affection, loyalty, fidelity, and undivided attention.
4. I get to decide which of the other rules are critical.

Battered women, criminal justice personnel, advocates, and batterer service providers around the country describe detailed lists of rules. Although few write down the rules for the "instruction" of battered women, batterers repeatedly articulate the rules as a reminder of their power and the allegiance owed them.

One story is told of a batterer who wrote thirteen pages of rules, ranging from prohibitions against contact with anyone without his express permission to directives for sexual services to be performed for him, specifications about how meals were to be prepared and served, guidelines for devotion to him in public, and procedures to mask, from him and others, the hurt and injuries caused by his assaults and degradation.

Another is told of a batterer, incarcerated for his domestic abuse, who provided his partner with a weekly schedule of activities for the family and who persuaded his brother and oldest son to monitor and report on the battered woman's compliance with his directives. He also gave instructions for punishing her for noncompliance, the penalties being routinely inflicted by her teenage son. Yet another specified that the battered woman must not touch, bathe, feed, or dress their daughter and forbade the mother and child from speaking with each other except in his presence.

Most batterers are like Sam Sipe. They create rules to assure that their interests are more than ascendant. Their interests are the *only* ones to be honored or to which resources should be dedicated. The interests of the battered woman are subordinated to those of the abuser and are typically entertained when they also advance the interests of the batterer.

Although all batterers believe in their right to enforce these rules, they do not necessarily select the same tactics of control. Batterers usually tailor the quantum of enforcement to the seriousness of the infraction, the batterer himself being the sole arbiter of the degree of punishment merited by the breach. This weighing of the import of the rule and the punishment to follow is not, however, rational or even necessarily predictable. The hierarchy of rules often varies with the batterer's assessment of the centrality of the rule to his power over the abused woman and the amount of rage "provoked" by the violation.

Furthermore, batterers are often strategic about enforcement of these rules. They engage in a cost/benefits analysis in exacting punishment for violation. Men evaluate the risks and likely consequences of controlling and violent enforcement. They take into consideration "the intervention factor," recognizing that violent conduct is a much lower risk to them if undertaken in private, either where third parties are not aware of the violence or will not intervene. They take into account "the injury factor," minimizing the amount of injury intentionally inflicted and the visibility of the injuries to reduce the likelihood of adverse consequences. They also use "the efficacy factor," employing those enforcers that have proven most reliable.

Beyond this, batterers mitigate risk by engendering profound fear and humiliation in the battered woman to persuade her not to reveal the violent and degrading enforcement techniques used. They isolate battered women socially so that people who might intervene to protect are not aware of the violence and injuries. They cast aspersions on the moral character, parenting, and mental health of battered women to discredit them with those who might intervene. They develop a convincing repertoire of reasons to justify violent and coercive controls, shifting responsibility to battered partners for both the rules and enforcement. They appeal to cultural teachings about the propriety of male dominance and female subservience in marriage and relationships. In doing so, many batterers are highly ingratiating and persuasive.

Rule making, rule enforcement, and strategies to avoid accountability and to mitigate risk often work for men who batter, or at least work for a long time in the life of the marriage or relationship. Success at rule making and enforcement through violent tactics may be prolonged when a batterer carefully constrains his conduct and the context in which he inflicts violent controls. On the other hand, should the community and the legal system not intervene to stop the violence when it is publicly disclosed, batterers conclude that the risks are minimal and thereafter exercise less caution and inflict escalated, life-imperiling violence, believing that they can continue to act with impunity. In fact, batterers too often find that community institutions will aid and abet them in controlling and intimidating battered women. Sam Sipe apparently learned from the indifference and collusion of his family, employers, friends, religious leaders, neighbors, mental health professionals, justice system actors, and educators that he could do with Beth as he pleased.

But the picture would be incomplete without understanding the experience of battered women living with rule-making and enforcing batterers. Battered women are actively engaged in stopping the violence and seeking relief from it. Like Beth Sipe, many battered women may initially conclude that full compliance with the directives of the batterer may win his love or respect and stop the violence. However, women soon learn that full compliance is not a safeguard. Violent, degrading, and controlling conduct is inflicted by abusers at whim—because the batterer had a difficult experience at work, lost a softball game, is mad that his favorite television show has been canceled, has no money for a fishing license, lost in video games with the children, or because the battered woman went to church to teach her Sunday School class, refused to send the children to school when they were sick, baked cookies for the Little League fund-raiser, and so on.

As battered women realize that compliance will not achieve safety and as they determine that compliance with unreasonable, immoral, unfair demands diminishes their integrity and jeopardizes the well-being of the children, they begin to engage in strategic rule resistance. The deliberation process for the battered woman considering whether to comply or resist is complex. She considers some of the following questions: Do I care enough to resist? Is it safe, practical, or important to resist? Is this a rule that must be broken to retain my integrity and self-worth? Is this a demand that will fundamentally endanger my children or myself? Is there a way around the rule? Is it possible to trick the batterer into believing I have complied when I have not? Can I live with this duplicity? Can I negotiate a modification that is less onerous? How can I mitigate the consequences of compliance and of resistance? Which is better in light of all the circumstances of my life and the consequences? Can I resist at a time and in a place where others will support me and prevent the violence? How, then, can I avoid retaliation once these potential intervenors are not around? How can I change my daily routines to avoid contact with the abuser? How can I protect the children when they have contact with the batterer? How can I improve the other circumstances of my life so that the violence and coercive controls don't defeat me? Who can I enlist as allies in support of me or to intervene with the batterer? What do I want them to do? Is it ethical to ask others to help me? Aren't I betraying the batterer in disclosing his violence and coercion? Is the violence worse than any betrayal from disclosure? Can I stop him myself or do I have to involve others? What can I do or ask others to do to convince this man that he has to change or he will lose this relationship? What will work?

Sometimes the resistance is immediate, not the product of a deliberative process, for example, when battered women act to defend themselves or their children from physical and sexual violence.

The resistance strategies of battered women work best when supported by a community that is intolerant of the violence, acts to safeguard battered women and children, rejects notions of men's authority over women, intervenes to stop the violence, and helps men choose to forsake violent, degrading, and coercive practices and the beliefs that rationalize domestic terrorism.

When, like Beth Sipe, battered women are confronted with lay and professional persons who act in concert with the batterer, who blame battered women for the violence, or who are merely indifferent, they may begin to despair, sometimes concluding that "shutting down" emotionally and physically or complying, rather than acting to resist or achieve helpful intervention, will enable them to endure and perhaps survive.

As we approach the twenty-first century, it shocks the conscience that entire communities in this country, including the justice, education, religious, and human services systems, remain aligned with batterers in their rule making, enforcement, and terrorism. It is time that communities act consistently to eschew violence, to hold batterers solely responsible for their violent and coercive conduct, to safeguard battered women and children, to compel economic and social restitution by batterers, and to shoulder the responsibility for stopping the violence; tasks that have been borne too long and exclusively by battered women.

Beth Sipe and the Health Care System

Jacquelyn C. Campbell

I have stopped reading Beth Sipe's story just after she has been released on bail after her initial incarceration. Tears are running down my face, and all I can think is, How many times does this kind of story have to happen? How can we call ourselves a civilized, even moral country, and the women and children of this nation are *still* not safe from such physical harm and emotional savagery, even with increasing public awareness about the problem? And as a health care professional, what shame I feel that Beth and her sons were so badly served over and over again by a system whose nurses and doctors have vows to help and to heal.

I first came into contact with cases like Beth's in late 1975. How can it be that twenty years later, we are doing only marginally better? I used to think that—after hearing hundreds of such stories, from women themselves and from police homicide files of women who were killed—that I would get used to it, that I would no longer cry. I've learned that such callousness will never develop. So instead, I am determined that it *will* get better, that we in the health care system will join in partnership with shelter advocates and the criminal justice system, will continue to improve in effectively helping and protecting battered women and their children so that this kind of story will no longer happen, so that men like Sam are stopped long before they are killed.

As a health care professional, I will comment in this response on how Beth's story illustrates both the failures and the opportunities of the health care system in the struggle against domestic violence. Beth Sipe's story is unusual both in its horrors (probably the far end of the continuum in terms of severity of abuse and sadism of the perpetrator) and in its sheer numbers of missed opportunities by both the health care system and the military and civilian criminal justice system. At the same time, it is all too typical in its dynamics of the battering relationship and the general pattern of responses of those systems.

Horrifically abusive behavior like Sam's tends to escalate in severity and frequency over time. Other abusers actually desist, some apparently spontaneously or when the woman leaves early on (as did Beth from her first marriage) or when the batterer successfully completes batterer treatment or other action is taken (Campbell, Pliska, Taylor, & Sheridan, 1994; Feld & Straus, 1989). We are not clear as to the proportions of each kind of abusive relationship. However, all battering relationships are characterized by repeated physical and/or sexual assault within a context of coercive control (Campbell & Humphreys, 1993). Most experts agree that from 2 million to 4 million women are battered each year by their husbands, boyfriends, ex-husbands, or ex-boyfriends. At least 1,500 battered women are killed each year by their husbands (FBI, 1994), many more if boyfriends or former partners are included. Women who are separated or divorced are at increased risk of violence (Daly & Wilson, 1988).

All aspects of abuse (physical, sexual, and controlling, including emotional degradation) are important to the resultant effects on women's health and opportunities for interventions in the health care system. All forms of abuse have effects on women's health, and all can be seen as important aspects of Beth's story.

Sexuality and Reproduction

Beth's sexual abuse was a significant part of both her physical problems and the emotional impact of the abuse. Approximately 40% to 45% of physically abused women are also forced into sex (Campbell, 1989a; Russell, 1990). Beth's sexual abuse was similar to that reported by other battered women, both in terms of Sam's belief that he was entitled to sex with her whenever and however he wanted it—that he owned her body—and in the emotional and physical consequences for Beth (Campbell & Alford, 1989). The extreme shame and reluctance to disclose the sexual abuse—the last thing she told her therapist and an experience omitted from the first version of this autobiography—are congruent with my own study showing that battered women also subjected to sexual abuse have significantly lower self-esteem than those "only" experiencing physical assault (Campbell, 1989b). Also congruent with other studies was Beth's contracting of sexually transmitted diseases (STDs) and realistic fear of HIV/AIDS (Campbell & Alford, 1989; Eby & Campbell, 1995). Beth states, "I knew I was being raped, but because he was my husband, I thought he had the legal right." In fact, in Virginia and Utah in the 1970s, he *did* have that legal right (Russell, 1990).

Not only are women sexually abused by being forced into sex and physically hurt and brutalized as part of the sexual act, but they also are sexually abused by their partners' infidelity with other women, increasing their risk for STDs. Another related issue is that abused women often report, as did Beth, that batterers refuse to take responsibility for birth control, but paradoxically want to control childbearing decisions and may force or emotionally coerce women to have or not have an abortion (Campbell, Pugh, Campbell, & Visscher, 1995).

Early Assessment and Intervention

One of the principles of public health is that a problem such as domestic violence can be addressed at three levels. Primary prevention, prevention before the fact, is the earliest and ideal level, before any damage is done. Secondary prevention, identification and treatment in the earliest stages, can also prevent permanent damage. Catching a health problem early is a hallmark of the public health approach, which has been applied successfully to such health care problems as cancer and heart disease.

In its sexual assault aspects, the Sipes' case presented several opportunities early in the relationship when domestic violence could have been identified and addressed. Beth was seen very early in her relationship and diagnosed with venereal disease (chlamydia), given birth control, and seen again during her first pregnancy. All of these encounters should have included a routine assessment for abuse (Campbell & Humphreys, 1993; McFarlane & Bullock, 1991; Parker, McFarlane, et al., 1992). The question, "Does your husband (or partner) ever force you into sex" (or sexual activities) would have been a way of asking Beth about sexual abuse in a way to which she could relate (Russell, 1990).

About 16% of pregnant women are abused during pregnancy, a higher prevalence than other complications of pregnancy (Parker et al., 1992). Several complications of pregnancy—including low birthweight, insufficient weight gain, substance abuse, inadequate prenatal care, and premature delivery—have also been associated with abuse during pregnancy (Parker, McFarlane, & Soeken, 1994). Although physical violence did not occur during Beth's first pregnancy, emotional and financial abuse was a stressor. The sexual assaults she endured just prior to delivery may well have contributed to her high blood pressure and first pregnancy labor inducement; they clearly caused the episiotomy tearing after each delivery. At Beth's six-week checkup after James's delivery, she had bruises, vaginal, bladder, and uterine infections, and vaginal tearing. The physician "made no comment" (p. 21).

The connections between abuse during pregnancy and miscarriages have been clearly established by research. Sam wanted her to get an abortion when she thought she was pregnant when James was about seven months old. When she refused, he beat her so badly that she miscarried. Here was another lost opportunity on the part of the health care system for early assessment and intervention with Beth. At another point, Beth was diagnosed as "malnourished" during her pregnancy with Daniel, a condition related to both Sam's financial abuse (allowing very little money for the family) and the stress caused by Sam's sexual abuse. These factors may have contributed to Daniel's premature delivery, relatively small size, and infant health problems.

Battered women are frequently seen in emergency departments (EDs) for injuries related to abuse. In fact, depending on the method of survey, between 8% and 25% of female patients in EDs are abused by their male partner (McLeer, Anwar, Herman, & Maquilling, 1989; Stark, Flitcraft, & Frazier, 1979). On at least two occasions, Beth went to an ED with acute injuries, and on both occasions, Sam warned her specifically that if she told how she was hurt, he would kill her. Although the established prevalence of abuse-related injuries seen in EDs warrants routine screening of traumatized women for domestic violence, the reality of how much danger any disclosure may involve for these women must be taken into account by health care professionals.

Mandatory Reporting

The issue of mandatory reporting to police by health care professionals is relevant here. The state of California has passed a law formalizing such a mandate, and reporting is also now mandatory in military health care settings. Most advocacy and health care domestic violence organizations have advised against such mandates precisely because of such threats and the chance that such reporting may endanger women's safety and decrease the chances that abused women will turn to health care professionals for help because of their fears of such reporting (Family Violence Prevention Fund, 1995). Confidentiality has always been one of the hallmarks of interactions with the health care system, and it is one of the reasons women may feel they can turn there for help. In addition, mandated reporting fails to recognize women's autonomy in making their own decisions about pursuing their options through the criminal justice system.

The military mandated reporting may be especially problematic because of the effect on men's military careers if domestic violence is on their record. In fact, Sam's threats when Beth went to the ED were specifically about his fear of jeopardizing his career. As long as an abused military wife has hope for the marriage, she will be extremely reluctant to hurt her husband's career by reporting the abuse, even though this situation also gives her leverage. Some military installations have mandated health care professionals to report suspected woman abuse to Family Assistance personnel, who will keep the first offense confidential as long as the perpetrator enters (and completes) batterer treatment. This appears to be an excellent strategy, leveraging career pressure to mandate intervention with a clear consequence for subsequent offenses.

Conditions That Appear Unrelated

Another lesson regarding assessment and intervention in Beth's story is her recounting of a visit to the ED not for an injury but for a migraine headache. Frequently unrecognized in many health care problems are the effects of domestic violence, even when no obvious injury is present. A condition such as migraine headaches may be caused by the stress of the abuse or aggravated by the situation. Although a direct link with migraine headaches has not been established, one study found chronic pain to be the primary reason that domestic violence survivors sought health care in an ED (Goldberg & Tomlanovich, 1984). Increased risk for other stress-related physical conditions, such as chronic irritable bowel syndrome, has been established by other studies (Drossman, Leserman, Nanhman, et al., 1990). Beth also had hypertension, another medical condition with known stress components that has not been established as directly resulting from domestic violence. Another sequela of stress is suppression of the immune system. Although we cannot be certain from Beth's story, she seems to have experienced an unusually high number of infections.

Just as medical research has not yet or only recently established links between domestic violence and specific health care problems, so do battered women often fail to make that connection. Therefore, health care professionals need to conduct abuse assessments with *all* females seeking health care interventions, rather than waiting for a certain profile or set of symptoms to appear or waiting for the women themselves to make that link.

Beth's history also reminds us of the need to ask about domestic violence in privacy. She describes having extensive and visible scar tissue and damage in her anal area from the sexual abuse, which was noticed by her physician during her workup for endometriosis. She says, "the doctors asked me pointed questions about anal sex . . . with Sam standing there" (p. 85), so that she clearly could not be honest about her abuse.

In Beth's story, I counted at least twenty encounters with the health care system for major *physical* health problems. These ranged from pneumonia (twice), to myocarditis (infection around the heart), cystic breast disease, complications of pregnancy, endometriosis, several surgeries (including surgery for hemorrhoids that may have been related to the sexual abuse), and hepatitis. She also reports losing consciousness several times during beatings, after which it appears she never had a complete neurological workup. Beth also describes frequent stress-related vomiting and weight loss.

Such an extensive medical history is unusual for a relatively young woman, but it reflects statistics that show battered women (and their children) use health maintenance organization medical services six to eight times more often than nonabused women (Rath & Jarrett, 1990). Other studies also show battered women with significantly more stress-related physical problems than women who are not battered (e.g., Campbell, 1989a).

The lessons for the health care system are that a complicated and extensive medical history warrants a particularly careful assessment for domestic violence and that appropriate interventions for domestic violence at the secondary prevention level can decrease health care costs later. Another lesson is how important it can be to make accurate medical documentation of the abuse. Beth had a great deal of trouble getting access to her medical records after Sam's death. How much more empowering it would be if battered women were told of the potential usefulness of medical documentation of battering and exactly how to access those records!

Mental Health Issues

Beth was seen in a variety of settings for mental health concerns. As she stated so eloquently, "my emotional pain was even greater than the physical pain" (p. 41). She was prescribed tranquilizers after James's birth and then (on Sam's orders) faked a suicide attempt and was hospitalized. Depression is the most common affective response to battering; as a result, abuse is considered a significant risk factor for suicide (Gleason, 1993; Stark & Flitcraft, 1991). All women, especially those depressed and/or having made a suicide attempt, should be carefully screened for domestic violence. Certainly any relationship violence should be addressed in the treatment of depression and taken into account in the prescription of medications for mental health problems. Beth also saw a psychiatrist when she first separated from Sam, a point in time when appropriate intervention to stop the abuse could have made a tremendous difference.

Beth's children also demonstrated the effects of battering. They were described as "cranky and nervous," and they exhibited school problems, bed-wetting, nightmares, asthma, and substance abuse (James, at age ten). Such health and behavior problems in children have been documented as linked to battering of their mothers (Jaffe & Wolf, 1989) and should prompt an assessment of the child's exposure to violence if noted by health care professionals and/or school personnel.

The overlap between child abuse and wife abuse is noted in several studies (e.g., Straus & Gelles, 1990b) and illustrated by Beth's story. Matt was another man's child and therefore particularly at risk. Sam kicked him through a window and otherwise abused him. There was also an incident of child neglect: Daniel ate cigarettes when Sam was not properly supervising him. Still another incident occurred when Sam "slapped" Daniel, then an infant, *in front of a nurse practitioner* and yelled at Beth, calling her a "vicious little bitch." Whenever health professionals suspect child abuse, they need also to assess for wife abuse (and the reverse).

Conclusion

In summary, I found it difficult to fathom how we in the health care system could have missed so many opportunities to be helpful to Beth. I find it incomprehensible that the surgeon who operated on her nose could have failed to inquire carefully, gently, and appropriately as to exactly how it had been struck so that the cartilage had again separated from the bone. I find it inexplicable that the surgeon who operated on her breasts could not recognize that she had been beaten there postoperatively to cause the kind of damage she describes. At the same time, I know from research and other battered women's stories, that health care professionals often seem blind to obvious as well as subtle signs of abuse.

We are doing a better job at including indicators of abuse in the basic curricula for health care professionals and in continuing medical and nursing education programs. We need to develop and test better interventions for the health care system so that professionals feel confident that their interventions will be useful. We also need to change health care policy so that domestic violence assessment and interventions are mandated, legitimatized, and paid for.

Beth's story is incredibly eloquent as a story of abuse, but it is also significant in terms of its lessons for those of us in the health care system. We often see women for regular health care visits when they are first starting to be battered, often not for problems resulting from their abuse. If we routinely assess for abuse, we may be able to help the woman recognize it sooner and get help before the pattern becomes entrenched. Later in abusive relationships, we will see women both for injuries and for stress- or injury-related physical conditions. We will also see them in mental health settings and see their children for a variety of health problems. There are a wealth of opportunities to assess abuse and intervene to stop it. If the health care system can work in conjunction with the criminal justice and shelter system, there will be fewer stories like Beth's. We owe her an apology, an apology that we can make meaningful only by changing our policies and practice with women in the future.

"Let's Get Out; I Can't Stand It Here Anymore"

Jeffrey L. Edleson

Beth Sipe's story is very moving, even for those of us who have long worked in this field. I am always shocked by what battered women are forced to endure. But then again, after working in the field for any length of time, one is not at all surprised at what Beth and women like her have to endure during their relationships and even after their partners' deaths. Parts of Beth's story are heard every day in the over 1,200 battered women's shelters in this country.

Beth's story is also one shared by her three sons as they grew up in a terror-filled environment. Their feelings are encapsulated in Daniel's statement at the end of Chapter 8, which is the title of this commentary: "Let's get out; I can't stand it here anymore." Reading this story often brought my thoughts back to my own two sons and how a parent's behavior affects their development. I want to respect the Sipe children's desire for privacy by turning my attention away from their specific stories and by focusing more generally on battered women's efforts to protect their children, on the high degree of overlap between child maltreatment and woman battering in the same families, on the effects of witnessing violence on a child's development, and on both battered women and abusive men as parents.

Battered Women's Efforts to Protect Children

Battered women's stories often elicit questions asking why she stayed. Beth answers clearly that she stayed in large part for her children's well-being. Whether one agrees or not with her judgment, it is clear that Beth felt that staying in her relationship with Sam was the best for her children's safety and economic well-being. It was clear that Sam and others didn't allow much room for alternative choices.

Several published studies tend to support the fact that Beth is not the only battered woman who has taken many active steps to protect her children despite unpredictable violence and the effects such violence had on her and her children. Hilton's (1992) study of twenty battered women found that many of them were deeply concerned for their children. In fact, almost one third of the women interviewed remained with their abusers out of concern for their children. Women stayed, despite the violence, in order to ensure necessary financial support for their children or because of threats by their violent partners to harm the children and wage lengthy custody battles if they did leave. Beth's experience was much the same.

A study of battered women's decisions to leave their violent partners (Syers-McNairy, 1990) found that women go through a process of reevaluation before leaving their abusive partners. Over half the women interviewed in this study cited concern for their children as the major factor that led to reevaluating their relationships. Beth went through this same process of re-evaluation over the years. She understood that the environment at home was becoming increasingly dangerous for her children and took steps to create an alternative for them, against great odds.

Battered mothers face many new challenges when they leave their abusers and create a new home for their children. Bilinkoff (1995) suggests four areas of parenting with which battered women struggle as they work to establish their parental role independent of an abusive partner: reasserting appropriate power and control with children; making up for an often absent father; relying upon children as allies or confidants; and seeing a father's behavior reflected in one or more children. Beth's task of reestablishing herself as a parent was made all the more difficult by Sam's manipulation of rewards for the child who lived with him and punishment of the other who resided with Beth.

Woman Battering and Child Maltreatment

The Sipe children are not alone in having to endure abuse similar to their mother's. Estimates of the number of abused children who live in homes where their mothers are also being physically abused are uniformly high. For example, child protection workers in the Massachusetts Department of Social Services (Hangen, 1994) reported statewide that an average of 32.5% of their cases also involved domestic violence. A somewhat higher estimate was obtained in Straus and Gelles's 1985 national survey of over 6,000 American families (see Straus & Gelles, 1990a). They found that 50% of the men who frequently assaulted their wives also frequently physically abused their children. They also found that mothers who were beaten were at least twice as likely to physically abuse their children as were mothers who were not abused. Walker's (1984) study of 400 battered women revealed that 53% of the fathers and 28% of the mothers physically abused their children.

Child abuse studies also show that although the majority of perpetrators are women, perpetrators of the most severe forms of child abuse are men. Pecora, Whittaker, Maluccio, Barth, and Plotnick (1992) reviewed several sets of data and concluded that "most families involved in child fatalities were two-person caretaker situations where a majority of the perpetrators were the father of the child or the boyfriend of the mother" (p. 110). Data on sixty-seven child fatalities in families previously identified by the Massachusetts Department of Social Services found that twenty-nine (43%) were in families where the mother also identified herself as a victim of domestic violence (Felix & McCarthy, 1994).

The risk of violence toward mothers and children continues during separation and after divorce, raising concerns about safe custody visitation arrangements (see Saunders, 1994). Beth found this to be true in Nevada, and Minnesota police reported that almost half (47%) of battered women were victimized by an ex-spouse or friend, exceeding the percentage of those married to their abuser (44%) (Minnesota Department of Corrections, 1987). A quarter of the women in another study (Leighton, 1989) reported threats against their lives during custody visitations. Women are, in fact, at a greater risk of homicide when they have separated from their partners (Wilson & Daly, 1993).

Effects of Witnessing Violence

In most states, the majority of people residing in battered women's shelters are children. Battered women have always fled with their children, and as in Beth's case, sometimes they will not seek safe shelter if their children cannot accompany them.

The most widely cited estimates of the number of children who witness violence (but are not themselves abused) come from the works of Carlson and Straus. Somewhere between 3.3 million (Carlson, 1984) and 10 million (Straus, 1991) children in the United States are said to be at risk of witnessing woman abuse each year.

"Witnessing" abuse may involve a variety of experiences for a child. It may involve viewing or hearing an actual violent event, as well as seeing the aftermath (e.g., injuries to mother, police intervention) of such violence.

There is a small but growing literature on the effects of witnessing violence at home. Studies have found that child witnesses exhibit more aggressive and antisocial as well as fearful and inhibited behaviors (Christopherpoulos et al., 1987; Jaffe, Wilson, & Wolfe, 1986), and show lower social competence than other children (Wolfe, Zak, Wilson, & Jaffe, 1986). Children who witnessed violence were also found to show more anxiety, depression, and temperament problems (Christopherpoulos et al., 1987; Forsstrom-Cohn & Rosenbaum, 1985; Holden & Ritchie, 1991; Hughes, 1988; Westra & Martin, 1981), less empathy and self-esteem (Hinchey & Gavelek, 1982; Hughes, 1988), and lower verbal, cognitive, and motor abilities (Westra & Martin, 1981) than children who did not witness violence at home. There is also some support for the hypothesis that children from violent families of origin carry violent and violence-tolerant roles to their adult intimate relationships (Cappell & Heiner, 1990; Rosenbaum & O'Leary, 1981; Widom, 1989).

Several recent studies have also linked youth violence in the community to witnessing violence at home. For example, Carlson (1990) found that males who witnessed spouse abuse were significantly more likely to use violent behavior than nonwitnesses, but that there were no significant differences for females. DuRant, Cadenhead, Pendergrast, Slavens, and Linder (1994) found the strongest statistical predictor of the use of violence by 225 urban black adolescents was their previous exposure to violence and victimization.

There is no consensus whether witnessing violence is a form of child abuse and neglect. Does witnessing violence involve mental and emotional injury, a reportable form of child abuse in the majority of U.S. jurisdictions (Younes & Besharov, 1988)? Child witnessing is reported to Child Protection Services in some jurisdictions, and sometimes children are placed in temporary care outside of a home if the mother discloses she is a victim of domestic violence. In other localities, the mother's victimization is not a determining factor in out-of-home placements, and a child who witnesses domestic violence is seldom reported to authorities.

Abusive Men as Fathers

Peled (1993) found that "children's relationships with their fathers were the single most problematic and difficult aspect of their adjustment to changes in the aftermath of violence" (p. 173). All the children Peled interviewed experienced long separations from their fathers. How children came to understand their relationships with abusive fathers varied depending on a variety of factors, for example, whether the father was their biological parent or a stepfather or boyfriend. All children had to deal with both "bad" and "good" views of their abusive fathers. Many found ways to deemphasize the violence in contrast to other aspects of their relationships with their fathers.

Mathews (1995) suggests that failing to work with abusive fathers in tailored programs aimed at changing their parenting styles is an often-missed opportunity to help children. The reality is that many fathers, regardless of their abusiveness, will maintain visitation with and even custody rights over their children. Mathews (1995) has described a parenting program developed specifically for batterers by the Amherst H. Wilder Foundation in St. Paul, Minnesota. Too seldom are an abusive father's parenting skills addressed in other batterer treatment programs.

Another strategy aimed at improving safety for women and children as well as increasing the father's parenting skills has been the development of supervised visitation centers in which battered women may safely exchange children during a father's visit, batterers may visit with their noncustodial children, and both parents may individually learn—through supervised experiences—new styles of parenting. One of the first such centers is the Duluth Visitation Center in Duluth, Minnesota (see McMahon & Pence, 1995).

It is sad that Sam Sipe was never pressured or persuaded to seek help through a batterer's program. It may have benefited Sam, Beth, and her children. Had a supervised visitation center been available, some of Sam's violence might also have been curbed.

Conclusion

The danger to which women and children are exposed in their homes is still not taken seriously by many family members, friends, and professional helpers. It is inexcusable that people hesitate to help battered women or even actively block their efforts to gain safety. There were so many opportunities to avoid the horrible outcome of this story. So many times Beth attempted to elicit the help of others, and so many times we all failed her.

Informal and professional helpers' reluctance to come to battered women's aid reflects deeply ingrained social biases against women and sadly contributes to maintaining intimate violence at epidemic levels in this country. In the Sipes' case, Sam rarely received a message from any intervenor that his behavior was illegal or inappropriate or would not be tolerated. This tended to reinforce Beth's isolation and give Sam license to endlessly increase the severity of his violence toward her.

Beth was confronted with many more horrors after Sam's death, but she is still very lucky the nightmare ended so soon after his death. The National Clearinghouse for the Defense of Battered Women (1995), located in Philadelphia, estimates that about 2,000 women—one of three women in prison for homicide—have been convicted of killing an intimate partner. They also estimate that from 59% to 67% of these women were being abused by their partner at the time of the killing. Beth's story is most likely similar to many of these women's stories.

Reflections on Our Work With Battered Women

Deborah D. Tucker

I was very moved by the experiences of Beth and her children, both by the uniqueness of their particular struggle and the familiarity of so much of what they went through. The experiences relayed by battered women often begin to run together for those of us who have had the opportunity to really hear women describe them. What a gift to have this strong woman share with us who she was and what she felt, all the way from childhood to the aftermath of sixteen years of incredible violence, and to know that she and her children have survived to make lives for themselves.

No words can be better than hers to describe what she felt, and her plain-spoken manner of relaying physical, psychological, and sexual violence powerfully illuminates the all-encompassing nature of woman battering. No one approach satisfied Sam in his need for complete power and control of Beth. All forms of violence were employed, as were the tactics of intimidating, economically abusing, using the children, minimizing, denying, blaming, and threatening, all of which we have come to see as the essential elements of a battering relationship. The domination and degradation that Beth survived is representative of the struggles faced by women throughout America.

Unfortunately, the fact that Beth's marriage ended through Sam's death is also too common, and it shows how domestic violence services must be improved and made more responsive to the real needs of victims. It is my hope that shelter staff, board members, and volunteers, as well as other direct providers of services, will read Beth's story and reexamine the effectiveness of programs and services.

We derive our real strength as a movement from the philosophy that what women want from us guides our programs. In this essay, I want to address those whom I think will read and benefit most from this book—those working in the battered women's movement as well as other allied professionals who actually see and talk with more battered women than we who work in shelters do. Finally, I want to discuss the military policies and belief systems that support rather than confront woman abuse; these are illuminated quite clearly in this book. The starkness of the military callousness to Beth and her children is only a sharper vision of what we see within the civilian world. Much more must be done by military and civilian institutions to intervene effectively in and prevent domestic violence.

Battered Women's Movement

Beth indicates that she called the domestic violence hot line on Friday, April 8; the incident resulting in Sam's death occurred on Saturday, April 9. Beth tells us that she was listened to, but not much could be done because the boys were too old to be admitted to the shelter, and she wasn't willing to leave without them. Programs throughout the country have adopted policies limiting the age of boys who may be admitted with their mothers to emergency shelters. This policy grew from concerns that older boys from violent homes often represented a threat to the safety of others within the shelter, particularly younger children.

Beth's experience reveals the tension many shelters around the country confront when making a choice between serving a woman and her children's need for safe shelter and protecting other shelter residents from the very real dangers that young men raised by violent fathers may present. This issue will become more important as shelters increasingly benefit from funds being channeled to the states through the Violence Against Women Act and other public funding sources. Federal and state policies prohibit limiting or denying services on the basis of age. Shelters across the country would be well-advised to revisit any policies that discriminate on the basis of age.

Women serving in Texas prisons for offenses against their battering partners have named their group WAVE—Women Against Violent Endings. These women have helped us to understand that they perceived battered women's shelters in much the same way as the other bureaucracies from which they sought help or information. This is, of course, a real disappointment to us. We must be ever vigilant about that which is clearly within our responsibility and acknowledge our shortcomings. Our deficiencies can include the way we ourselves choose to describe our programs in the public media and the policies we adopt.

We have learned from the women in WAVE that shelter names are often very off-putting to battered women. If we call ourselves the Family Crisis Center or Family Violence Center, or describe ourselves in our public materials without demonstrating our commitment to helping women, we may inadvertently give the message that we view the problem as that of a dysfunctional family rather than an act of violence being committed by one person against another. Battered women are so often burdened with the belief that if they could just do something differently (or everything differently), the abuse would stop. We need to let them know—before they risk calling our hot lines or arrive at the front door—that we are advocates for them and we do not believe that the abuse they have suffered is due to their failures as wives or mothers. I believe our public education approaches must move beyond the question, Why does *she* stay? to Why does *he* hit?

I know we worry about the discussion of battering of men, and of women being violent, too. We worry that funders will see us as radicals and won't support us. I often discuss this topic with local shelter directors and boards, as well as with my sister coalitions' staffers. In reality, if the Federal Bureau of

Investigation is correct that 95% of the reported cases of domestic assault are committed by men against women, and the other 5% includes homosexual partnerships as well as defensive assaults committed by women against men, then we get down to a very small number of cases that might in fact represent acts of violence committed by women against men. As Ellen Pence, Michael Paymar, and the other incredible folks in Duluth at the Domestic Abuse Intervention Project (DAIP) have shown us, there are very few cases in which a male who is being battered is truly afraid to leave, or where, when he does try to get out of the relationship, he is subject to the same escalation of threats and violence that battered women often experience. We do need to be responsive to these victims and to encourage men to become involved in providing assistance to their brothers in these circumstances. But our organizational names or our advertising and promotion should not lead women to think that we practice couples counseling or other victim-blaming approaches. Can we be confident, as Congress was in passing the Violence Against Women Act? Can we be creative in communicating our mission so as to include same-sex battering victims and battered men (few though they may be), while still reaching the women who have so often asked others for help and may fail to ask us without reassurance of our intent?

Finally, I submit that in this country, success is often equated with financial resources. Do we in the shelter movement not have much greater money, resources, volunteers, and community involvement than ever before? We have been successful, not because we are well-hidden wolves in sheep's clothing, but because we "run with the wolves," and our mission of ending violence against women is supported by battered women and our communities. When we do what we set out to do, we gather allies who know full well who we are. It is much more dangerous to set aside our passion, to "run with the poodles" and become part of the problem. Without battered women who will help us to advocate for effective public policy, raise funds, and design responsive programs, we will never attract public and private support. And battered women will never join us or will leave our side if they see us as institutions more concerned with ourselves than our ultimate goals. Money is power and more money should not co-opt us; it should encourage us to continue to tell the truth about the dynamics of family violence and its connection to sexism.

Other policies that we all struggle with, policies that affected Beth, are limits on length of stay and the reporting of child abuse. Beth indicated that in 1976, she fled to a shelter, taking her youngest son with her and returning later for the older children. Matt had a black eye caused by Sam, and the shelter reported that abuse to the authorities. Beth indicates that she was concerned about the abuse being reported, and the investigator ultimately accepted Sam's story that his son was injured by a softball. She tells us that she "caught hell when my time at the shelter ran out and I had no place to go except back to Sam" (p. 69).

With regard to the practice of limiting the length of stay within a shelter, certainly we all understand the tremendous need and how frequently we must turn away women and children who are in danger due to lack of space within our facilities. We must repeat in public, to funders and lawmakers, the number of women and children we had to turn away due to lack of space. We must also look at the other end of our services and provide transitional housing for women who are clear that they must, for themselves and their children, separate permanently from the batterer. These women, as we all know, often need more than the two- to four-week stays our policies permit.

Battered women's shelters also need to reexamine their own investment in length-of-stay policies. Do we pit battered women against each other by placing strict limits on lengths of stay? Placing guilt on a woman because she and her children may be keeping someone else from getting help is most obvious when we are hung up on our house rules and making sure everyone is complying equally with required chores or our program approach. Whose needs are we meeting when we terminate a woman and force her and her children to leave the shelter for failing to attend support groups or to do chores?

Beth demonstrated two things to me most strongly. First, that she would work as hard as was necessary to feed, clothe, and house her children. Second, that her dedication to those children kept her motivated to survive, even in her darkest moments of abuse, and even after the threat of the abuse had been removed and the remorse almost swallowed her. She kept going. Beth and women like her are the ones we must put forward in our communities to explain that having a twenty-five- or even a fifty-bed shelter is not enough. Long-term stays must be possible until legal measures can be taken or enough money accumulated for her and the children to depart safely. We can't let ourselves or our communities off the hook by accepting an inadequate response. Only by keeping open minds and hearts will we help women escape violence and raise up a society that abhors it.

Allied Professions

Reform of Child Protective Services (CPS) and the manner in which child abuse complaints are handled by those agencies and law enforcement is central to the work of this movement. We must look at the betrayal of women and children that occurs every day when reports are made. The investigations seem more often to place the victims at greater risk of harm than to result in consequences for the abusers.

I believe that the basic structure of CPS is inherently the problem. CPS staff are perceived as "the people who take your kids away" and not the agency that stops violence against children and holds perpetrators accountable for their behavior. I believe CPS should be redesigned, either to employ only specialized workers to conduct investigations or to use law enforcement units to gather evidence of whether or not a crime has been committed. If no crime has occurred or can be substantiated, then caseworkers trained to provide assistance to the family could be assigned to work with them. These caseworkers would have a "clean slate" with the family and could be considered trustworthy.

When abuse of a child is substantiated, one of the first questions must be, Is the woman also being abused? When investigators, be they CPS or law enforcement, fail to take into account the woman's vulnerability to abuse and instead treat the parents together as "the parental unit," they are failing the child. The best way to protect a child from abuse is to protect his or her mother from abuse. In Texas, the lowest estimate of any studies done of the incidence of both woman and child abuse existing together has been 45%. If we can say that half of the cases currently being investigated by CPS involve abuse of women, and in most of those cases, CPS is doing nothing to assist the women, then this system is failing women and children, and we must advocate for change.

If CPS sees that its mission to stop and prevent abuse of children necessitates a partnership with us, we will have achieved something as remarkable as the establishment of 1,200 shelters for battered women and their children in less than twenty years. To do that, we must get at the underlying beliefs that separate us. Battered women widely distrust CPS. And can you blame them? Why should a battered woman trust a caseworker when the word on the street is not that this person can help you and your children to safety, but is "if you can't keep your kids safe, then we'll take them away"? This challenge seems insurmountable to us some days, yet think back to how the law enforcement community viewed us and domestic violence ten years ago. Because we focused so much of our energy on training and policy change through legislation and local advocacy, law enforcement has become our strongest ally in many communities. The same commitment must be made to CPS.

We have achieved progress with the criminal justice system. We have also seen a groundswell of interest from professionals in social services, mental health, the medical community, attorneys, clergy, and educators. This is vitally important because battered women usually seek help from these "outside professionals" before approaching shelters or other domestic violence programs. We estimate in Texas that 4% of the women being battered come to the shelter as residents or nonresidents for legal information and support. More than 20% of women call the police or seek legal help, and the vast majority of women talk to a minister, a counselor, nurse or doctor, teacher, or someone they perceive to have information and advice for them.

We must put more resources into preparing all professionals for these encounters. Law enforcement personnel no longer deny that at least 30% of their street time goes to domestic violence. In fact, some think the proportion is greater. Other professionals in emergency rooms or in mental health clinics are starting to notice what an incredible percentage of their cases involve domestic violence. The best thing that happened to move the battered women's movement ahead during the Reagan years was Surgeon General C. Everett Koop's assertion that intentional injury to women through rape and domestic violence represents a significant health problem—an epidemic. This announcement brought requests for training, materials development, policy analysis, and collaboration in combating violence against women.

In conjunction with our efforts to handle the success of being discovered by these professions, we must also ask them to assist us by going back to the colleges, universities, or other settings in which they obtained credentials for the positions they now hold. All of us within and without the battered women's movement must seek to influence the preparation various professionals receive to do their work and to reduce the time it takes for each profession to hear battered women and to examine their profession's role in decreasing this experience so common in our society.

Beth stated that her minister's support and reinforcement that no husband has the right to beat his wife was so important to her. This was valuable, but shortly after, he informed her that he would no longer visit their home because Sam was a "heathen." Something is severely lacking when ministers are not really trained in the dynamics of violence and do not understand that comfort for the victim is only the first step. We must also have their help to confront the behavior of the batterer, to educate their congregation and the community to the lengths that batterers will go to isolate the family.

Beth also mentioned how she and Sam went for marriage counseling after a particularly brutal beating in 1973. Both counselors offered practical suggestions that might have reduced the conflicts in a nonviolent marriage. But neither counselor addressed Sam's violence and alcoholic behavior. Beth drew some comfort from the counselors, but Sam dismissed them as "outsiders" and "just a bunch of bull" (p. 36). Today, knowledgeable counselors would not see them as a couple until Sam had completed his own programs to eliminate his violence and drinking problems. We must continue to spread the word in the mental health field until all those in practice are knowledgeable about how to work with domestic violence. Only through prevention and early appropriate intervention can we hope to avert such tragic endings.

Beth was very fortunate to have Evelyn, the woman who became her counselor and true friend. Evelyn listened to Beth closely and was able to modify her practice based on Beth's needs. Evelyn was respectful of Beth in ways both large and small, educating her and accompanying her at difficult moments. Evelyn went beyond what most counselors are willing to do and became an advocate for Beth.

Battered women are very rarely rendered helpless, and many in the domestic violence field have rejected the use of the term *learned helplessness* to describe battered women's responses. Usually, like Beth, battered women continually struggle to meet the challenges of violence, medical problems, bills to be paid, and children to parent. Like Beth, they often reach for more education and better work, however long it takes. The forces used against Beth by this one man were joined by so many others. Beth was truly a survivor of this man's violence, not someone who learned helplessness.

Military Services

We talk about denying how lethal men can be to women; no one does it better than the U.S. military. After growing up in an Air Force family, then having the opportunity to work with people from all branches and to do specialized training on domestic violence for the military, I have come to understand that some of my original assumptions about the military's response to violence against women were naive.

I first thought that the military's hard work to eliminate racism would help them to see that ending sexism is also essential to the future. I also knew that the Family Advocacy Program is federally funded 400% more than the civilian world to combat domestic violence: $40 is spent per military service and family member for every ten cents per civilian in the population. I expected that greater resources would mean greater understanding of the problem and that some of the solutions that are being proven to work would be employed.

Sadly, I found a culture that has not embraced much change. There are still military clubs with belly dancers and stripteases. Even though the new vernacular is *spouse,* many seem to find it impossible to use that term and refer to a service member's wife as his *dependent.* Military personnel still use the sentence Sam used, "If the military had wanted me to have a wife, they would have issued me one" (p. 23). This lets women know that this supposedly family-oriented organization still teaches that they are "surplus baggage."

All the training given to ameliorate the effects of family violence and other significant problems like alcohol abuse are couched in the need to reduce distractions from the soldiers' ability to concentrate on performing the mission. Although many large employers have initiated employee assistance programs for much the same reason, few are incorporating them into a culture that has told women and children they are part of the employer's community as well. When performance awards or other achievements are given out, the military recognizes that the spouse has contributed to the individual's success, but when that spouse is being battered, this attitude flips around on her to become blaming—somehow, if something is going wrong, it must be her fault.

Until very recently, most within the military were trained to see family violence as a relationship or communication problem. What is she doing that is causing him to behave this way? Many hold the beliefs that we have worked so hard to eradicate, such as "some women like being hit" and "men hit women because they won't shut up" or "women provoke men to violence." As policy is changing and men who commit acts of violence are experiencing consequences—including occasional court-martial—Sam's threat of "you get me kicked out of the military and I'll kill you" (p. 41) is not an uncommon one for battered military wives to hear. It is a difficult shift for the military to make: Official policy states that family violence is wrong, but all the belief systems that seem to make the behavior understandable cannot be challenged.

For example, military men are responsible for the behavior of their wives and children. Any "infraction" committed by a member of the family reflects on the service member. How can a man who can't control his family control his troops? This attitude underscores quite clearly the support of the military culture for a man's having undisputed power and control in his family.

Military men who batter are truly surprised when they are arrested or punished for abusive behavior because it has been viewed for so long as an entitlement, even a responsibility. Total control of the money is expected by both the military and civilian batterer, and practices of the military can severely limit a battered woman's ability to survive. Beth talked of the difficulty she had in receiving the allotment pay while Sam was in Vietnam, and in obtaining medical or base exchange services when her military ID card was taken. It is common practice for batterers to control access to the military ID card as a way to limit their victims' contact with family or base command functions, information, or services. Practices like requiring Beth to live away from the base are very common in order to decrease potential contact with others. Soldiers who have training in weapons and commonly keep weapons in their homes are particularly frightening to their partners. Yet, rarely will the weapon of a soldier be confiscated after a domestic violence incident is reported.

Perhaps the most consistent disappointment in the military policy for intervening is the use of couples counseling. Battered women, batterers, counselors, and researchers have all noted the ineffectuality and dangers of couples counseling, but the military, particularly the Army, clings to it. Most counselors were trained by Dr. Peter Neidig, who has urged that most violence against women is really "mutual violence." He minimizes the suggestion that women are often acting to defend themselves from abuse when they are violent and stresses that both partners have the problem (Neidig & Friedman, 1984). This works well for the batterer, who wants the victim to believe the violence is about her behavior and not his own.

Women who come to shelters in Texas are often very conflicted. On the one hand, when requesting help from the military, they are often discouraged. Questions such as "Do you really want to do this to his career? He's a good soldier, he's under stress, can't you be patient and help him out more?" let battered women know that their experience doesn't count for much to the military authorities. On the other hand, if they ask us for help, confidentiality is essential, because these women know what the abuser will do if the military is advised of the true nature of the violence from outsiders. Because shelters that contract for services with the military are required to give the family's name, civilian shelters provide significant services to military family members without reimbursement.

First sergeants, company commanders, and military leaders, who are often without any training in domestic violence issues, are the ones who make many of the real decisions concerning the intervention. I thought of the military as a true hierarchy, but it is more a collection of individual fiefdoms. In the training I've done, counselors, doctors, and social workers have let me know over and over that I'm preaching to the choir. Some feel that they have done everything possible to stop couples counseling from being the Army's preferred response, and many express jealousy of the training being done for the Marine installations by DAIP in Duluth.

The Duluth model and its training involve everyone who has a role. Because the company or post commanders are like the boss and the judge rolled into one, they are desperately in need of training if any real change is to occur in the military community. Military commanders can choose to follow recommended policy or not, depending on their own evaluation of the circumstances and their own belief systems. Recommendations prepared by multidisciplinary teams for these boss/judges can be readily swept aside if the service member is considered a valuable soldier.

Family Advocacy staff work for the command, and many are frustrated by their limitations. I have reassured them that there are parallels within the civilian world. For example, a well-respected, wealthy batterer often faces fewer consequences for his behavior than an unknown, less affluent individual. Classism and racism are found just as readily within the civilian world. Judges are often untrained in the issues, and employers may not have sanctions for employees who commit family violence. But just because we don't have it working too well out here does not excuse the military from persisting in outmoded and even dangerous practices in how they intervene. Can we not expect, with the much greater resources that have been invested through our tax dollars, that the military can lead the way, rather than drag behind? Can we not ask the military to help us build a new concept of family life, where each family member is encouraged "to be all he or she can be?"

Conclusion

Women in WAVE in the Texas prisons have also helped us to see a number of commonalities that are important for us to consider. Most of the women who ultimately killed in self-defense were women who experienced horrific sexual violence that no one knew about. Doctors, counselors, and others who seemed to know clearly that the women were being abused usually never asked about the kinds of things Beth described and other battered women have told us about: the stitches torn out after childbirth, the damage to her breasts, the anal intercourse resulting in injury apparent to those who were to care for her. The reluctance of victims to discuss sexual violence with their counselors or other helping professionals is so powerful that we must all find a way to ask about it and draw it out. I don't know what the relationship is between the women who are forced to defend themselves and sexual violence, and maybe we could understand more clearly if we knew also how many of the women who die at the hands of their batterers were also sexually abused. Could it be that those men who commit sexual violence are on a continuum of batterers who are more likely to create a lethal situation?

The women also talk of the final incident in which they defended their lives in much the same manner as Beth described it: the man's eyes glaring with hate, the complete lack of concern for the presence of children (which might mean an intent to also kill those children), the continuation of the attack on them even when they had acted defensively and injured their batterer. They also tell similar stories of what followed: being arrested and not being allowed to change out of clothes with urine or blood, receiving no medical care, being manipulated into giving their statements, being kept from their children and having no opportunity to comfort them. All of these issues could be handled so differently without compromising an investigation. Women who allege that they have killed in self-defense and who bear the obvious signs of injury, as Beth did, should certainly be allowed to get fresh clothing, to go immediately to the hospital, to have the clothes that are forensically valuable removed as part of a medical exam of their condition, to attend to basic physical needs such as dry underwear before questioning, and to see and comfort their children, even if that is done in the presence of an officer.

Over and over when we talk with women who killed in self-defense, they say, "It didn't have to be. No one should have died." We must look at every aspect of our services, the intervention offered by helping professions and reach out to the military. We must continue to strive for a criminal justice system that offers safety for victims and accountability for batterers, regardless of class, race, or performance in their workplace. Rarely is the first act of domestic violence life-threatening. We must come to understand either how to prevent that first act or to intervene so thoroughly that it is never repeated. This challenge is one that will require work by all of us, including battered women like Beth who will help us to continue learning.

References

American Psychiatric Association. (1994). *Diagnostic and statistical manual of mental disorders* (4th ed.). Washington, DC: Author.

Bachman, R., & Saltzman, L. E. (1995). *Violence against women: Estimates from the redesigned survey.* Washington, DC: U.S. Department of Justice, Office of Justice Programs, Bureau of Justice Statistics.

Barnard, G. W., Vera, H., Vera, M. I., & Newman, G. (1982). Till death do us part: A study of spousal murder. *Bulletin of American Academy of Psychiatry and Law, 10,* 271.

Barnett, O. W., & LaViolette, A. D. (1993). *It could happen to anyone: Why battered women stay.* Newbury Park, CA: Sage.

Bernstein, S. E. (1993). Living under siege: Do stalking laws protect domestic violence victims? *Cardozo Law Review, 15, 525-567.*

Bilinkoff, J. (1995). Empowering battered women as mothers. In E. Peled, P. G. Jaffe, & J. L. Edleson (Eds.), *Ending the cycle of violence: Community responses to children of battered women* (pp. 97-105). Thousand Oaks, CA: Sage.

Browne, A. (1987). *When battered women kill.* New York: Free Press.

Campbell, J. C. (1989a). A test of two explanatory models of women's responses to battering. *Nursing Research, 38,* 18-24.

Campbell, J. C. (1989b). Women's responses to sexual abuse in battering relationships. *Women's Health Care International.*

Campbell, J. C., & Alford, P. (1989). The dark consequences of marital rape. *American Journal of Nursing, 89,* 18-24.

Campbell, J. C., & Humphreys, J. (1993). *Nursing care of survivors of family violence.* St. Louis: Mosby.

Campbell, J. C., Pliska, M. J., Taylor, W., & Sheridan, D. (1994). Battered women's experiences in emergency departments: Need for appropriate policy and procedures. *Journal of Emergency Nursing, 20*(4), 280-288.

Campbell, J. C., Pugh, L. C., Campbell, D., & Visscher, M. (1995). The influence of abuse on pregnancy intention. *Women's Health Issues, 5*(4), 214-223.

Caplan, P. J. (1985). *The myth of women's masochism.* New York: E. P. Dutton.

Cappell, C., & Heiner, R. B. (1990). The intergenerational transmission of family aggression. *Journal of Family Violence, 5,* 135-152.

Carlson, B. E. (1984). Children's observations of interparental volence. In A. R. Roberts (Ed.), *Battered women and their families* (pp. 147-167). New York: Springer.

Carlson, B. E. (1990). Adolescent observers of marital violence. *Journal of Family Violence, 5,* 285-299.

Chez, R. A. (1988). Woman battering. *American Journal of Obstetrics & Gynoecology, 158,* 1-4.

Christopherpoulos, C., Cohn, A. D., Shaw, D. S., Joyce, S., Sullivan-Hanson, J., Kraft, S. P., & Emery, R. E. (1987). Children of abused women: I. Adjustment at time of shelter residence. *Journal of Marriage and the Family, 49,* 611-619.

Daly, M., & Wilson, M. (1988). *Homicide.* New York: Aldine deGruyter.

Drossman, D. A., Leserman, J., Nanhman, G., Li, Z., Gluck, H., Toomey, T. C., & Mitchell, M. (1990). Sexual and physical abuse in women with functional or organic gastrointestinal disorders. *Annals of Internal Medicine, 113*(11), 828-833.

DuRant, R. H., Cadenhead, C., Pendergrast, R. A., Slavens, G., & Linder, C. W. (1994). Factors associated with the use of violence among urban black adolescents. *American Journal of Public Health, 84,* 612-617.

Eby, K. K., & Campbell, J. C. (1995). Health effects of experiences of sexual violence for women with abusive partners. *Women's Health Care International, 14.*

Elliot, D. S. (1989). Criminal justice procedures in family violence crimes. In L. Ohlin & M. Tonry (Eds.), *Family violence.* Chicago: University of Chicago Press.

Ewing, C. P. (1987). *Battered women who kill.* Lexington, MA: Lexington Books.

Family Violence Health Resource Center. (1995). *Protocol of care.* San Francisco: Family Violence Prevention Fund.

Farr, K. A. (1988). Dominance bonding through the good old boys' sociability group. *Sex Roles, 18*(5/6), 259-277.

Feld, S. L., & Straus, M. A. (1989). Escalation and desistance of wife assault in a marriage. *Criminology, 27*(1), 141-161.

Felix, A. C., III, & McCarthy, K. F. (1994). *An analysis of child fatalities 1992.* Boston: Massachusetts Department of Social Services.

Ferraro, K. (1995). Criminology, deviance, law. *Contemporary Sociology, 24*(4), 382-385.

Forsstrom-Cohn, B., & Rosenbaum, A. (1985). The effects of parental marital violence on young adults: An exploratory investigation. *Journal of Marriage and the Family, 47,* 467-472.

Forward, S., & Torres, J. (1986). *Men who hate women and the women who love them.* New York: Bantam.

Franklin, C. W. (1984). *The changing definition of masculinity.* New York: Plenum.

Gillespie, C. K. (1989). *Justifiable homicide: Battered women, self-defense, and the law.* Columbus: Ohio University Press.

Gleason, W. J. (1993). Mental disorders in battered women: An empirical study. *Violence and Victims, 8*(1), 53-68.

Goldberg W. G., & Tomlanovich, M. C. (1984). Domestic violence victims in the emergency department. *Journal of the American Medical Association, 251,* 3259-3264.

Gondolf, E. W. (1988). *Battered women as survivors: An alternative to treating learned helplessness.* Lexington, MA: Lexington Books.

Graham, D., Rawlings, E., & Rimini, K. (1988). Survivors of terror: Battered women, hostages, and the Stockholm syndrome. In K. Yllö & M. Bograd (Eds.), *Feminist perspectives on wife abuse* (pp. 217-233). Newbury Park, CA: Sage.

Groesbeck v. Housewright, 657 F.Supp. 798 (D.Nev. 1987) aff'ed, 844 F.2d 791 (9th Cir. 1988).

Hangen, E. (1994). *D.S.S. Interagency Domestic Violence Team Pilot Project: Program data evaluation.* Boston: Massachusetts Department of Social Services.

Hilton, N. Z. (1992). Battered women's concerns about their children witnessing wife assault. *Journal of Interpersonal Violence, 7,* 77-86.

Hinchey, F. S., & Gavelek, J. R. (1982). Empathic responding in children of battered women. *Child Abuse and Neglect, 6,* 395-401.

Hoff, L. A. (1990). *Battered women as survivors.* New York: Routledge.

Holden, G. W., & Ritchie, K. L. (1991). Linking extreme marital discord, child rearing, and child behavior problems: Evidence from battered women. *Child Development, 62,* 311-327.

Hughes, H. M. (1988). Psychological and behavioral correlates of family violence in child witness and victims. *American Journal of Orthopsychiatry, 58,* 77-90.

Island, D., & Letellier, P. (1990). *Men who beat the men who love them: Battered gay men and domestic violence.* New York: Harrington Park Press.

Isaac, N. E., & Sanchez, R. L. (1994). Emergency department response to battered women in Massachusetts. *Annals of Emergency Medicine, 23,* 855-858.

Jaffe, P., Wilson, S., & Wolfe, D. (1986). Promoting changes in attitudes and understanding of conflict among child witnesses of family violence. *Canadian Journal of Behavioral Science, 18,* 356-380.

Jaffe, P., Wolfe, D., Wilson, S., & Zak, L. (1986). Emotional and physical health problems of battered women. *Canadian Journal of Psychiatry, 31,* 625-629.

Jaffe, P. G., Wolfe, D. A., & Wilson, S. K. (1990). *Children of battered women.* Newbury Park, CA: Sage.

Jaffe, P. G., Sudermann, M., Reitzel, D., & Killip, S. M. (1992). An evaluation of a secondary school primary prevention program on violence in intimate relationships. *Violence and Victims,* 7(2), 129-146.

Jones, A., & Schechter, S. (1992). *When love goes wrong.* New York: Harper Collins.

Jones, R. F. (1993). Domestic violence: Let our voices be heard. *Obstetrics & Gynecology, 81,* 1-4.

Karmen, A. (1982). Women as crime victims: Problems and solutions. In B. R. Price & N. Sokoloff (Eds.), *The criminal justice system and women.* New York: Clark Boardman.

Larson v. State, 104 Nev. 961, 766 P.2d 261 (1988).

Leighton, B. (1989). *Spousal abuse in metropolitan Toronto: Research report on the response of the criminal justice system* (Report No. 1989-02). Ottawa: Solicitor General of Canada.

Lerman, L. (1986) Prosecution of wife beaters: Institutional obstacles and innovations. In M. Lystad (Ed.), *Violence in the home: Interdisciplinary perspectives.* New York: Brunner/Mazel.

Mahoney, M. A. (1991). Legal images of battered women: Redefining the issues of separation. *Michigan Law Review, 90,* 1-94.

Mahoney, M. A. (1994). Victimization or oppression? Women's lives, violence, and agency. In M. A. Fineman & R. Mykitiuk (Eds.), *The public nature of private violence.* New York: Routledge.

Mathews, D. (1995). Parenting groups for men who batter. In E. Peled, P. G. Jaffe, & J. L. Edleson (Eds.), *Ending the cycle of violence: Community responses to children of battered women* (pp. 106-120). Thousand Oaks, CA: Sage.

McFarlane, J., Parker, B., Soeken, K., & Bullock, L. (1992). *Journal of the American Medical Association, 267,* 3176-3178.

McLeer, S., Anwar, R. A., Herman, S., & Maquiling, K. (1989). Education is not enough: A systems failure in protecting battered women. *Annals of Emergency Medicine, 18*(6), 651-653.

McMahon, M., & Pence, E. (1995). Doing more harm than good? Some cautions on visitations centers. In E. Peled, P. G. Jaffe, & J. L. Edleson (Eds.), *Ending the cycle of violence: Community responses to children of battered women* (pp. 186-206). Thousand Oaks, CA: Sage.

Miedzian, M. (1991). *Boys will be boys: Breaking the link between masculinity and violence.* New York: Doubleday.

Miller, S. L. (1989). Unintended side effects of pro-arrest policies and their race and class implications for battered women: A cautionary note. *Criminal Justice Policy Review, 3,* 299-317.

Miller, S. L., & Barberet, R. (1994). A cross-cultural comparison of social reform: The growing pains of the battered women's movements in Washington, D.C., and Madrid, Spain. *Law and Social Inquiry, 19*(4), 601-644.

Miller, S. L., & Forest, K. B. (1994). *It's all in the name: Reexamining the victim discourse.* Paper presented at the American Society of Criminology annual conference, Miami, FL.

Miller, S. L., & Iovanni, L. M. (1994). Determinants of perceived risk of formal sanctions for courtship violence. *Justice Quarterly, 11*(2), 281-312.

Minnesota Department of Corrections. (1987). *Summary data presentation on information obtained from law enforcement agencies 1984-1985.* St. Paul: Minnesota Department of Corrections Program for Battered Women.

Montemurri, P. (1989, December 3). Leaving an abusive husband can spark deadly outburst of rage. *Las Vegas Review-Journal.*

National Clearinghouse for the Defense of Battered Women. (1995). *Battered women in prison for homicide* (compiled August 1995). Philadelphia, PA: Author.

Neidig, P. H., & Friedman, D. H. (1984). *Spouse abuse: A treatment program for couples.* Champaign, IL: Research Press.

Nevada Revised Statute § 48.061

NiCarthy, G. (1987). *The ones who got away: Women who left abusive partners.* Seattle, WA: Seal Press.

Parker, B., McFarlane, J., & Soeken, K. (1994). Abuse during pregnancy: Effects on maternal complications and birth weight in adult and teenage women. *Obstetrics and Gynecology, 84*(3), 323-328.

Pecora, P. J., Whittaker, J. K., Maluccio, A. N., Barth, R. P., & Plotnick, R. D. (1992). *The child welfare challenge: Policy, practice, and research.* New York: Aldine De Gruyter.

Peled, E. (1993). *The experience of living with violence for preadolescent witnesses of woman abuse.* Unpublished doctoral dissertation, University of Minnesota, Minneapolis.

Pence, E. & Paymer, M. (1993). *Education groups for men who batter.* New York: Springer.

Prato, L., & Braham, R. (1991). Coordinating a community response to teen dating violence. In B. Levy (Ed.), *Dating violence: Young women in danger.* Seattle: Seal Press.

Rath, G. D., & Jarrett, L. G. (1990). Battered Wife Syndrome: Overview and presentation in the office setting. *South Dakota Journal of Medicine, 43*(1), 19-25.

Renzetti, C. M. (1992). *Violent betrayal: Partner abuse in lesbian relationships.* Newbury Park, CA: Sage.

Rosenbaum, A., & O'Leary, D. K. (1981). Children: The unintended victims of marital violence. *American Journal of Orthopsychiatry, 51,* 692-699.

Russell, D. (1990). *Rape & marriage.* Bloomington: Indiana University Press.

Saunders, D. G. (1994). Child custody decisions in families experiencing woman abuse. *Social Work, 39,* 51-59.

Schechter, S. (1987). *Guidelines for mental health practitioners in domestic violence cases.* Washington, DC: National Coalition Against Domestic Violence.

Sheriff v. Gleave, 104 Nev. 496, 761 P.2d 416 (1988).

Smith, D. K. (1987). *The everyday world as problematic: A feminist sociology.* Boston: Northeastern University Press.

Stanko, E. A. (1985). *Intimate intrusions: Women's experience of male violence.* London: Routledge.

Stark, E., & Flitcraft, A. (1991). Spouse abuse. In M. L. Rosenberg & M. A. Fanley (Eds.), *Violence in America: A public health approach.* New York: Oxford University Press.

Stark, E., Flitcraft, A., & Frazier, W. (1979). Medicine and patriarchal violence: The social construction of a private event. *International Journal of Health Services, 9,* 461-492.

Straus, M. A. (1991, September). *Children as witnesses to marital violence: A risk factor for life-long problems among nationally representative sample of American men and women.* A paper presented at the Ross Roundtable on Children and Violence, Washington, DC.

Straus, M. A., & Gelles, R. J. (1990a). *Physical violence in American families.* New Brunswick, NJ: Transaction.

Straus, M. A., & Gelles, R. J. (1990b). *Violence in American families.* New York: Transaction Press.

Syers-McNairy, M. A. (1990). *Women who leave violent relationships: Getting on with life.* Unpublished doctoral dissertation, University of Minnesota, Minneapolis.

Symposium on Domestic Violence. (1992). *Journal of Criminal Law and Criminology, 83*(1), 1-253.

Walker, L. E. (1979). *The battered woman.* New York: Harper & Row.

Walker, L. E. (1984). *The battered woman syndrome.* New York: Springer.

Walker, L. E. (1989). *Terrifying love: Why battered women kill and how society responds.* New York: Harper & Row.

Westra, B., & Martin, H. P. (1981). Children of battered women. *Maternal Child Nursing Journal, 10,* 41-54.

Widom, C. S. (1989). *The intergenerational transmission of violence.* New York: Harry Frank Guggenheim Foundation.

Wilson, M., & Daly, M. (1993). Spousal homicide risk and estrangement. *Violence and Victims, 8,* 3-16.

Wolfe, D. A., Zak, L., Wilson, S., & Jaffe, P. (1986). Child witnesses to violence between parents: Critical issues in behavioral and social adjustment. *Journal of Abnormal Child Psychology, 14,* 95-104.

Younes, L. A., & Besharov, D. J. (1988). State child abuse and neglect laws: A comparative analysis. In D. J. Besharov (Ed.), *Protecting children from abuse and neglect: Policy and practice* (pp. 353-490). Springfield, IL: Charles C Thomas.

About the Authors

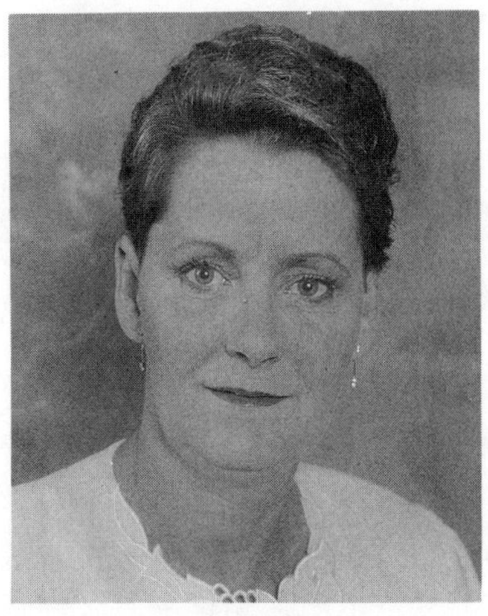

Beth Sipe is a formerly battered woman who has become a survivor. After seventeen years of abuse, she left her violent husband, only to be more severely harassed and threatened when she became independent. The mother of three adult children, she has reclaimed her identity and lives a quiet, productive life.

Photograph by Nancy Santullo, Los Angeles, California.

Evelyn J. Hall, Ph.D., is a Licensed Marriage and Family Therapist in private practice for fourteen years. Concurrently, she has served as Clinical Supervisor of the Counseling Office for Temporary Assistance for Domestic Crisis (TADC), a program dealing specifically with domestic violence. A guest speaker for various national and local groups, she has taught continuing education classes at the University of Nevada, Las Vegas, such as Women and Violence, and Families in Crisis.

About the Commentators

Jacquelyn C. Campbell is the Anna D. Wolf Endowed Professor at the Johns Hopkins University School of Nursing, with a joint appointment in the Hopkins Injury Control Center. She has authored or coauthored more than fifty articles and chapters, mostly on battered women and family violence. She has worked directly with wife abuse shelters for the last ten years, and her clinical experience includes a variety of community health nursing positions in the inner city of Dayton, Ohio. Currently, she is on the Board of Directors of the Family Violence Prevention Fund, a national organization located in San Francisco. She received her doctorate in nursing from the University of Rochester, New York.

Jeffrey L. Edleson is Professor in the University of Minnesota School of Social Work. He is an Associate Editor of the journal, *Violence Against Women,* and has published over fifty articles and several books on domestic violence, groupwork, and program evaluation. He has conducted intervention research at the Domestic Abuse Project in Minneapolis for almost twelve years and is its Director of Evaluation and Research. He has provided technical assistance to domestic violence programs and research projects across North America as well as in Israel, Singapore,

Tamil Nadu (India), and Bucharest (Romania). He received his master's degree and doctorate in Social Work from the University of Wisconsin at Madison. He is a Licensed Independent Clinical Social Worker in Minnesota and has practiced in elementary and secondary schools and in several domestic violence agencies.

Barbara J. Hart, Esq., is Legal Director of the Pennsylvania Coalition Against Domestic Violence, Associate Director of the Battered Women's Justice Project, and Legal Consultant to the National Resource Center on Domestic Violence. Her work includes public policy making, training, and technical assistance on a broad range of issues, including crafting coordinated community intervention systems, development and critique of legislation, court procedures and program standards for batterer treatment services, impact litigation on behalf of battered women and children, and designing training curricula for effective intervention against domestic violence. She has written several books and coproduced two documentaries. She has a private consultation and training practice, providing assistance to lawmakers, business leaders, battered women's programs, and treatment programs for battering men.

Susan L. Miller is Associate Professor of Sociology at Northern Illinois University. Her research interests include victimology, gender and social control, and theoretical and policy implications of gender, social inequality, and crime. She is the author or co-author of several recent articles that address these issues. She is currently at work on an analysis of gendered power and social relations among community police officers; she also continues to examine how victim labeling overlooks women's resiliency and resistant behaviors. She received her Ph.D. in Criminology from the University of Maryland.

William H. Smith, Esq., graduated from Davidson College in 1975 and Loyola University School of Law in Los Angeles in 1978. He is admitted to practice in California and Nevada and is a member of the National Association of Criminal Defense Lawyers, California Attorneys for Criminal Justice, Nevada Trial Lawyers Association, and Nevada Attorneys for Criminal

Justice. He has tried more than 75 jury trials, including several capital murder cases.

Deborah D. Tucker began working on violence against women in 1974 as a volunteer with the first rape crisis center in Texas. In 1977, she helped form Austin's Center for Battered Women, the first battered women's shelter in Texas, and served as the Center's Executive Director for its first five years. Since 1982, she has been the Executive Director of the Texas Council on Family Violence, a statewide membership association of battered women's shelters, batterer's treatment programs, organizations, and individuals working together to end violence against women. She has also been active in the national battered women's movement and is Vice-Chair of the National Network to End Domestic Violence. She holds a master's degree in public administration. For over three years, she has provided domestic violence training for military personnel from all four branches of the service.